LANGUAGE!®
The Comprehensive Literacy Curriculum

Reading
Writing
Spelling
Vocabulary
Grammar
Speaking

Jane Fell Greene, Ed.D.

Cambium
LEARNING®
Group

Voyager
LEARNING

9 10 11 12   SKY   23 22 21

Authors:
Jane Fell Greene, Ed.D.
Nancy Chapel Eberhardt

For acknowledgements of permissioned materials, see Sources, page 171.

ISBN 13: 978-1-60218-693-4
ISBN 10: 1-60218-693-6
169990

Printed in the United States of America

Published and distributed by

17855 Dallas Parkway, Suite 400 • Dallas, TX 75287 • 800 547-6747
www.voyagersopris.com

Table of Contents • Handbook

Table of Contents • Handbook

STEP 5
Listening and Reading Comprehension — H71

STEP 6
Speaking and Writing — H81

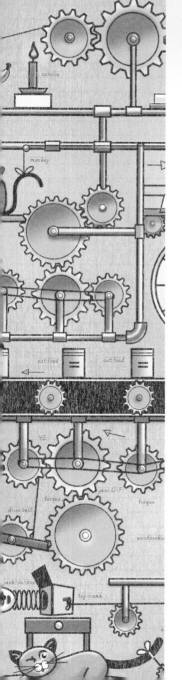

Table of Contents • Text Selections

Unit 13

Invent It

Independent
Build Knowledge
Fluency

Instructional
Use Text Features
Author's Purpose
Predict
Build Knowledge
Build Vocabulary
Clarify Meaning
Apply Vocabulary

Challenge
Build Knowledge
Build Vocabulary
Clarify Meaning
Literary Terminology

Table of Contents · Text Selections

Unit 14
Make Art

Independent
Build Knowledge
Fluency

Instructional
Use Text Features
Author's Purpose
Predict
Build Knowledge
Build Vocabulary
Clarify Meaning
Apply Vocabulary

Challenge
Build Knowledge
Author's Purpose
Build Vocabulary
Clarify Meaning
Literary Terminology

Unit 15
Be a Hero

Independent
Build Knowledge
Fluency

Instructional
Use Text Features
Author's Purpose
Predict
Build Knowledge
Build Vocabulary
Clarify Meaning
Apply Vocabulary
Literary Terminology
Elements
    of Literature

Challenge
Build Knowledge
Author's Purpose
Build Vocabulary
Clarify Meaning

Unit 16

Cheer an Athlete

Independent
Build Knowledge
Fluency

Instructional
Use Text Features
Author's Purpose
Predict
Build Knowledge
Build Vocabulary
Clarify Meaning
Apply Vocabulary
Literary Terminology

Challenge
Build Knowledge
Author's Purpose
Build Vocabulary
Clarify Meaning
Literary Terminology

Unit
17
Go to Egypt

Independent
Build Knowledge
Fluency

Instructional
Use Text Features
Author's Purpose
Predict
Build Knowledge
Build Vocabulary
Clarify Meaning
Apply Vocabulary

Challenge
Build Knowledge
Author's Purpose
Build Vocabulary
Clarify Meaning

Table of Contents • Text Selections

Unit 18

Explore a Continent

Independent
Build Knowledge
Fluency

Instructional
Use Text Features
Author's Purpose
Predict
Build Knowledge
Build Vocabulary
Clarify Meaning
Apply Vocabulary

Challenge
Build Knowledge
Author's Purpose
Build Vocabulary
Clarify Meaning
Literary Terminology

Table of Contents · Resources

Handbook

Handbook

To find information in this Handbook, you can use the Handbook Table of Contents, pages iii–iv, or the Handbook Index, pages 164–170. Below are some tips for using both features.

Table of Contents

A table of contents lists **general** topics in the order they are presented in a book. Use a table of contents when you are looking for a general topic.

Index

An index lists **specific** topics in alphabetical order.

Use an index when you are looking for a specific topic.

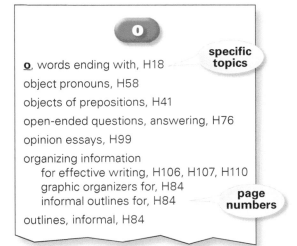

STEP 1

Phonemic Awareness and Phonics

Consonants and Vowels (Unit 1)

Languages have two kinds of sounds: **consonants** and **vowels**.

- **Consonants** are closed sounds. They restrict or close the airflow using the lips, teeth, or tongue.

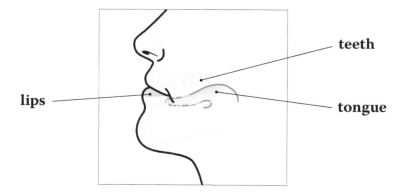

- **Vowels** are open sounds. The air doesn't stop.

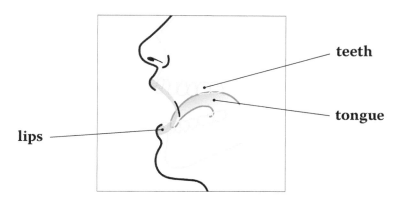

English Consonant Chart

(Note the voiceless/voiced consonant phoneme pairs)

Mouth Position

Type of Consonant Sound		Lips (Bilabial)	Lips/Teeth (Labiodental)	Tongue Between Teeth (Dental)	Tongue Behind Teeth (Alveolar)	Roof of Mouth (Palatal)	Back of Mouth (Velar)	Throat (Glottal)
	Stops	/p/ /b/			/t/ /d/		/k/ /g/	
	Fricatives		/f/ /v/	/th/ /<u>th</u>/	/s/ /z/	/sh/ /zh/		/h/[1]
	Affricatives					/ch/ /j/		
	Nasals	/m/			/n/		/ng/	
	Lateral				/l/			
	Semivowels	/ʰw/ /w/[2]			/r/	/y/		

1 Classed as a fricative on the basis of acoustic effect. It is like a vowel without voice.

2 /ʰw/ and /w/ are velar as well as bilabial, as the back of the tongue is raised as it is for /u/.

English Consonant Chart based on Bolinger, D. 1975. *Aspects of Language* (2nd ed.). Harcourt Brace Jovanovich, p. 41.

Consonant Letter Combinations (Unit 8, 11)

di = 2
graph = letter

Digraphs are two letters that represent one sound.

| c | + | h | = | / *ch* / as in **ch**op, su**ch** |

| t | + | h | = | / *th* / as in **th**is |

| s | + | h | = | / *sh* / as in **sh**op, di**sh** |

| w | + | h | = | / *wh* / as in **wh**en |

| t | + | h | = | / *th* / as in **th**in, ma**th** |

| n | + | g | = | / *ng* / as in si**ng** |

tri = 3
graph = letter

Trigraphs are three letters that represent one sound.

| t | + | c | + | h | = | / *tch* / as in ma**tch** |

Blends are consonant sound pairs in the same syllable. The consonants are not separated by vowels. In blends, each consonant is pronounced.

Initial blends are letter combinations that represent two different consonant sounds at the beginning of a word.

l blends: **bl-**, **cl-**, **fl-**, **gl-**, **pl-**, **sl-**	black
r blends: **br-**, **cr-**, **dr-**, **fr-**, **gr-**, **pr-**, **shr-**, **thr-**, **tr-**	brick
s blends: **sc-**, **sk-**, **sm-**, **sn-**, **sp-**, **st-**	scare
w blends: **dw-**, **sw-**, **tw-**	dwell

Final blends are letter pairs that represent two different consonant sounds at the end of a word.

| **-mp**, **-nd**, **-sk**, **-st**, **-ct**, **-lk**, **-lt**, **-sp** | band |

Clusters consist of three or more consonants in the same syllable. The consonants are not supported by vowels. Each consonant is pronounced.

| **scr**, **spl**, **spr**, **str** | spray |

English Vowel Chart

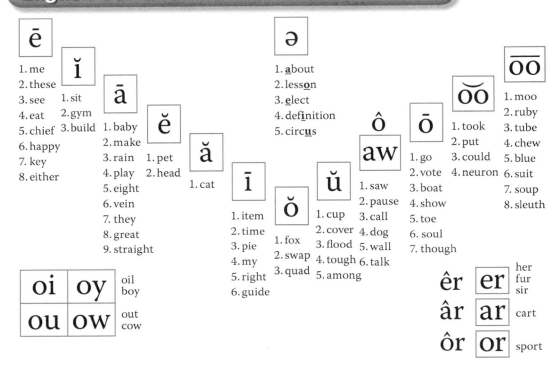

ē
1. me
2. these
3. see
4. eat
5. chief
6. happy
7. key
8. either

ĭ
1. sit
2. gym
3. build

ā
1. baby
2. make
3. rain
4. play
5. eight
6. vein
7. they
8. great
9. straight

ĕ
1. pet
2. head

ă
1. cat

ī
1. item
2. time
3. pie
4. my
5. right
6. guide

ŏ
1. fox
2. swap
3. quad

ŭ
1. cup
2. cover
3. flood
4. tough
5. among

ə
1. about
2. lesson
3. elect
4. definition
5. circus

ô

aw
1. saw
2. pause
3. call
4. dog
5. wall
6. talk

ō
1. go
2. vote
3. boat
4. show
5. toe
6. soul
7. though

o͝o
1. took
2. put
3. could
4. neuron

o͞o
1. moo
2. ruby
3. tube
4. chew
5. blue
6. suit
7. soup
8. sleuth

oi **oy** oil boy
ou **ow** out cow

êr **er** her fur sir
âr **ar** cart
ôr **or** sport

Note: The order of spelling examples reflects the relative frequency of incidence for that spelling of the phoneme.

Vowel Sounds

The same vowel letter can represent different sounds.

Diacritical mark: The breve (˘) signals short vowel sounds.

Short sounds

Letter	a	e	i	o	u
Sound	/ ă /	/ ĕ /	/ ĭ /	/ ŏ /	/ ŭ /
	cat	egg	sit	fox	up

Long sounds

The long vowel sound for **a**, **e**, **i**, and **o** is the same as the name of the letter that represents it. The long vowel sound for **u** can be pronounced two ways.

Diacritical mark: The macron (¯) signals long vowel sounds.

Letter	a	e	i	o	u	
Sound	/ ā /	/ ē /	/ ī /	/ ō /	/ o͞o /	/ yo͞o /
	cake	Pete	bike	nose	tube	cube

Sounds of y as a vowel   (Unit 17)

The letter **y** represents three different vowel sounds. The position of the letter in the syllable determines the sound it represents.

Letter	y	y	y	y	y
Sound	/ ī /	/ ī /	/ ī /	/ ē /	/ ĭ /
	sky	deny	type	happy	gym
Syllable type	end of a one-syllable word (an open syllable)	end of a two-syllable word, when the second syllable is stressed	final silent **e** syllable	end of a two-syllable word, when the second syllable is unstressed	closed syllable

Syllable Types

Words are made up of **syllables**.

- A syllable is a word or word part that has one vowel sound.
- Every word has at least one syllable.
- The syllable's type is determined by the syllable's vowel sound.

Syllable Type	Pattern	Vowel Sound	Diacritical Mark
Closed (Unit 13)	A syllable that ends with a consonant sound. **dig, trans-mit**	The vowel sound is short.	ă
r-controlled (Unit 14)	A syllable that has a vowel followed by **r**. **car, mar**-ket	The vowel sound is r-controlled: / âr /, / ôr /, or / êr /.	âr
Open (Unit 15)	A syllable that ends with a vowel. **she, my, o**-pen	The vowel sound is long.	ā
Final silent e (Unit 16)	A syllable that ends in a final silent **e**. de-**fine**, ath-**lete**	The vowel sound is long.	ā

Schwa   (Unit 13)

Stress in words and the **schwa** go together. Stress is the emphasis that syllables have in words.

- If a syllable is stressed, the vowel is usually long or short.
- If the syllable is not stressed, the vowel is usually reduced to **schwa**. Schwa sounds like / ŭ /, but is more reduced.

lesson = / lĕs´ən /

The **o** in **lesson** is reduced to schwa. The **o** does not have an / ŏ / sound; it is reduced. The **o** sounds like / ə /.

STEP 2

Word Recognition and Spelling

Building Words from Sounds and Letters   (Unit 1)

We put vowels and consonants together to make words.
Two words in English are made of just one vowel.

i = I   a = a

All other words combine consonants and vowels.

a + t = at

m + a + t = mat

m + a + s + t = mast

l + a + s + t = last

b + l + a + s + t = blast

Syllables

For more about **Syllable Types**, see Step 1, page H8.

What Is a Syllable?   (Unit 3)

Words are made up of parts we call **syllables**.

- Some words have just one syllable.
- Every syllable has one vowel sound.
- A syllable may or may not be a word by itself.

	How many syllables?		
	1	**2**	**3**
map	map		
bandit	ban	dit	
inhibit	in	hib	it

When a syllable has a vowel followed by at least one **consonant**, the vowel sound (v) is usually short.

ĭt   mă<u>p</u>   bĕ<u>nd</u>

VC   VC   VCC

Syllable Patterns

Note the pattern of vowels (v) and consonants (c).

VC/CV Pattern (Unit 3)

ban + dit = bandit
vc   cv = vc/cv

atlas	sudden
basket	problem
random	

Some two-syllable words have a different pattern.

VC/V Pattern (Unit 5)

rob + in = robin
vc   v = vc/v

finish	solid
lemon	melon
seven	

V/CV Pattern (Unit 15)

si + lent = silent
v   cv = vcv

legal	acorn
moment	equip
music	

VR/CV Pattern (Unit 14)
If the first vowel is followed by an **r**, the syllable is **r**-controlled.

mar + ket = market
v   cv = v/cv

corner	target
current	orbit
perhaps	

V/V Pattern (Unit 15)

ne + on = neon
v v = v/v

diet	poem
fuel	quiet
lion	

Compound Words

For more about **Compound Words**, see Step 3, page H26.

What Is a Compound Word?   (Unit 3)

A **compound word** is made up of two or more smaller words.

In a compound word, both words have to be real words that can stand on their own.

sand	+	bag	=	sandbag

Unit 13	catnap	checklist	laptop	matchbox
Unit 14	backyard	grasshopper	landmark	starfish
Unit 15	leftover	ongoing	paperback	supermarket

Prefixes   (Unit 13)

For more about **Prefixes**, see Step 3, page H24.

We can build longer words and change their meaning by adding prefixes. Prefixes are word parts added to the beginning of words.

un	+	lock	=	unlock

Unit 13	dis-, in-, non-, un-	Unit 16	anti-, sub-
Unit 14	inter-, under-	Unit 17	con-, trans-
Unit 15	pre-, re-, super-		

Contractions

Contractions are two words combined into one word. One or more letters are left out and are replaced by an **apostrophe** (').

For other uses of an **Apostrophe**, see Step 4, page H36.

Contraction with **not**   (Unit 7)

is + nøt = isn't

The letter <u>o</u> in **not** is replaced by the apostrophe (').

Contractions with **would**   (Unit 9)

I + woul̶d = I'd

The letters <u>woul</u> in **would** are replaced by the apostrophe (').

Contractions with **will**   (Unit 10)

it + w̶i̶ll = it'll

The letters <u>wi</u> in **will** are replaced by the apostrophe (').

Contractions with **am**, **is**   (Unit 13)

I + a̶m = I'm

The letter <u>a</u> in **am** is replaced with the apostrophe (').

she + i̶s = she's

The letter <u>i</u> in **is** is replaced with the apostrophe (').

I'm	she'll	he's	it's

Contractions with **are**   (Unit 14)

they + a̶re = they're

The letter <u>a</u> in **are** is replaced with the apostrophe (').

we're	you're	they're

Contractions with have (Unit 15)

they + ~~ha~~ve = they've

The letters **ha** in **have** are replaced with the apostrophe (').

I've	we've	you've	they've

Contractions with had or has (Unit 16)

you + ~~ha~~d = you'd

she + ~~ha~~s = she's

The letters **ha** in **had** or **has** are replaced with the apostrophe (').

had:	I'd, you'd, he'd, she'd, it'd, we'd, you'd, they'd
has:	he's, she's, it's

Abbreviations

An **abbreviation** is a shortened form of a word.

Doctor	= Doctor	= Dr.	**Period**
October	= October	= Oct.	
California	= California	= CA (postal abbreviation)	
Department of Motor Vehicles	= Department Motor Vehicles	= DMV	

* See the Unit 12 **Essential Word** list for more abbreviations.

Spelling Conventions

Spelling conventions are tips that help us remember how to spell English words.

Words ending with v or s + e

Almost no English words end in **v**. At the end of a word, **v** is almost always followed by **e**: have, give, live.

Often the **e** follows a single **s** at the end of the word. The **e** does not signal a long vowel. Examples:

promise	purchase

Double Consonants   (Unit 5)

Use double letters **-ss, -ff, -ll, -zz**

- at the end of many words.
- in many one-syllable words.
- after one short vowel.

pass	stiff	will	jazz

Ways to Spell / k /   (Unit 4)

The sound / k / is spelled three ways. The position of / k / in the word signals how to spell it:

- use **c** at the beginning of words before the vowel **a**: **c**at.
- use **k** at the beginning of words before the vowel **i**: **k**id.
- use **-ck** after one short vowel in one-syllable words: ba**ck**, si**ck**.

Adding -es (Unit 7)

Nouns and verbs ending in **s**, **z**, or **x** add **-es** to form plural nouns or singular present tense verbs.

Plural Nouns: dresses fizzes boxes

Singular Present Tense Verbs: presses buzzes waxes

Using ch or -tch (Unit 8)

The sound / *ch* / is represented two ways. The position of / *ch* / in a word helps you spell it:

- Use **ch** at the beginnings of words.

| ch | i | p |

- Use **-tch** after a short vowel at the ends of one-syllable words.

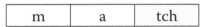

| m | a | tch |

There are four exceptions: **much, such, rich,** and **which**.

Think of this sentence to remember these words: A **rich** person gave so **much**, **which** was such good news!

/ ŭ / Spelled o (Unit 9)

Some words keep an Old English spelling for the / ŭ / sound.

In these words, the vowel sound is spelled with the letter **o**: front, short, ton.

Final Silent e (Unit 10)

The **e** at the end of the word is a signal to use the long vowel sound. The final **e** is silent. This is called the **final silent e** pattern.

The use of the final silent **e** can make a big difference in meaning.

mǎn + e = mānȩ   pǐn + e = pīnȩ

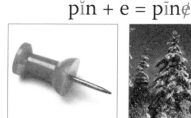

Spelling Rules

Spelling rules help us add endings to words.

Doubling Rule (Unit 6)

When a

- 1-syllable word   hop
- with **1** vowel   hop
- ends in **1** consonant   ho**p**

double the final consonant *before* adding a **suffix** that begins with a **vowel**.

$$\overset{v}{\text{hop} + p + \underset{\text{suffix}}{\text{ing}}}$$

Do not **double** the consonant when the **suffix** begins with a consonant.

$$\text{cap} + \underset{\text{suffix}}{\overset{c}{\text{ful}}} = \text{capful}$$

Drop e Rule (Unit 10)

When adding a suffix to a **final silent e** word:

If the suffix begins with a vowel, drop the **e** from the base word.

v

| hope | + | ing | = | hoping |

But, if the suffix begins with a consonant, **do not** drop the **e** from the base word.

c

| hope | + | ful | = | hopeful |

Words Ending in o (Unit 15)

For words ending in a consonant + **o**: Add **-es** to form plural nouns and singular present tense verbs. The **-es** keeps the sound for **o** long.

Add -es to Words Ending in Consonant + o.

| hero | + | es | = | heroes | | go | + | es | = | goes |

For words ending in a vowel + **o**: Add **-s** to form noun plurals.

Add -s to Words Ending in Vowel + o.

| video | + | s | = | videos |

The Change y Rule (Unit 17)

When a base word ends in **y** preceded by a consonant, change **y** to **i** before adding a suffix, except for **-ing**.

Change y to i when adding a suffix unless the suffix is -ing.

| try | + | ed | = | tried | | try | + | ing | = | trying |

Vocabulary and Morphology

Adding certain letters to words can add to or change their meanings.

Multiple Meanings

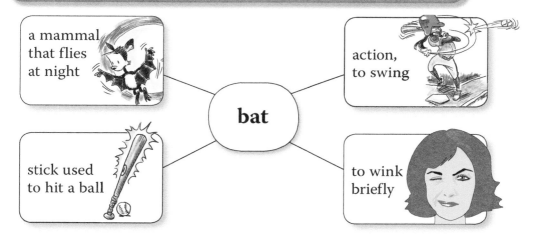

a mammal that flies at night

action, to swing

bat

stick used to hit a ball

to wink briefly

Meaning Parts • Noun Endings

See also
Noun Forms Step 4, page H35.

Adding -s or -es / Plural Nouns   (Units 1, 7)

Singular means "one of something." **Plural** means "more than one."

Adding -s changes a singular noun to a plural noun.

-s means more than one.

cat	cats

Nouns ending in certain letters use -es to make them plural.

- Singular nouns ending in <u>s</u>, <u>z</u>, or <u>x</u>: **dresses, fizzes, boxes**
- Singular nouns ending in <u>ch</u>, <u>sh</u>, or -<u>tch</u>: **riches, dishes, matches**

Adding 's / Singular Possessive Nouns (Unit 2)

Adding 's (an apostrophe and an **s**) to a noun shows ownership, which means possession.

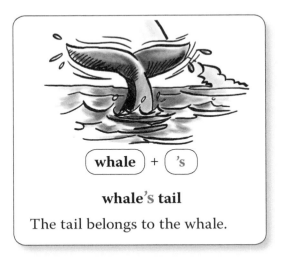

whale + 's

whale's tail

The tail belongs to the whale.

Adding s'/ Plural Possessive Nouns (Unit 11)

Adding s' signals plural possession. This means that more than one person or thing owns, has, or takes one or more things.

whale + s'

whales' tails

The tails belong to the whales.

Meaning Parts • Adjective Endings

Adding -er / Comparative Adjectives (Unit 14)

Adding -er signals comparison between two nouns or pronouns.

Adding -est / Superlative Adjectives (Unit 14)

Adding -est signals comparison among three or more nouns or pronouns.

Adjective	Comparative Adjective	Superlative Adjective

My little sister is **short**.	She is **shorter** than my older sister.	She is the **shortest** person in my family.

Before a multisyllabic adjective, we usually use **more** or **most** to make the comparative and superlative forms of the adjective.

Adjective	Comparative Adjective	Superlative Adjective

This is colorful art.	This art is **more** colorful than that one.	This is the **most** colorful art.

Handbook H21

See also
Verb Forms (Tense Timeline), Step 4, page H43.

Meaning Parts • Verb Endings

Adding -s or -es / Singular Present Tense Verb (Units 4, 8)

Adding -s or -es signals the number and tense (time) of a verb:

-s or -es means <u>singular</u> <u>present tense.</u>
one of something   happening now

> The ice **melts.**
>
> The runner **finishes** the race.

Adding -ed / Past Tense (Unit 7)

Adding -ed signals past tense.

Adding -ing / Progressive Form (Units 5, 9)

Adding -ing to a verb means an action is ongoing, or in progress.

The -ing ending signals the present progressive verb form when preceded by **am**, **are**, or **is**.

> am lock**ing**
>
> are lock**ing**
>
> is lock**ing**

The -ing ending signals the past progressive verb form when preceded by **was** or **were**.

> was push**ing**
>
> were push**ing**

Adding -ing / Present Participle (Unit 15)

When we add -ing to a verb, the new word can act as an adjective—a word that describes nouns.

The -ing form of a verb, which can be used to describe nouns, is called a **present participle**.

Present Progressive	Present Participle Acting as an Adjective
The sun is shining.	The shining sun is hot.
Shining is a verb, with the action in progress.	**Shining** answers the question *What kind?* of sun.

Adding -ed or -en / Past Participle (Unit 16)

When we add -ed or -en to some verbs, the new word can also act as an adjective—a word that describes nouns. The -ed or -en form of a verb, when it describes a noun, is called a **past participle.**

Past Tense	Past Participle Acting as an Adjective
The athlete injured his foot.	The injured athlete used crutches.
Injured is a verb, with the action in the past tense.	**Injured** is an adjective, answering the question *Which one?* about athlete.

Prefixes

A prefix can add to or change the meanings of a word.

A prefix + a base word = a new word with a new meaning.

attached

unattached

	Prefix	Meanings	Examples
Unit 13	dis–	apart, not, opposite of	disrupt
	in–	in, into	inform
	non–	without	nonstop
	un–	not, do the opposite of	unplug
Unit 14	inter–	between or among	interact
	under–	below or less	underpass, undersized
Unit 15	pre–	before	preset, prefer
	re–	back or again	return, restore, report
	super–	above, over; superior	superhero
Unit 16	anti–	opposite; against	antitoxin
	sub–	below, beneath, under	substandard
Unit 17	con–	with, together	conflict
	trans–	across, through	transfer
Unit 18	non–	not; without	nonsense
	pre–	before	preregister
	re–	back; again	revisit

Suffixes

What Is a Suffix?   (Unit 17)

A suffix can add to or change the meaning of a word.

A base word + a suffix = a new word with a new meaning.

	Suffix	Meanings	Examples
Unit 17	-ly	how something is done	quickly

Inflectional Suffixes

These endings are used at the end of words to change number, possession, comparison, and tense. They are inflectional suffixes:

For more about **Meaning Parts**, see page H19.

Number	Possession	Comparison	Tense
-s	-'s	-er	-ing
-es	-s'	-est	-ed, -en

Compound Words

For more about **Compound Words**, see Step 2, page H12.

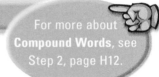

Understanding the Meaning of Compound Words (Unit 3)

- Often the last part of a compound word provides information about the meaning of the word.

  A **sandbag** is a type of **bag**.

- Sometimes the first part and the last part combine to form an entirely new meaning. (Unit 4)

  Both **hot** and **dog** are words, but **hotdog** is not a type of dog.

This is a **hot dog**,   but not a **hotdog**.

Three Kinds of Compound Words (Unit 13)

Compound words are written in three ways:

Closed: written without a space between the words

    downhill   The road to the school is all **downhill**.

    laptop   She took a **laptop** to the park.

Open: written with a space between the words

    jump shot Trina sank a **jump shot** to win the basketball game.

    base hit   He got a **base hit** in the ninth inning of the World Series game.

Hyphenated: written with a hyphen (-) between the words

    plug-in   We need a **plug-in** air freshener for the laundry room.

    left-hand Make a **left-hand** turn at the intersection

Expressions

Expressions are a common way of saying something. They are similar to idioms. Expressions do not have a specific form. They are simply a common way of saying something.

Expression	Meaning	Sample Sentence
all wet	mistaken; on the wrong track	Her idea about how to cook a turkey was *all wet*.
in the wind	likely to happen	The final vote is *in the wind*.
odds and ends	mixed things; leftovers; pieces	The desk drawer was filled with *odds and ends*.

An idiomatic expression, or **idiom**, is a common phrase that cannot be understood by the meanings of its separate words. The idiom can only be understood by knowing the meaning of the entire phrase. Its words cannot be changed, or the idiom loses its meaning.

Idiom	Meaning	Sample Sentence
be in hot water (Unit 13)	be in serious trouble with someone in authority	They *were in hot water* after breaking the store window.
make a drop in the bucket (Unit 13)	make an insufficient amount in comparison with what is required	The money I made during the summer *was a drop in the bucket* compared to what I needed to buy a car.
hold your horses (Unit 14)	slow down; wait a minute; be patient	"*Hold your horses!*" yelled the teacher as the children ran ahead to the playground.
pull the rug out from under you (Unit 14)	remove all support and help from you	Losing his job *pulled the rug out from under him.*
go to the dogs (Unit 15)	decline; come to a bad end	After the factory shut down, the area *went to the dogs.*
put the cart before the horse (Unit 15)	do things out of a logical order	Planning how to spend your first paycheck before starting the job is *putting the cart before the horse.*
be down-to-the-wire (Unit 16)	be almost out of time; at the very end	The student *was down to the wire* for turning in the exam before the bell rang.
take five (Unit 16)	take a short rest or break	The band decided to *take five* before continuing rehearsal.
see eye-to-eye (Unit 17)	be in agreement	The two coaches did not *see eye-to-eye* on the call.
saved by the bell (Unit 17)	rescued from a difficult situation just in time	I was about to say the wrong thing when I was *saved by the bell.* My cell phone rang.
make waves (Unit 18)	be uncalled for; improper; out of control	I don't want to *make waves*, but I need to report this to the police.
put your finger on something (Unit 18)	point out or describe exactly; find something	I can't *put my finger* on the reason why he didn't call me back.

Word Relationships

One way to understand the meaning of a word is to compare it to other words.

Word Relationships	What Is It?	Examples
antonyms	Words that have opposite meanings	top/bottom; expand/contract; connect/disconnect
synonyms	Words that have the same or similar meaning	connect/attach; finish/end
attributes	Words that tell more about other words such as size, parts, color, and function	atlas/maps; jacket/pocket; ribbon/red; cotton/soft; eggs/dozen
homophones	Words that sound the same but have different meanings	their/there; our/hour

Antonyms   (Unit 2)

Antonyms have opposite meanings.

Antonyms		
	above	below	
	dead	alive	

Synonyms (Unit 3)

Words that have the same or similar meaning are **synonyms**.

Synonyms				
	big	=	large	
	mad	=	angry	

Homophones (Unit 7)

homo = same
phone = sound

Homophones are words that sound the same but have different meanings. Context helps to clarify their meanings.

Homophones		
their	there	they're
belongs to them	names a place	contraction for they + are
_____ getting in_____car to get_____.		
__**They're**__ getting in____**their**_____car to get __**there**_____.		

Homophones		
Unit 14	fir/fur	your/you're
Unit 17	eye/I	lynx/links

Attributes (Unit 5)

Words can tell about objects' **attributes**, such as size, parts, color, and function.

Categories and attributes help us define words.

Size
A windmill is **tall**.

Parts
A windmill has a **base and blades**.

Shape
Windmills are **narrow**.

Function
Windmills **catch wind energy to make electric energy**.

Definition
A windmill is a machine with a **base and blades** that **catches wind energy to make electric energy**.

Water—In prehistoric times, long before Old English was spoken, there was a language that was the ancestor of English. In that ancestral language, Proto-Indo-European, the root for the word water was *wed-, "wet." With the suffix -r, it became *wod-r, and then *watar in Germanic. (Germanic was the next generation before Old English; the Germanic word, *otraz, is the source of our word otter, the water animal.) In Old English, it became wt, "wet," which became wet in modern English.

In modern English, it became water. The Greek word for water, hud-r, became the base for the English prefix hydro- (meaning water) and related words like hydrant. One thing we know for sure: water and all of its predecessors have always meant wet!

*unattested word or root

The thrid brid—Up until the 1500s, a common English word was brid. A brid was the name for any young animal with feathers. Today we call any animal with feathers a bird. The meaning of the word changed a little and so did its pronunciation. The name Bridget means "little bird."

The word third was once spelled and pronounced thrid. It sounded more like the word it came from: three.

Some other words with vowel + **r** also changed. Curd is the part of milk that coagulates (becomes solid) when it gets sour. We use curd to make cheese. The word curd was once pronounced crud. The word crud survived—but with a different meaning.

Hero—In Greek mythology and legend, a heros was a man who was endowed with great courage and strength, celebrated for his bold exploits, and favored by the gods. The female Greek mythological figure, Hero, was a priestess of Aphrodite, the goddess of love and beauty.

The contemporary definition has remained true to its Greek origins. A hero is a male or female individual who is admired for reasons of character, accomplishment, or feats of courage. It applies especially to those individuals who risk or sacrifice their lives for a noble purpose. The word heroine is often used to refer to the main female character of a literary work.

Athlete—Over 2500 years ago, the ancient Greeks held public competitions in horse racing, chariot racing, wrestling, running, javelin throwing, and other sports. They called the competitors *athletes* because they competed for prizes in the contests. The ancient Greek word for "prize" was *athlon*.

Even though the idea and the word *athlete* are very old, people in England did not use the word until the 1500s. That was the time that English began to borrow many Greek and Latin words. Before that time, English had no single word for someone who participated in sports.

Why y?—When **y** begins a word like *yet, yes,* or *yesterday*, it represents a consonant sound. Long ago, it was pronounced something like the **g** in *get*.

Sometimes, **y** at the end of a word represents the long / ī / sound, as in *my, spy,* or *sky*. Up until Shakespeare's time (1564–1616), these words were pronounced *me, spee,* and *skee*. They were spelled *mi, spi,* and *ski*. Other words, like *very, sorry,* and *merry*, were also spelled with **i**: *veri, sorri,* and *merri*.

As the use of the printing press increased, printers and writers needed to create spelling rules. One rule they made was this: No English word should end with the letter **i**. So they used the letter **y** to spell the ends of such words.

Continent—*The American Heritage Dictionary*, Fourth Edition (2002), defines *continent* as: "One of the principal land masses of the earth." These are usually regarded as Africa, Antarctica, Asia, Australia, Europe, North America, and South America. The prefix *con* means "with" or "together." The root *tenere* means "to hold." So, *continent* literally means "holding together."

Originally, it meant anything that is contained (the contents). Later, it meant any body of land contained within a boundary. By 1600, the word had obtained its modern meaning.

The origin of a word is often not the same as its meaning. Meanings can change over time, but a word's origin remains the same.

STEP 4

Grammar and Usage

When we understand words and their meanings, we can use them in sentences. Words have different jobs in sentences. Sometimes the same word can have different jobs depending on how it is used.

Nouns

> Nouns can be singular or plural. See **Meaning Parts** in Step 3, page H19.

What Is a Noun? (Units 1, 13)

A **noun** names a **person**, a **place**, a **thing**, or **idea**.

Person	Place	Thing	Idea
castaway	island	airplane	rescue

Common and Proper Nouns (Unit 3)

Nouns may be common or proper.

- A **common noun** names a *general* person, place, or thing.
- A **proper noun** names a *specific* person, place, or thing.

> Proper nouns begin with a capital letter.

Common Nouns	Proper Nouns
man	Mr. West
city	Boston
holiday	Independence Day
event	Olympics
historical period	Renaissance
days of the week	Saturday
months of the year	April

Concrete and Abstract Nouns   (Unit 3)

Nouns may be concrete or abstract.

- A **concrete noun** names a person, place, or thing that we *can see or touch*.

table	car	pencil	plate	teacher

- An **abstract noun** names an idea or a thought that we *cannot see or touch*.

love	Saturday	sports	democracy

Noun Forms

See also
Meaning Parts
Step 3, page H19.

Singular noun   (Unit 1)

Singular means "one of something."

Plural noun   (Unit 1)

Adding -**s** changes a singular noun to a plural noun.

Adding the suffix -**s** to a singular noun . . . . makes a plural noun.	
▪ lemon + s = lemons	▪ **Lemons** taste good in tea.
Adding the suffix -**es** to nouns ending in **s**, **z**, **x**, **ch**, **sh**, or **tch** . . . makes a plural noun.	
▪ dress + es = dresses ▪ fizz + es = fizzes ▪ box + es = boxes ▪ rich + es = riches ▪ dish + es = dishes ▪ match + es = matches	▪ Rose bought three new **dresses**. ▪ They drank cherry **fizzes**. ▪ The **boxes** were full of books. ▪ The safe contains many **riches**. ▪ The **dishes** fell to the floor. ▪ The wet **matches** would not light.

Singular Possessive Noun (Unit 2)

Adding **'s** to a noun shows possession.

Adding the suffix **'s** to a singular noun . . . . makes a possessive singular noun.	
■ Stan + 's = Stan's	■ **Stan's** stamps are at camp.
■ van + 's = van's	■ The **van's** mat is flat.
■ man + 's = man's	■ The **man's** cap is black.

Plural Possessive Noun (Unit 11)

Plural nouns show possession through the use of **s'**.

Adding the suffix **-s'** to nouns . . . . makes a possessive plural noun.	
■ boy + s' = boys'	■ **The boys' cards were missing.**
■ girl + s' = girls'	■ The **girls'** snacks are on the table.
■ dog + s' = dogs'	■ The **dogs'** bowls are empty.

Noun Functions

Nouns have several functions (jobs).

Noun as a Subject   (Unit 2)

Nouns can serve as the subjects of sentences.

The **subject**:

- is one of two main parts of English sentences.
- names the person, place, or thing that the sentence is about.
- usually comes before the verb.
- answers "Who (what) did it?"

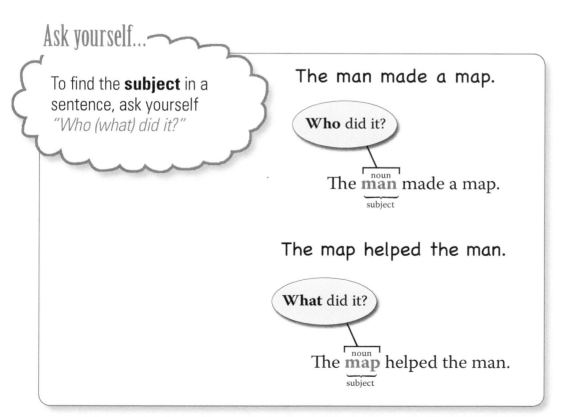

Ask yourself...

To find the **subject** in a sentence, ask yourself *"Who (what) did it?"*

The man made a map.

Who did it?

The **man** made a map.
noun
subject

The map helped the man.

What did it?

The **map** helped the man.
noun
subject

For **Compound Subjects**, go to Step 4, page H66.

Simple Subject   (Unit 8)

The noun that the sentence is about is the **simple subject** of the sentence.

> The blue egg fell from the nest.
>   simple subject

Complete Subject

The simple subject and all of its modifiers are called the **complete subject**.

> The blue egg fell from the nest.
>   complete subject

For **Compound Direct Objects**, go to Step 4, page H68.

Noun as a Direct Object   (Unit 3)

A noun can be the direct object—the person, place, or thing that receives the action.

The direct object:

- is in the predicate part of the sentence.
- answers "What did they (he, she, it) do it to?"

Ask yourself...

To find the **direct object**, ask yourself the following questions: *Who did it? What did it do?* Then ask: *Who did he do it to?*

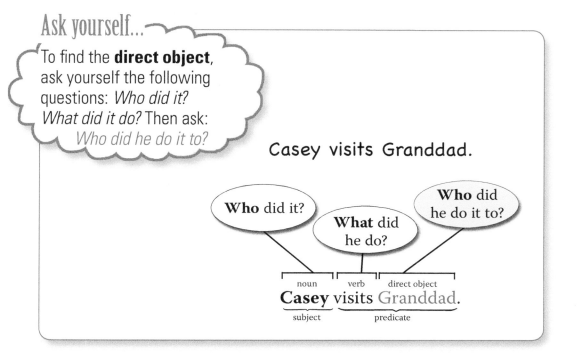

Casey visits Granddad.

Who did it?

What did he do?

Who did he do it to?

noun	verb	direct object
Casey	visits	Granddad.

subject — predicate

Noun as a Indirect Object   (Unit 17)

Ask yourself...

To find the **indirect object**, ask yourself the following questions: *Who did it? What did it do?* Then ask: *To whom did he do it to?*

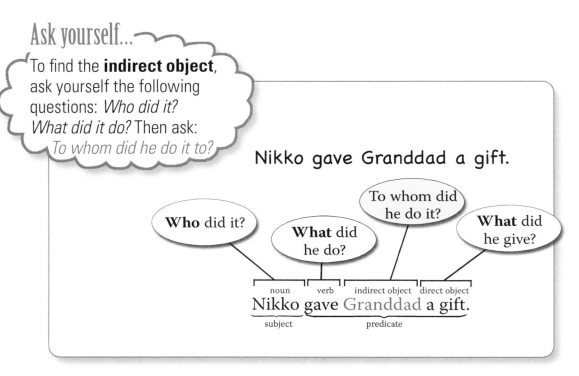

Nikko gave Granddad a gift.

Who did it?

What did he do?

To whom did he do it?

What did he give?

| noun | verb | indirect object | direct object |

Nikko gave Granddad a gift.

subject   predicate

Noun as an Object of the Preposition (Unit 4)

A noun can be the **object of the preposition** in a prepositional phrase.

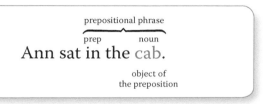

Noun as an Appositive (Unit 17)

A noun or noun phrase can also serve as an **appositive**.

An appositive:

- follows another noun or pronoun and explains, renames, or identifies it.
- may have one or more modifiers.
- is usually set off from the rest of the sentence with commas.

King Tut, an ancient **pharaoh**, was buried in a pyramid.
noun   appositive

Verbs

Verbs describe actions.   (Unit 1)

Every sentence has at least one verb or verb phrase.

We **can see** some actions:

jump   walk   clap

Some actions we **can't see**:

think   wish   dream

Verb Phrases   (Unit 9)

A phrase is a group of words that does the same job as a single word.

A verb phrase:

- does the job of a verb.
- conveys tense.
- has two parts: **helping verb** (HV) + **main verb** (MV).

Helping verbs	
am	were
is	will
was	

Verb Forms

Verbs describe action. Verbs also signal time. (Unit 4)

Tense Timeline (Unit 4)

A **tense timeline** shows three points in time—past, present, and future.

Yesterday	Today	Tomorrow
Past	Present	Future

Verb Forms • Present Tense (Unit 4)

If something is happening right now, it is the **present tense**.

Yesterday	Today	Tomorrow
Past	Present	Future

I sit.

He sits.

They sit.

For third person singular, add -s to the verb to signal present tense.

Person	Singular	Plural
First Person	I sit.	We sit.
Second Person	You sit.	You sit.
Third Person	He (She, It) sits.	They sit.

Verb Forms • Past Tense

If something happened yesterday, it is usually past time, or **past tense**.

Yesterday	Today	Tomorrow
Past	Present	Future

They helped.
They won.

Regular Verb Forms

Most English verbs form the past tense by adding -ed.
These are called **regular verbs.**

Person	Singular	Plural
First Person	I pass**ed**.	We pass**ed**.
Second Person	You pass**ed**.	You pass**ed**.
Third Person	He (She, It) pass**ed**.	They pass**ed**.

	Verb	Past Tense	Verb	Past Tense	Verb	Past Tense
Unit 13	adapt	adapted	connect	connected	select	selected
	assist	assisted	expand	expanded	suspend	suspended
	attach	attached	finish	finished	vanish	vanished
	collect	collected	punish	punished	visit	visited
Unit 16	admire	admired	complete	completed	devote	devoted
	erode	eroded				

Irregular Past Tense Verbs (Units 1-18)

Some verbs signal past time through **irregular verb forms**.

Irregular verb forms:

- Do not use **-ed**.
- Have different endings or spellings.

Verb	Past Tense	Verb	Past Tense	Verb	Past Tense
be (am, is, are)	was/were	go	went	shine	shone
become	became	have	had	sing	sang
begin	began	hit	hit	sit	sat
bend	bent	know	knew	spend	spent
bring	brought	lend	lent	spring	sprang
catch	caught	let	let	stand	stood
come	came	make	made	stick	stuck
cost	cost	mistake	mistook	string	strung
cut	cut	overcome	overcame	swim	swam
dive	dove	overtake	overtook	swing	swung
do	did	put	put	take	took
drink	drank	ride	rode	think	thought
drive	drove	ring	rang	thrust	thrust
fit	fit	rise	rose	wake	woke
fly	flew	run	ran	win	won
forget	forgot	say	said	withstand	withstood
forgive	forgave	sell	sold	write	wrote
get	got	send	sent		
give	gave	shake	shook		

Verb Forms • Future Tense

A verb phrase can convey future time. The verb **will** signals **future tense**.
Future verb phrase = **will** + **verb**

Yesterday	Today	Tomorrow
Past	Present	Future
		I will vote.
		They will ride.

Person	Singular	Plural
First Person	I will ride.	We will ride.
Second Person	You will ride.	You will ride.
Third Person	He (She, It) will ride.	They will ride.

	Verb	Future Tense	Verb	Future Tense	Verb	Future Tense
Unit 13	adapt	will adapt	connect	will connect	select	will select
	assist	will assist	expand	will expand	suspend	will suspend
	attach	will attach	finish	will finish	vanish	will vanish
	collect	will collect	punish	will punish	visit	will visit

Verb Forms • Progressive

The **progressive form** of verbs means ongoing action. The **-ing** ending on a main verb with a helping verb signals the tense and ongoing action.

Yesterday	Today	Tomorrow
Past	Present	Future
was/were + verb + **-ing**	am/is/are + verb + **-ing**	will be + verb +**-ing**
I was sitting.	I am sitting.	I will be sitting.

Present Progressive   (Unit 5)

Present progressive word phrases means that the action is ongoing in present time.

Person	Singular	Plural
First Person	I am sitting.	We are sitting.
Second Person	You are sitting.	You are sitting.
Third Person	He (She, It) is sitting.	They are sitting.

	Verb	Present Progressive	Verb	Present Progressive
Unit 15	begin	am/is/are beginning	open	am/is/are opening
	depress	am/is/are depressing	relax	am/is/are relaxing
	evolve	am/is/are evolving	restrict	am/is/are restricting

Past Progressive (Unit 9)

Past progressive verb phrases means that the action was ongoing in past time.

Person	Singular	Plural
First Person	I was passing.	We were passing.
Second Person	You were passing.	You were passing.
Third Person	He (She, It) was passing.	They were passing.

	Verb	Past Progressive	Verb	Past Progressive
Unit 9	brush	was/were brushing	hunt	was/were hunting
	cut	was/were cutting	instruct	was/were instructing
	duck	was/were ducking	rush	was/were rushing

Future Progressive (Unit 11)

Future progressive verb phrases mean that the action will be ongoing in future time.

Person	Singular	Plural
First Person	I will be passing.	We will be passing.
Second Person	You will be passing.	You will be passing.
Third Person	He (She, It) will be passing.	They will be passing.

	Verb	Future Progressive	Verb	Future Progressive
Unit 11	act	will be acting	skate	will be skating
	camp	will be camping	solve	will be solving
	drive	will be driving	stand	will be standing
	plant	will be planting	swim	will be swimming

Verb Forms for *Be, Have,* and *Do*

For more about **Subject/Verb Agreement**, see Step 4, page H62.

- **Be, have,** and **do** can be main verbs or helping verbs.

- Different forms of **be, have,** and **do** are used with different personal pronouns to achieve **subject–verb agreement** in sentences.

Be	Past		Present		Future	
Person	**Singular**	**Plural**	**Singular**	**Plural**	**Singular**	**Plural**
First Person	I **was**	we **were**	I **am**	we **are**	I **will be**	we **will be**
Second Person	you **were**	you **were**	you **are**	you **are**	you **will be**	you **will be**
Third Person	he, she, it **was**	they **were**	he, she, it **is**	they **are**	he, she, it **will be**	they **will be**

Main Verb: He <u>is</u> an inventor.
MV

Helping Verb: He <u>is inventing</u> a car.
HV   MV

Have	Past		Present		Future	
Person	**Singular**	**Plural**	**Singular**	**Plural**	**Singular**	**Plural**
First Person	I **had**	we **had**	I **have**	we **have**	I **will have**	we **will have**
Second Person	you **had**	you **had**	you **have**	you **have**	you **will have**	you **will have**
Third Person	he, she, it **had**	they **had**	he, she, it **has**	they **have**	he, she, it **will have**	they **will have**

Main Verb: I <u>have</u> a secret.
MV

Helping Verb: I <u>have kept</u> the secret.
HV   MV

Do	Past		Present		Future	
Person	Singular	Plural	Singular	Plural	Singular	Plural
First Person	I **did**	we **did**	I **do**	we **do**	I will **do**	we will **do**
Second Person	you **did**	you **did**	you **do**	you **do**	you will **do**	you will **do**
Third Person	he, she, it **did**	they **did**	he, she, it **does**	they **do**	he, she, it will **do**	they will **do**

Main Verb: I do my homework.
                MV

Helping Verb: I do rely on my friends.
               HV   MV

Verb Functions

Predicate (Unit 2)

The **predicate** is the second of the two main parts of a sentence.

The **predicate:**

- contains the main verb of the sentence.
- describes the action.
- usually comes after the subject.
- answers "What did they (he, she, it) do?"

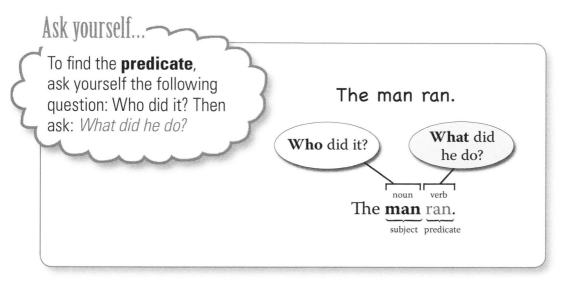

Ask yourself...

To find the **predicate**, ask yourself the following question: Who did it? Then ask: *What did he do?*

The man ran.

Who did it?

What did he do?

noun | verb

The **man** ran.

subject | predicate

Simple Predicate   (Unit 8)

For **Compound Predicates**, see Step 4, page H67.

The verb that tells what the subject did is the **simple predicate**.

The class clapped during the song.
simple predicate

Complete Predicate

The simple predicate and all its objects and modifiers are called the **complete predicate**.

The class clapped during the song.
complete predicate

Adjectives   (Unit 6)

Adjectives describe nouns.

They answer:

- *how many?*
- *what kind?*
- *which one?*

Some prepositional phrases act like adjectives because they can also tell about attributes of a noun. These phrases begin with a preposition and end with a noun.

The subject of the sentence can have adjectives and prepositional phrases that act as adjectives describing the person, place, or thing that the sentence is about.

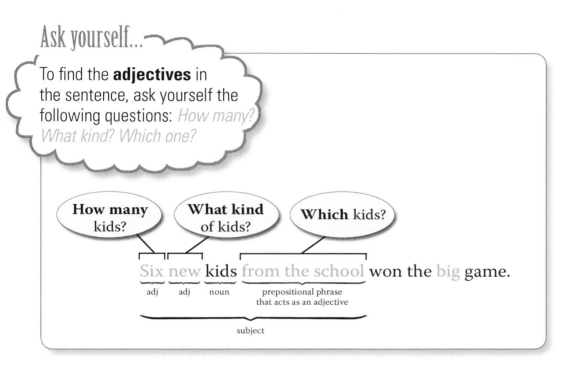

Ask yourself...

To find the **adjectives** in the sentence, ask yourself the following questions: *How many? What kind? Which one?*

How many kids?　　**What kind** of kids?　　**Which** kids?

Six new kids from the school won the big game.

adj　adj　noun　prepositional phrase that acts as an adjective

subject

Adjectives can also describe other nouns in the sentence.

　　What kind of game? big

Types of Adjectives (Unit 16)

- Single words　　　　　The **red** apples fell from the tree.
- Prepositional phrases　The truck, **with the metallic finish**, was cool.
- Present participles　　The **eroding** hillside put the homes in danger.
- Past participles　　　The **injured** athlete limped.

Participial Phrases Acting as Adjectives (Unit 16)

A participle can introduce a **participial phrase**.

- The entire phrase acts as an adjective to modify a noun.
- A participial phrase can come before or after the noun it modifies.
- In a participial phrase, the first word is the participle.
- Commas are used to set off a participial phrase.

Answers the question
Which one?

The athlete, **injured** by his fall, used crutches.

participial phrase

Adjectives with Conjunctions (Unit 16)

Two adjectives of the same kind that modify the same noun are joined by a conjunction: **and, or,** or **but**.

and: The **dark** and **stormy** night frightened me.

or: **Hot** or **cold** meals were choices on the menu.

but: The **tired** but **determined** athlete finished the game.

Adjectives for Comparison   (Unit 14)

Adjective endings signal a comparison between nouns or pronouns.

Comparative: Add **-er** to compare two nouns or pronouns using the word **than**.

Superlative: Add **-est** to compare three or more nouns or pronouns.

Adjective: He was **short.**

Comparative: He was **shorter** than his brother.

Superlative: He was the **shortest** member of the band.

Adverbs (Unit 6)

For more about **Prepositions**, see Step 4, page H56.

Adverbs are words that describe verbs.

Adverbs and prepositional phrases that act as adverbs tell:

- *when?*
- *where?*
- *how?*

Some prepositional phrases act like adverbs. Prepositional phrases begin with a preposition and end with a noun. **On Monday**, **in the house**, **with a bang**, and **to the class** are prepositional phrases.

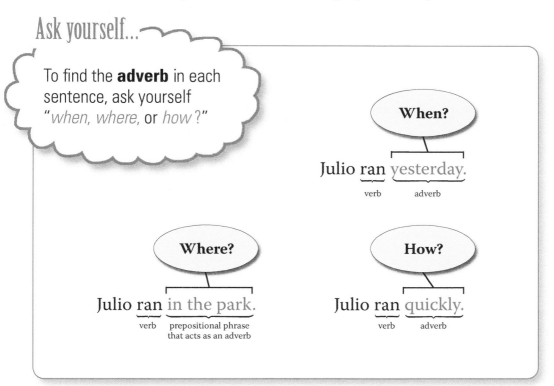

Ask yourself...

To find the **adverb** in each sentence, ask yourself "*when, where,* or *how* ?"

When?

Julio ran yesterday.
verb   adverb

Where?

Julio ran in the park.
verb   prepositional phrase
       that acts as an adverb

How?

Julio ran quickly.
verb   adverb

Prepositions   (Unit 4)

A **preposition** is a function word that begins a prepositional phrase.

A **prepositional phrase** is a group of words that begins with a preposition and ends with a noun or pronoun that is the **object of the preposition**.

Prepositions show the position or relationship between the noun or pronoun and some other word in the sentence.

In this sentence, **in** (the preposition) shows a relationship between **van** (the object of the preposition) and **Pam** (the subject of the sentence).

Some of the **Unit Words** and **Essential Words** in Units 1–12 are prepositional: **in, as, at, from, of, past, to, into, for.**

Prepositions Show Relationship   (Unit 6)

Most prepositions show a position in

- space (inside, over, under)

- time (during, since, until)

- space and time (after, from, through)

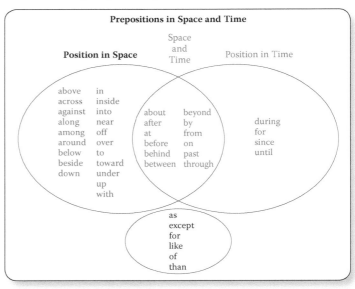

Pronouns

Pronouns are function words that are used in place of nouns. Different groups of pronouns have different functions.

Subject (Nominative) Pronouns (Unit 4)

Nominative pronouns take the place of the subject in a sentence.

> **I**, **you**, **he**, **she**, **it**, **we**, **you**, and **they** are nominative pronouns.

Jack sat in a cab.

He sat in a **cab**.

(**He** replaces **Jack** in the sentence.)

Subject Pronouns		
Person	**Singular**	**Plural**
First Person	I	we
Second Person	you	you
Third Person	he, she, it	they

Object Pronouns   (Unit 6)

Some pronouns take the place of **objects**. They are called **object pronouns**.

> **Me, you, him, her, it, us**, and **them** are object pronouns.

Carla is handing the plant to **Sally**.

Carla is handing the plant to **her**.

(**Her** replaces **Sally** in the sentence.)

Object Pronouns		
Person	**Singular**	**Plural**
First Person	me	us
Second Person	you	you
Third Person	him, her, it	them

Possessive Pronouns   (Unit 7)

These pronouns show ownership (possession). They are called **possessive pronouns**.

my	mine	your	yours	our	ours
his	her	hers	its	their	theirs

Sometimes a possessive pronoun functions as an adjective.

> **My desk** is a mess.

Or, sometimes the possessive pronoun replaces the noun.

> **Mine** is a mess.

Conjunctions

See also
Compound Subjects,
page H66, and
Compound Predicates,
page H67.

Conjunctions join words, phrases, or clauses in a sentence. They also join sentences.

Coordinating Conjunctions (Unit 7)

Coordinating conjunctions are the most common type of conjunction. They connect words that have the same function. Two common coordinating conjunctions are **and** and **but**.

- The conjunction **and** relates two similar ideas.

> Ellen rested. Her friends rested.
> Ellen **and** her friends rested.
>
> compound subject

- The conjunction **but** signals contrasting ideas.

> The hurricane hit land. The people escaped.
> The hurricane hit land, **but** the people escaped.
>
> compound sentence

- The conjunction **or** signals an alternative or choice.

> An artist can sculpt stone. An artist can carve stone.
> An artist can carve **or** sculpt stone.
>
> compound predicate

The predicates, *sculpt* and *carve*, are joined by the conjunction **or** to build a compound predicate.

Multiple Functions of Words

Words in Context

In English, words have different functions (jobs).   (Unit 3)
> **Nouns** are words that name people, places, or things.
> **Verbs** are words that describe action.
> **Adjectives** describe nouns.   (Unit 6)

Sometimes the same word can have multiple functions. The context helps determine the function of the word.

For example, the word **dig** can be a noun or a verb. **Dig** can also be an adjective.

Noun	Verb	Adjective

The **dig** was a success in Africa.	Scientists **dig** to find bones.	The scientists went to the **dig** site.

Syllable Stress   (Unit 13)

Sometimes words can look the same but be pronounced two different ways by shifting the syllable stress. Shifting the stress changes the meaning and function of the word.

Noun	Verb
	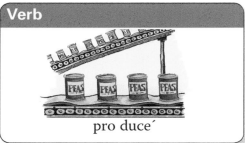
pro´ duce	pro duce´

Sentences

What Is a Sentence? (Unit 1)

A **sentence** conveys a complete thought by answering two questions:

- Who (What) did it?
- What did they (he, she, it) do?

We put nouns and verbs together to make **sentences**.

Simple Sentences (Unit 2)

A **simple sentence** has one subject and one predicate.

- The subject answers: "Who (What) did it?"
- The verb in the predicate answers: "What did they (he, she, it) do?"

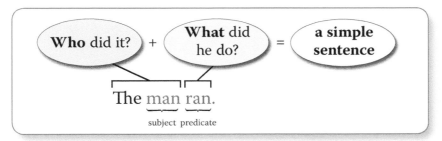

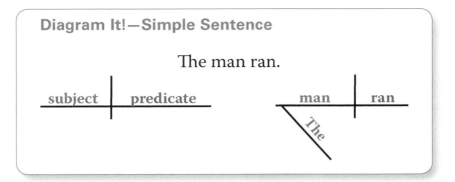

Subject/Verb Agreement (Unit 7)

The sentence subject and predicate verb must agree in number.

Singular verbs are used with singular subjects, and plural verbs are used with plural subjects.

My <u>sister</u> <u>chats</u> online with her friends.
    singular   singular
    subject   verb

My <u>brothers</u> <u>play</u> games on the Internet.
   plural subject plural verb

Don't be confused by the -s.

A singular subject (without adding -s) agrees with a singular verb (with an -s).

My brother chats.
    singular   singular
    subject   verb

A plural subject with an -s agrees with a plural verb (without an -s).

My brothers chat.
   plural subject plural verb

Sentence Expansion

For more about **Noun as a Direct Object**, see Step 4, page H39.

Predicate Expansion with Direct Object   (Unit 3)

You can expand the predicate in a sentence by adding a direct object.

Diagram It!—Direct Object

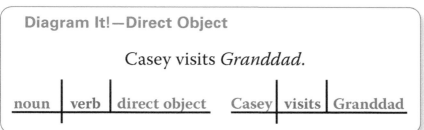

Predicate Expansion with Adverbs   (Unit 4)

See also **Writing Sentences**, Step 6, page H86, **Adverbs**, Step 4, page H55.

You can expand the predicate in a sentence by adding adverbs or prepositional phrases that act like adverbs.

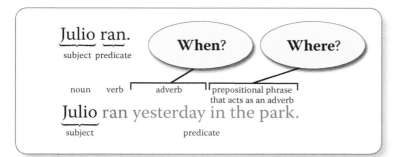

Moving Adverbs in a Sentence (Unit 5)

Words or phrases that answer the questions "when, where, or how" can be moved within the sentence.

Julio ran in the park yesterday.

noun   verb   prepositional phrase   adverb
                that acts as an adverb

Yesterday, Julio ran in the park.

adverb   noun   verb   prepositional phrase
                                  that acts as an adverb

Diagram It!—Adverbs

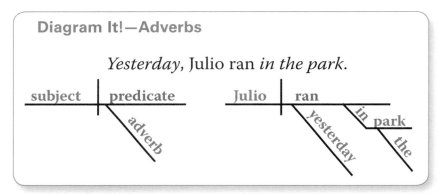

Yesterday, Julio ran *in the park*.

subject | predicate   Julio | ran

adverb   yesterday   in park
                                     the

Subject Expansion with Adjectives (Unit 6)

You can expand the subject of a sentence by adding adjectives.

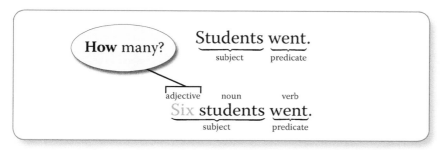

Diagram It!—Adjectives

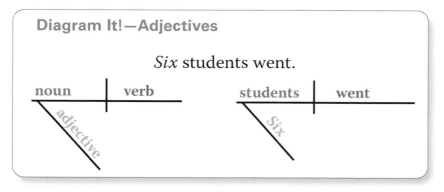

Compound Sentence Parts

> For more about **Coordinating Conjunctions**, see Step 4, page H59.

Compound Subject (Unit 7)

A **compound subject** is two subjects joined by a **conjunction**.

Ellen rested. Her friends rested.
 subject   subject

Ellen **and** her friends rested.
         compound subject

Diagram It!—Compound Subject

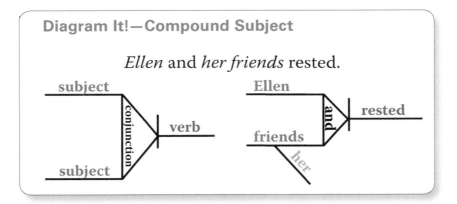

Ellen and her friends rested.

Compound subjects require plural verbs.

Compound subjects joined by **and** are plural subjects, since they name more than one person, place, or thing.

Ezra and Fred send emails.
 compound subject   plural verb

Compound Predicate   (Unit 8)

A **compound predicate** is two simple predicates joined by a **conjunction**.

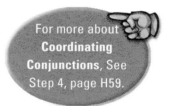

For more about **Coordinating Conjunctions**, See Step 4, page H59.

> The class *sang*. The class *clapped*.
>   predicate   predicate
>
> The class *sang and clapped*.
>   compound predicate

The predicates, *sang* and *clapped*, are joined by the conjunction **and** to build a compound predicate.

Diagram It!—Compound Predicate

The class *sang* and *clapped*.

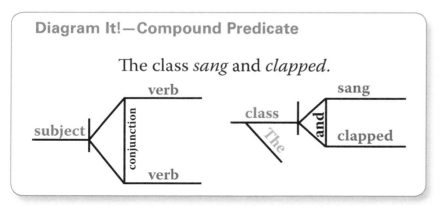

Compound Direct Object   (Unit 9)

A **compound direct object** is two direct objects joined by a **conjunction**.

For more about **Coordinating Conjunctions**, see Step 4, page H59.

> The bugs infest *crops*. The bugs infest *animals*.
>   direct object   direct object
>
> The bugs infest *crops* **and** *animals*.
>   compound direct object

The direct objects, *crops* and *animals,* are joined by the conjunction **and** to build a compound direct object.

Diagram It!—Direct Objects

The bugs infest *crops* and *animals.*

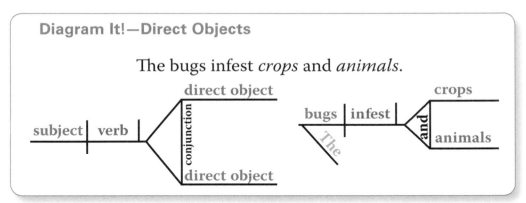

Compound Sentence   (Unit 10)

A **compound sentence** is two sentences joined by a conjunction.

- The **conjunction** *and*

   The word **and** is a conjunction that relates two similar ideas.

Julio walked.

Dan ran.

Julio walked **and** Dan ran.

In this **compound sentence**, *Julio walked* and *Dan ran* are joined by the conjunction **and**.

Diagram It!—Compound Sentences

Julio walked and *Dan ran.*

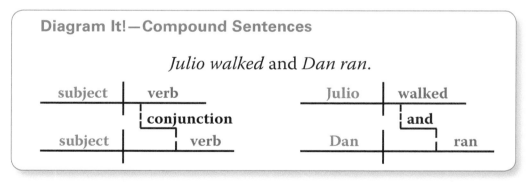

Mechanics

Apostrophes	
An apostrophe is used with the letter <u>s</u> to show possession. (Unit 2)	Tyrone's map the whales' fins
An apostrophe shows where letters are left out in a contraction. (Unit 7)	I am — I'm

Commas	
Phrases: Commas can be used to set off phrases at the beginning of sentences. (Unit 5)	At the end of the song, Juan clapped.
Adjectives of the same kind: A comma can be used to separate adjectives of the same kind. (Unit 16)	The big, black cat sat.
Appositives: Commas are usually used to separate the appositive and its modifiers from the rest of the sentence. (Unit 17)	Sam, my pet cat, is black.
In dates: A comma separates the day from the year in a date. (Unit 16)	December 1, 2009
In addresses: A comma separates the city from the state in an address. (Unit 16)	Denver, CO 80020
In letters: A comma is often used after the greeting and the closing.	Dear Uncle Tran, Thank you,

Sentence Signals	
Capital letters are used at the beginning of all sentences. (Unit 1)	The cat sat.
Punctuation marks—**periods, question marks,** and **exclamation points**—can be used to end a sentence. (Unit 1)	Where did it sit? It sat on my lap!

STEP 5

Listening and Reading Comprehension

Vocabulary Strategies

The context provides clues to figure out the meaning of vocabulary words you don't know. Here are five **Use the Clues** vocabulary strategies:

---

❶ Meaning Cues:

Look for meaning cue words. They provide cues to the definition of a word in context. Meaning cue words include *is/are, it means, which stands for, can be defined as*, and more.

The <u>Internet</u> is <u>a network of computers</u>.

Punctuation marks, including commas and dashes, can also set off the meaning of a word.

The <u>Internet</u>, <u>a network of computers</u>, transmits information quickly.

---

❷ Substitutions:

Look for words or phrases that rename nouns. Substitutions are often synonyms or distinctive features of the noun.

The Internet <u>links</u>, or <u>connects</u>, computers around the world.

The word **connects** renames the word **links**.

---

❸ Pronoun Referents:

Use pronouns to identify meaning clues to define unknown vocabulary words in context.

Oliver Zompro is an <u>entomologist</u>.

He is <u>a scientist who studies insects</u>.

❹ Context Cues:

Look for cues to the meaning of an unfamiliar word. Add up the cues to define the word.

It is a movie <u>review</u>. The writer <u>gives an opinion</u> about a new movie.

❺ Visual Information:

Use pictures, charts, and other visual information that accompanies the text to understand the meaning of new vocabulary words.

Also, the Web is organized in a special way. It is made up of home pages. A <u>home page</u> is usually the <u>first page</u> you see <u>on a Web site</u>.

This first page on the NASA Web site is its home page.

Types of Text

Reading selections, also called text, come in different types. There are two main categories of text: **expository** and **narrative**. All types of writing have a purpose. Some text may have more than one purpose.

Type of Text	Author's Purpose	Media (print or online)
expository text informational nonfiction	to inform, to describe, to persuade, to entertain	textbooks encyclopedias newspapers magazines Web sites
narrative text tells a story	to describe an event or experience; to teach us something about our lives; to entertain	novels anthologies magazines Web sites

Types of Imaginative Literature

There are different types of narrative text called imaginative literature. Each type is defined by its characters, setting, and purpose.

Type	Characters	Setting	Purpose
science fiction	fantastic or futuristic people or other things	fantastic or futuristic place and time	comments on current society; describes future science and technology
folktale	fictional, everyday people	imagined place and time, often associated with a group of people or culture	makes sense of the world and human existence through stories passed down from one generation to another
legend	a particular person	a particular time and place in history, often based on real events	explains, often using exaggeration, how something came about in history
myth	supernatural beings and superheroes	a time before recorded history	describes how the world, people, and creatures came to be the way they are

Text Features (Unit 1)

Writers of **informational text**—also called **nonfiction**—use text features to provide clues to the topic and other important information.

Title–indicates the topic of the informational text

Heading–names the topics of each subsection of the informational text

Pictures and Captions–provide visual and textual information that supports or adds to the information in the text

Margin Information–defines vocabulary or offers short explanations or illustrations of some part of the text

Text Features of a Newspaper

Every newspaper, whether published in print or online, is divided into **sections**.

Print Newspaper

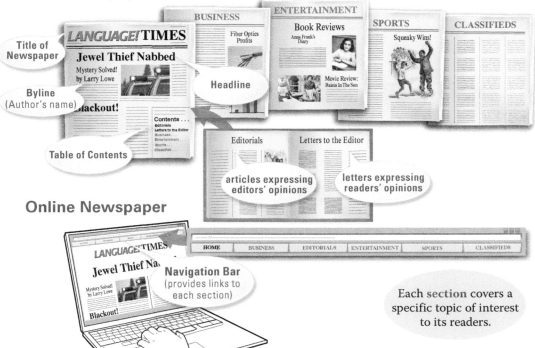

Title of Newspaper

Byline (Author's name)

Table of Contents

BUSINESS

Fiber Optics Profits

ENTERTAINMENT

Book Reviews

Anne Frank's Diary

Movie Review: Raisin In The Sun

SPORTS

Squeaky Wins!

CLASSIFIEDS

LANGUAGE! TIMES

Jewel Thief Nabbed

Mystery Solved! by Larry Lowe

Blackout!

Headline

Contents . . .
Editorials
Letters to the Editor
Business
Entertainment
Sports
Classified

Editorials

Letters to the Editor

articles expressing editors' opinions

letters expressing readers' opinions

Online Newspaper

LANGUAGE! TIMES

Jewel Thief Na...

Mystery Solved! by Larry Lowe

Blackout!

HOME BUSINESS EDITORIALS ENTERTAINMENT SPORTS CLASSIFIEDS

Navigation Bar (provides links to each section)

Each **section** covers a specific topic of interest to its readers.

Text Features of a Play

Writers of plays use specific text features to guide the people who direct and act in the play.

❶ **Preface:** sets up the theme of the play

❷ **List of characters:** names who is in the play

❸ **Set:** tells how the stage will look for each section of the play

❹ **Props:** tell what furniture or other items are needed on the sets

❺ **Costumes:** tell what the actors will wear

❻ **Bold names:** tell who performs the dialog or actions following each name

❼ **Parenthetical references:**

■ are not read aloud

■ tell what happens before the actors speak, or tell about a change in the stage set

■ tell the actors what to do, how to do it, or how to say the words

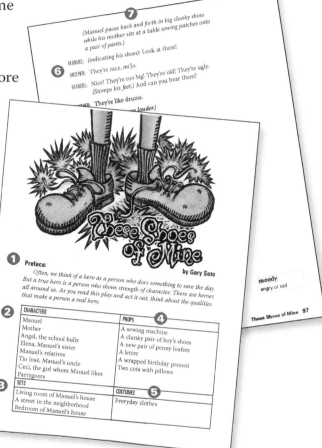

❼ (Manuel paces back and forth in big clunky shoes while his mother sits at a table sewing patches onto a pair of pants.)

MANUEL: (indicating his shoes): Look at them!

❻ MOTHER: They're nice, mi'jo.

MANUEL: Nice! They're too big! They're old! They're ugly. (Stomps his feet.) And can you hear them?

_____ They're like drums.

_____ _____ louder.)

❶ Preface:
Often, we think of a hero as a person who does something to save the day. But a true hero is a person who shows strength of character. There are heroes all around us. As you read this play and act it out, think about the qualities that make a person a real hero.

by Gary Soto

These Shoes of Mine

moody
angry or sad

These Shoes of Mine 97

❷

CHARACTERS	PROPS ❹
Manuel	A sewing machine
Mother	A clunky pair of boy's shoes
Angel, the school bully	A new pair of penny loafers
Elena, Manuel's sister	A letter
Manuel's relatives	A wrapped birthday present
Tío José, Manuel's uncle	Two cots with pillows
Ceci, the girl whom Manuel likes	
Partygoers	

❸

SETS	COSTUMES ❺
Living room of Manuel's house	Everyday clothes
A street in the neighborhood	
Bedroom of Manuel's house	

Comprehension Questions

How to Answer Open-Ended Questions   (Unit 1)

Use these steps to answer a short-answer question
with a complete sentence:

1. Look for a signal word to know what the question is asking.
2. Find information in the text to answer the question.
3. Plan and write the answer.
4. Check the answer.

Example question:

**Look for the
signal word**

Are <u>all</u> bats bug-eaters?

No, some bats eat
fruits or flowers.

**Find answer
in text**

mammals
warm-blooded
animals

Flying and Feeding
Bats can fly. They are the only ma ̶ ̶
can fly. Bats use wings to fly. Skin conn ̶
hands, and ankles of the bat. The skin m ̶
Wings are important to a bat. They n ̶ ̶ ̶m to fly
5 and find food.
Flying takes lots of energy, s ̶ ̶ bats eat a lot. Bats
eat half their weight each da ̶ ̶. Bats eat a lot of things.
Some eat fruits and flowers. Some eat frogs and fish.
Some eat bugs. They eat mosquitoes and flies. They eat
10 moths and even termites!

sonar
ways to locate
objects using
sound; echolocation

Super Sonar
Did you think bats were blind? They are not. They
can see. Some even have good vision. Bats fly at night.
How do they find their way in the dark? Bats can "see"
with sound. They use sonar. Bats can "hear" where
15 they are. Bats cry out. We can't hear these sounds. Bats
find their way by listening to the echoes. Bats use other

24 Unit 1 • Going to Bat

Signal words help you know how to answer the question.

See page H78
for more
signal words.

Signal words	How to answer
If the question asks...	Your answer must include...
Is/are	A "yes" or a "no"
Who	Information about a person or group
Do	A "yes" or a "no"
What	An action or name of a thing
When	A specific time, date, or event
Why	A reason or explanation
Where	A general location or specific place
How	The way something is done

How to Answer Multiple-Choice Questions   (Unit 3)

Use these steps to answer multiple-choice questions:

1 Read carefully for signal words.

2 Look back in the text for information.

3 Try to eliminate distracter items.

Example question:

The Touareg are

A a tribe of people who live in Niger.

B special dinosaurs in Africa.

C big animals that live in Africa.

D scientists who work in Niger.

Africa Digs

Dr. Paul Sereno digs dinosaur bones. He gets a thrill when he digs up the bones of dinosaurs who lived thousands of years ago. In 1997, Dr. Sereno led a dig to **Niger**, Africa. He took 18 scientists with him.
5   The Touareg tribe helped his team look for bones. The Touareg people live in Niger. They know their **desert** land best. They know where to look for bones.

The dig was a success. Dr. Sereno's team had a fantastic find. They found a new dinosaur. The
10 Touareg told them a legend about a very big animal. They call it *Jobar*. The Touareg showed them where to look for the bones. The scientists named the dinosaur *Jobaria*. It means giant. How did they dig up the *Jobaria*? Let's follow the dig step by step.

Niger
a country of west Africa

desert
a dry place with little rainfall

Step 1: We've Got One!
15   The Touareg lead the team to a special place. Bones stick out of desert rock. The Touareg tell the scientists their legend. These bones belong to the giant beast, *Jobar.*

Step 2: Digging In
20   The dig begins. They use hammers, chisels, and drills. They work for 10 weeks. A huge skeleton **emerges**. It has been buried for 135 million years! Fifteen tons of rock cover it. The team carefully
25 takes the bones from the rock.

emerges
comes out of; appears

The Touareg tribe helped the team.

80 Unit 3 • **Dig It!**

Signal Words

Signal words	How to answer
If the question asks...	Your answer must include...
state	say or write specific information
recognize	use information you have learned
name	label specific information
locate	find specific information or show the position of something
list	state a series of names, ideas, or events
choose	make choices from specific information
describe	state detailed information about an idea or concept
tell	say or write specific information
define	tell the meaning
predict	use known information to say what might happen in the future
conclude	put information together to reach an understanding about something
illustrate	present an example or explanation in pictures or words
identify	give the name of something or select information from the text
explain	express understanding of an idea or concept
tell when	state a specific time or a period of time
discuss	present detailed information or examine a subject
paraphrase	restate information in different words to clarify meaning
contrast	state the differences between two or more ideas or concepts
categorize	create groups and place information into those groups based on certain shared characteristics
compare	state the similarities between two or more ideas or concepts
sort	place or separate into groups
match	put together or connect things that are alike or similar
classify	arrange or organize information into groups with similar characteristics

Remember Units 7–8 — applies to rows from *state* through *describe*.

Understand Units 9–12 — applies to rows from *tell* through *classify*.

	Signal words	How to answer
	If the question asks...	**Your answer must include...**
Apply Units 13–15	infer	provide a logical conclusion using information or evidence
Apply Units 13–15	generalize	draw a conclusion based on presented information
Apply Units 13–15	show	demonstrate an understanding of information
Apply Units 13–15	use	apply a procedure
Analyze Units 16–18	select	choose from among alternatives
Analyze Units 16–18	distinguish	find differences that set one thing apart from another
Analyze Units 16–18	organize	arrange in a systematic pattern
Analyze Units 16–18	outline	arrange information into a systematic pattern of main ideas and supporting details

Listening Tips

- Demonstrate active listening by:
    - Asking thoughtful questions and responding to relevant questions
    - Identifying main ideas of an informational presentation
    - Retelling the plot of a story
    - Taking notes
- Distinguish between fact and opinion (from a presentation or a media source).
- Evaluate the accuracy of information (from a presentation or a media source).
- Determine the purpose for listening (to obtain information, to solve problems, for enjoyment).

Structure of Text   (Unit 1)

Well-written text has organization. Informational text is organized using main ideas and supporting details.

The main idea tells what the paragraph is about.
The supporting details give more specific information about the main idea.

Ask yourself...

Which sentence tells what all of the sentences are about?

Ask yourself...

Which sentences support the main idea?

The bat can fly. It is the only mammal that can fly. Bats use wings to fly. Skin connects parts of the bat. It joins its hands, arms, and ankles. The skin makes wings. Bats fly to look for food. They fly at night. They need their wings to eat.
    Bats eat a lot. Bats eat half their weight each day! Food makes energy. Flying takes energy. Bats eat a lot of things. Some eat fruits. Some eat flowers. Some eat frogs and fish. Some eat lizards. Some eat bugs. They eat mosquitoes. They eat flies. They eat moths. They even eat termites!

STEP 6

Speaking and Writing

Structure of Writing (Unit 1)

Graphic organizers can show the structure of text. The **Blueprint for Writing** is a graphic organizer that shows the relationship between the main ideas (walls) and supporting details (pictures on the walls).

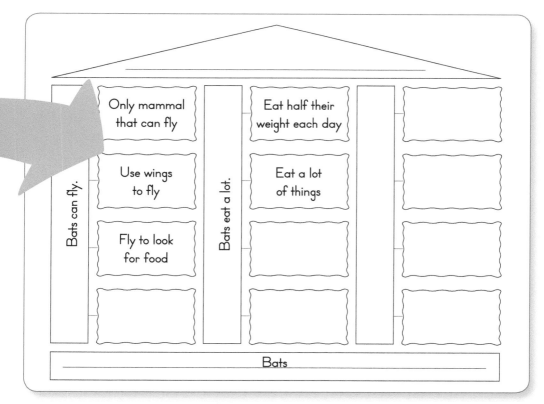

Summary Writing

Simple Summary (Unit 1)

A summary tells the most important ideas from a text selection.
A **simple summary** uses only the main ideas (walls).

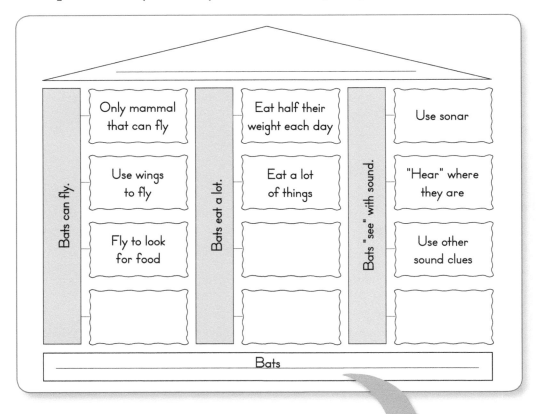

Bats can fly.

Only mammal that can fly

Use wings to fly

Fly to look for food

Bats eat a lot.

Eat half their weight each day

Eat a lot of things

Bats "see" with sound.

Use sonar

"Hear" where they are

Use other sound clues

Bats

"Batty About Bats!" explains facts about bats. Bats can fly. They eat a lot. Bats "see" with sound.

Expanded Summary   (Unit 1)

Sometimes a summary has more detail. An **expanded summary**
uses main ideas (walls) and some supporting details (pictures).

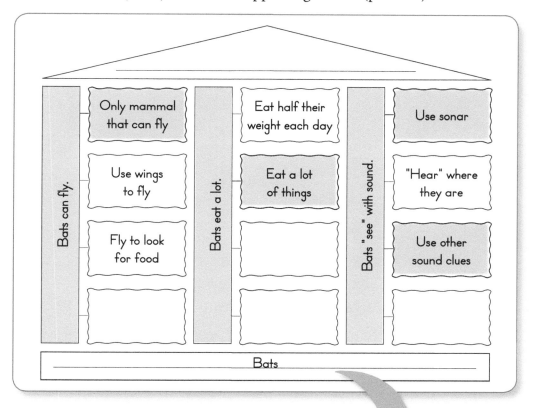

Bats can fly.

Only mammal that can fly	Eat half their weight each day	Use sonar
Use wings to fly	Eat a lot of things	"Hear" where they are
Fly to look for food		Use other sound clues

Bats eat a lot.

Bats "see" with sound.

Bats

   "Batty About Bats!" explains facts about
bats. Bats can fly. They are the only mammals
that fly. Bats eat a lot of things each day. Bats
"see" with sonar and other sound clues.

Graphic organizers and outlines help organize information to plan to write.

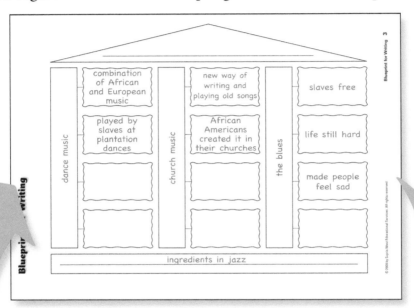

Both graphic organizers can organize the same information.

Informal (Two-Column) Outline (Unit 5)

Topic: ingredients in jazz

☆ dance music	—combination of African and European music —played by slaves at plantation dances
☆ church music	—new way of writing and playing old songs —African Americans created it in their churches
☆ the blues	—slaves free —life still hard —made people feel sad

Speaking Tips

Organization and Content

- Stay on topic.
- Organize content in a logical sequence.
- Provide a beginning, middle and end.
- Emphasize important points and details that support ideas.
- Use examples to clarify meaning.
- Use specific vocabulary.

Delivery

- Speak clearly and at an appropriate pace.
- Use volume, pitch, and phrasing to enhance meaning.
- Make eye contact with listener.
- Use correct grammar.
- Use props, visuals, or media to make points.

Sentences are pictures in words. To write a **Masterpiece Sentence** follow these steps:

Stage 1: Prepare Your Canvas (Unit 1)

Write the base sentence. Answer these questions:

Who (what) did it?	What did they (he, she, it) do?
the man	ran

Stage 2: Paint Your Predicate (Unit 3)

Expand the predicate. Use these questions:

When?	Where?	How?
during the race	on the track	fast

the **man ran** fast on the track during the race

Stage 3: Move the Predicate Painters (Unit 5)

Vary the sentence. Move the predicate painters. Notice the picture *doesn't* change!

during the race the **man ran** fast on the track

Stage 4: Paint Your Subject   (Unit 6)

Expand the subject. Use these questions:

How many?	Which are?	What kind?
	in the red	
	shirt	

during the race the **man** in the red
shirt **ran** fast on the track

Stage 5: Paint Your Words

Improve your words. Be descriptive.

During the race the **man** in the
red shirt ran fast on the track .

During the last lap of the race the
track star wearing his team's red
shirt **sprinted** around the track as fans cheered.

Stage 6: Finishing Touches

Check spelling and punctuation.

During the last lap of the race, the track star,
wearing his team's red shirt, sprinted around the
track as fans cheered.

Writing Paragraphs

Parts of a Paragraph

A paragraph is a group of sentences. Each sentence in the paragraph has a specific job.

Indent paragraphs

The Benefits of Exercise

Regular exercise benefits people's health in two important ways. (One) benefit is that exercise improves people's physical health. **It makes the heart, lungs, bones, and muscles stronger and keeps people at a healthy weight.** Exercise is (also) good for the mind. **It makes people feel better about themselves and calms them down when they are angry or stressed.** When people regularly do physical activities they enjoy, their bodies and minds stay fit, happy, and healthy.

The **Topic Sentence** tells what the paragraph is about.

Supporting Details give facts or reasons about the topic.

(Transition words) link one supporting detail to the next.

E's add interest for the reader. E's are:
- **explanations**
- **examples**
- **evidence**

The **conclusion** ties the parts together. Often it restates the topic.

Topic Sentence

The **topic sentence** in a paragraph states the topic of the paragraph. It is often the first sentence.

There are many types of topic sentences. Here are three of them:

IVF Topic Sentence   (Unit 1)

An **IVF topic sentence** has three parts. It is a good type of topic sentence for a summary paragraph.

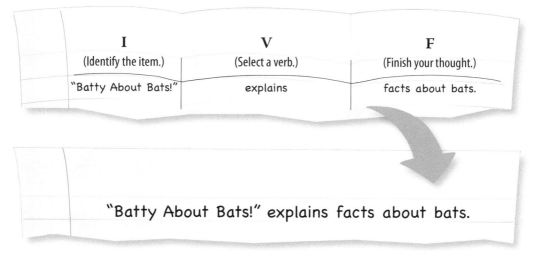

I	V	F
(Identify the item.)	(Select a verb.)	(Finish your thought.)
"Batty About Bats!"	explains	facts about bats.

"Batty About Bats!" explains facts about bats.

Verb Reference List for Summaries

explains	compares	tells	provides	presents
describes	gives	shows	lists	teaches

Number Topic Sentence (Unit 3)

A **Number topic sentence** includes the topic and a number word. The **topic** tells what the whole paragraph will be about. The **number** tells how many supporting details to include about the topic.

Three problems led to the Big Dig project in Boston.

Boston leaders identified **several** traffic problems.

Number Words

two	three	four	several	some
a number of	a few	a couple	many	

 Don't start a topic sentence with **there are**.

Start with:

    Who: *People in Boston* had several traffic problems.

    What: *Several traffic problems* led to the Big Dig project.

    When: *After years of traffic troubles,* three issues led to the Big Dig project.

    Where: *In Boston,* a number of traffic problems led to the Big Dig.

Turn Prompt Topic Sentence   (Unit 4)

A **Turn Prompt topic sentence** works well to answer a specific question. Part of the prompt becomes part of the topic sentence. Direction words, such as **explains**, tell you what you need to do.

Prompt:

Write a paragraph that <u>explains</u> how maps are made.

Topic sentence:

Maps are made in several layers.

Supporting Details

Supporting Details   (Unit 3)

Supporting details are sentences that provide **facts** or **reasons** to support a topic sentence.

Transition words link supporting details within a paragraph. Transition words and phrases also link ideas between paragraphs.

Transition Sets

First of all ▶	The next ▶	Another
One ▶	Also	
One ▶	Another ▶	Finally
One example ▶	Another example	
The first ▶	The second ▶	Last
To begin ▶	However	

E's Are Elaborations

The E's (Unit 5)

The E's are sentences that support the topic and supporting details in a paragraph.

Here are three kinds of E's. There are more!

*E*xamples give **illustrations**.

> With a punch of a button, we can download a favorite song to a mini computer.

*E*xplanations give **additional information**.

> We can get almost any music we want from the World Wide Web.

*E*vidence is data or facts that prove **something is true**.

> In 2006, one company said it sold three million music downloads a day!

Find these E's in "Computer Music" on the next page. Look for the supporting details on which they elaborate.

Conclusion

Concluding Sentence (Unit 5)

The concluding sentence in a paragraph often restates the topic sentence.

Computer Music

Computers are changing the way we make and listen to music. For one thing, the computer has changed how we create songs. For example, composers can write concert music on laptops. Musicians can even make their computers "sing" like a huge choir. And DJs can use computer "drum machines" to lay down beats for their next hip hop show. Computers are also changing the way we listen to tunes. We can get almost any music we want from the World Wide Web. With a punch of a button, we can download a favorite song to a mini computer. These mini computers are called MP3 players. They let us take music almost anywhere. In 2006, one company said it sold three million music downloads a day! According to a computer magazine, the number of downloads will keep growing. New technology offers new ways to make and hear beautiful music.

Topic Sentence

Conclusion

A paragraph can be stretched to become a report.
Each part of a paragraph can expand to write a report.

Parts of a Report

Indent Paragraphs

The Benefits of Exercise

Regular exercise benefits people's health in two important ways. One benefit is that exercise improves people's physical health. It makes the heart, lungs, bones, and muscles stronger and keeps people at a healthy weight. Exercise is also good for the mind. It makes people feel better about themselves and calms them down when they are angry or stressed. When people regularly do physical activities they enjoy, their bodies and minds stay fit, happy, and healthy.

The **Introductory Paragraph** states the topic of the entire report.

Body Paragraphs tell more about the topic.

The **Concluding Paragraph** links to the introductory paragraph and ties the whole report together.

The Benefits of Exercise

Regular exercise can benefit your health in two important ways. It improves your physical health and is good for your mind.

(First,) exercise improves people's physical health. It makes the heart, lungs, bones, and muscles stronger. The heart and lungs work together day and night to keep the body alive. Exercise strengthens them. It improves blood flow. Blood carries food and oxygen to the rest of the body. Exercise also helps to keep calcium in the body. Calcium is needed to build strong bones and muscles. Since bones grow the most during childhood, exercise is very important for young people. Exercise also helps people maintain a healthy weight. This lowers the risk of developing diseases such as diabetes.

Exercise is (also) good for the mind. It makes people feel better about themselves. It calms them down. When people exercise, their brains produce chemicals. These chemicals make people feel happier! They also provide natural pain relief, and help people to relax. A workout or even a brisk walk can greatly reduce feelings of anger and stress. Exercise helps people's minds in another way, too. When people are fit, they feel more positive about themselves.

It is clear that exercise is great for both the body and the mind. The benefits of exercise are just too important to ignore.

Parts of a Report

A report is made up of a group of paragraphs. Each paragraph in the report has a specific job.

Introductory Paragraph

An **introductory paragraph** states the topic for the entire report. There are different ways to write an introductory paragraph. One way is a Two-Sentence Introductory paragraph.

State the Topic: The first sentence tells the *topic* of the report.

Exercise can benefit your health in two ways.

State the Plan: The second sentence tells how the report will address the topic. It usually tells the *ideas* that will be covered in the body paragraphs.

Regular exercise improves your physical health and is good for your mind.

Combine these two sentences to write an introductory paragraph.

Exercise can benefit your health in two ways. Regular exercise improves your physical health and is good for your mind.

Body Paragraphs

Body paragraphs tell more about the topic. Often a body paragraph begins with a transition topic sentence. It also includes E's (elaborations) — explanations, examples, and evidence —that support the topic sentence. Transition words are important to link ideas between paragraphs. Find the transition topic sentences and E's in "The Benefits of Exercise" report on page H95.

Concluding Paragraph

A **concluding paragraph** links to the introductory paragraph and ties the whole report together.

Look at this concluding paragraph and see how it restates the introductory paragraph on page H95.

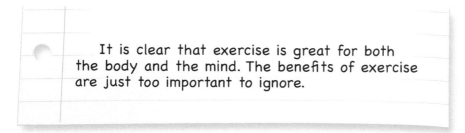

It is clear that exercise is great for both the body and the mind. The benefits of exercise are just too important to ignore.

The concluding paragraph for an Opinion Essay should **reinforce the opinion or position taken** in the essay. This paragraph should also sum up the reasons in the body paragraphs.

Another strategy for writing a concluding paragraph is to provide **food for thought**; that is, to leave readers with a question or an idea that keeps them thinking about the topic or helps them understand what makes the topic so interesting.

Attributes of Different Types of Writing

How are Reports and Personal Narratives Alike? (Unit 9)

- A report focuses on one topic and a personal narrative describes one experience.
- Both have an introductory paragraph, body paragraphs, and a concluding paragraph.

How are Reports and Personal Narratives Different?

Report	Personal Narrative
■ The body paragraphs of a report tell different points about the topic. Each point is stated in a transition topic sentence. ■ A report gives information about a topic; it does not include any personal details.	■ The body paragraphs of a personal narrative tell a story. The story has a beginning, middle, and end. ■ A personal narrative shares a true story that happened to the writer. The writer uses "I" to tell the story. ■ A personal narrative includes a message. The message may be a lesson that the writer learned from the experience he or she is writing about.

Transitions for Stories

while	the following day	later	that night
when	some time later	next	hours went by
after	the next morning	suddenly	at first I saw
during	after that		

Look for the transitions in the personal narrative on page H101.

Personal Narratives Let the Writer...

Describe events in a clear, interesting way	■ Show rather than tell the events of the story. ■ Include details to show what people, places, or things looked like. ■ Write sentences to entertain readers. ■ Choose words that express your feelings.
Use your own personal voice	■ Use "I" to write your story. ■ Tell your story as you would tell it to a friend or family member. ■ Include your personal opinions and feelings about events.
Share your feelings	■ Use language to express how you felt: "I was so **happy** that...!" "I was **worried** about..." "It made me **proud** that..." "I was **disappointed** that..." "Wow! It was so **exciting** that..."
Tell readers a message	■ Share a lesson about life. ■ Tell what you learned about yourself or someone else. ■ Tell what you gained from the experience.

Opinion Essays Let Writers...

■ Share an opinion or position about a question or issue; that is, agree (pro) or disagree (con) with an issue or question.

■ Use words that signal to the reader the position the writer is taking.

Pro	Con
I am in favor	I do not think
I agree	I don't favor
I support	I disagree

Personal Narrative Planner

Title: One Sport I Like

Introduction: I never thought I was good at sports because I can't throw a ball or run very fast.

Story

Beginning
- moved to a new neighborhood
- I was bored
- Carlos invited me to go running

Middle
- I ran around the block, I got really tired
- Carlos gave me lots of encouragement
- I became a stronger runner

End
- can run twenty times around my block
- I tried out for the cross-country team
- running practice every afternoon
- have met lots of other kids on the team

Conclusion: You've got to find the sport that is right for you.

One Sport I Like

Title

I never thought I was good at sports because I can't throw a ball or run very fast. Then last summer I found a sport I like.

Introduction

Last June my family moved to a new neighborhood. I didn't know anybody, and I was bored, bored, bored. One day I saw a boy across the street. He was wearing jogging shorts. I saw him stretch out and then take off down the street. In about five minutes he came around the block. He kept on running. As I sat on my lawn, I counted him circle the block ten times. When he finished, he came over and introduced himself. His name was Carlos. He invited me to go running the next day.

Beginning of the Story

The next morning I put on a pair of shorts and tennis shoes and met Carlos out in front of my house. I wasn't sure about running, but I figured I had nothing better to do. The first time I ran around the block, I got really tired. I was huffing and puffing. My sides hurt. Carlos gave me lots of encouragement, and he told me funny stories while we were running. He took my mind off how tired I was. I met Carlos every morning for the next few weeks. Little by little, I became a stronger runner.

Middle of the Story

Now I can run twenty times around my block! This fall I tried out for the cross-country team with Carlos. I made the team! I was so surprised. We have running practice every afternoon. It has been really great. I have met lots of other kids on the team. Now I have new friends as well as a sport I like.

End of the Story

What I learned was that not everybody is good at every sport. You've got to find the sport that is right for you.

Conclusion (with message)

Writing Compare and Contrast Paragraphs

Compare and Contrast Organizer

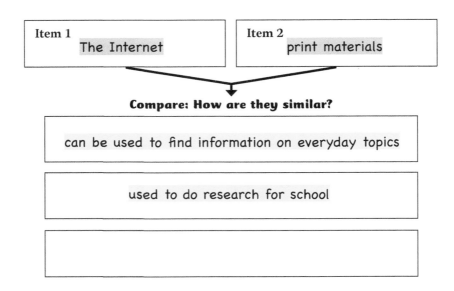

Item 1	Item 2
The Internet	print materials

Compare: How are they similar?

can be used to find information on everyday topics

used to do research for school

Contrast: How are they different?

find more information on the Internet- maps, store hours etc.	info	basic info in phone book
find a lot of information quickly on the Internet	speed	looking through many books can take more time

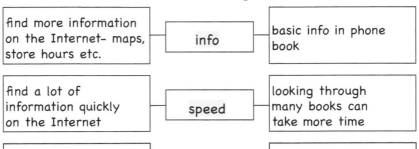

Compare and Contrast Words

alike	uncommon	different	unlike
and	also	contrast	differ
both	similar	but	vary

Internet or Print

When people need information, they can look in print materials such as books, or they can look on the Internet. The Internet and print materials share a lot in common, but they have many differences as well.

Introductory Paragraph

The Internet and print materials are alike in some ways. First, both the Internet and print media can be used to find information on everyday topics. People who want a telephone number for a business can look for it on the Internet. They can use a phone book, which is print material, too. If you want the schedule for the movies for Saturday night, you can look up the times in the newspaper and on the Internet. What if you are looking for directions to get someplace? You can buy a map to see how to get there. You can also find a map on the Internet. Second, both the Internet and print media can be used to do research for school. For example, students can read magazines, newspapers, or even books on the Internet just as they can in print. Students can find encyclopedias and dictionaries online, too. If they want information on a person or a place or need to know the meaning of a word, people have a choice of using a computer or looking up the information in a book.

The Internet and print materials also have many differences. First, people can often find more information on the Internet than they can in print media. For example, in a phone book, you can find some basic information about a place to order pizza, but on the Internet, you can find a lot more information. The Internet provides the telephone number of the restaurant, as well as the address and the hours it is open. You may also be able to read the pizza menu and look at a map to see how to get to the restaurant. Second, students can often find information they need for school faster on the Internet. It can take them a long time to find information for a report by looking through books. In contrast, they can usually find a lot of information quickly on the Internet. Although students still have to read the information, they can search for it much faster. That's because the Internet provides information from so many different sources.

Note the compare and contrast words circled in the paragraph.

The Internet and print media share a lot in common. However, they are really more different than they are similar.

Concluding Paragraph

Informal Letters   (Unit 16)

An **informal letter** is written to someone the writer knows well, such as a friend or relative. It is also called a friendly or personal letter.

Informal letters can be handwritten or typed.

Return address: Address for the person sending the letter. This is placed towards the right margin.

1010 Main Street
Writersville, VA 11111
September 10, 2009

Date: Date the letter is written.

Use a comma after the greeting.

Greeting: Name of the person who is going to receive the letter.

Hi Uncle Joe,

Indent paragraphs

    Guess what? I took your advice and entered the skateboarding competition in Writersville. The competition will be over a weekend. It would be great if you could come and watch.

Body: The message the writer wants to send. In an informal letter, less formal language is used.

    Thanks for encouraging me to do this. I hope that you can come to see the contest. Let me know if you can make it.

Closing: Signal for the end of the letter.

Love,
Manuel

Signature: Name of the person who wrote the letter.

Business Letters   (Unit 16)

A **business letter** is written to someone the writer does not know or who is in a position of authority, such as a government agency, teacher, minister, or other person of authority. It is also called a formal letter.

Business letters are usually typed.

Alex Ramirez
USA Middle School
Writersville, VA 11111
September 10, 2009

Martha Washington, Athletic Coordinator
City of Writersville
500 Main Street
Writersville, VA 11111

Dear Ms. Washington:

I'm interested in participating in the extreme sports competition. I have been a skateboarder for many years and would like to test my skills by competing. Please send me an application and information about how to signup.

Thank you,
Alex Ramirez
Alex Ramirez

Return address: Address for person sending the letter. This is placed at the left margin.

Date: Date the letter is written.

Inside Address: Address for the person who is getting the letter.

Use a colon after the greeting.

Greeting: Name for the person who is going to receive the letter. This can be a name or Sir or Madam.

Do **not** indent paragraphs

Body: The message conveyed in the letter. In a business letter, formal language is used.

Closing: Signal for the end of the letter.

Signature: Name of the person who wrote the letter.

Six Traits of Effective Writing (Unit 2)

Trait		What does this mean?
	Ideas and Content	Focus on the main ideas or story line. Supporting details (expository) or images/events (narrative) build understanding.
	Organization	Order of ideas and supporting details (expository) or clear beginning, middle, and end (narrative) make sense. Introduction, transitions, and conclusion help keep the reader hooked on the writing.
	Voice and Audience Awareness	Style suits both the audience and purpose of the writing.
	Word Choice	"Just right" words for the topic and audience.
	Sentence Fluency	Varied sentence use; no run-on sentences and sentence fragments.
	Conventions	Spelling, punctuation, grammar and usage, capitalization, and indenting paragraphs.

Editor's Marks
∧ add or change text
✄ delete text
↶ move text
¶ new paragraph
≡ capitalize
/ lowercase
⊙ insert period
○ check spelling or spell out word

Writer's Checklist for Book C

Key: Blue=expository only   Red=narrative only   Black=expository and narrative

Trait	Did I...?	Unit
Ideas and Content	Expository writing	
	❏ Clearly state the topic of the composition	7
	❏ Focus each paragraph on the topic	7
	❏ Include examples, evidence, and/or explanations to develop each paragraph	7
	Personal Narrative	
	❏ Tell a single true story	9
	❏ Include enough description and detail to develop the message/lesson learned	9
Organization	Write paragraphs:	
	❏ Tell things in an order that makes sense	1
	❏ Include all parts of a paragraph	6
	Write an expository essay:	
	❏ Write an introductory paragraph that states the topic and the plan	7
	❏ Use transition topic sentences to connect paragraphs	7
	❏ Write a concluding paragraph that restates the introductory paragraph	8, 14
	Write a personal narrative:	
	❏ Write an introductory paragraph that hints at the message/ lesson learned	9
	❏ Write three middle paragraphs that form the beginning, middle, and end of the story	9
	❏ Use story transitions to connect anecdotes/events	9
	❏ Write a concluding paragraph that explains the message/ lesson learned	9
Voice and Audience Awareness	❏ Think about my audience and purpose for writing	6
	❏ Write in a clear and engaging way that makes my audience want to read my work; can my reader "hear" me speaking	6
	❏ Use the word *I* to write about myself	9
Word Choice	❏ Try to find my own way to say things	2
	❏ Use words that are lively and specific to the content	2

Trait	Did I...?	Unit
Sentence Fluency	❏ Write complete sentences	1
	❏ Expand some of my sentences by painting the subject and/or predicate	3–18
	❏ Write a compound sentence part or a compound sentence	7–18
	❏ Write a sentence with a direct object	3–18
Conventions	Capitalize words correctly:	
	❏ Capitalize the first word of each sentence	1
	❏ Capitalize proper nouns, including people's names	3
	Punctuate correctly:	
	❏ Put a period or question mark at the end of each sentence	1
	❏ Put an apostrophe before the **s** for a singular possessive noun	2
	❏ Put an apostrophe after the **s** for a plural possessive noun	11
	❏ Use an apostrophe with contractions	7
	❏ Use a comma after a long adverb phrase at the beginning of a sentence	5
	❏ Use a comma to separate the appositive and its modifiers from the rest of the sentence	10–12
	Use grammar correctly:	
	❏ Use the correct verb tense	4
	❏ Make sure the verb agrees with the subject in number	4
	Spell correctly:	
	❏ Spell all **Essential Words** correctly	1–18
	Apply spelling rules	
	❏ The doubling rule (1-1-1)	6
	❏ The drop **e** rule	10, 16
	❏ The words ending in **o** preceded by a consonant rule	15
	❏ The change **y** rule	17

Using the Six Traits to Revise a Paragraph (Unit 12)

Draft Paragraph

Editor's Marks

∧	add or change text
ℓ	delete text
◯→	move text
¶	new paragraph
≡	capitalize
/	lowercase
⊙	insert period
◯	check spelling or spell out word

First, the Egyptians used very simple tools to cut the stone blocks for the pyramids. The Egyptans did not have things like electric drills. They could not blast the stone from a mountain with dynamite. Instead, they used wedges. Then they poured water on the wedges. The wedges soaked up the water like a sponge the water made the wedges expand. Amazing! They drove the wooden wedges into the surface of a huge stone. As they expanded, the wedges split the rock. Once each stone was cut, the workers used other tools to cut it into perfect block shapes.

Draft Paragraph with Edits

First, the Egyptians used very simple tools to cut the stone blocks for the pyramids. The Egyptians did
modern tools such as
not have ~~things like~~ electric drills. They could not blast the stone from a mountain with dynamite. Instead, they used wedges. Then they poured water on the wedges. The wedges soaked up the water like a sponge and the water made the wedges expand. ~~Amazing!~~ They drove the wooden wedges into the surface of a huge stone. As they expanded, the wedges split the rock. Once each stone was cut, the workers used other tools to
They used copper chisels and stone
cut it into perfect block shapes. ∧ hammers to do this work.

Revised Paragraph

First, the Egyptians used very simple tools to cut the stone blocks for the pyramids. The Egyptians did not have modern tools such as electric drills. They could not blast the stone from a mountain with dynamite. Instead, they used wedges. They drove the wooden wedges into the surface of a huge stone. Then they poured water on the wedges. The wedges soaked up the water like a sponge, and the water made the wedges expand. [Deleted "Amazing!" because it was not in a proper voice.] As they expanded, the wedges split the rock. Once each stone was cut, the workers used other tools to cut it into perfect block shapes. They used copper chisels and stone hammers to do this work.

Six Traits	Problem	Revision
Ideas and Content	The writer did not provide detailed information about the tools used to cut stone blocks.	A sentence was added to describe the tools workers used to cut stone into perfect blocks.
Organization	The fifth sentence was out of order.	The misplaced sentence was moved so that it described the process of using wedges in the proper sequence.
Voice	The exclamation *Amazing!* is too informal for this expository writing topic.	*Amazing!* was deleted.
Word Choice	The writer used the word *things* instead of a more specific word.	More precise words were used to replace *things* (*modern tools*).
Sentence Fluency	The sixth sentence was a run-on.	The sentence was changed into a compound sentence.
Conventions	*Egyptian* was misspelled once.	The spelling was corrected.

Pronunciation Key

Consonants

p	pup, rapped, pie	zh	vision, treasure, azure
b	bob, ebb, brother	h	hat, here, hope
t	tire, jumped, hurt	ch	church, match, beach
d	deed, mad, filed	j	judge, enjoy, jell
k	cat, kick, cut	m	mop
g	get, gill, magazine	n	not
f	fluff, rough, photo	ng	sing
v	valve, every, eleven	l	land
th	thin, three, math		
th	this, there, mother	w	with, wagon, west
s	sod, city, list	r	ramp
z	zebra, has, bees	y	yard, yes, yellow

Vowels

ē	beet	(bēt)	ō	boat	(bōt)
ĭ	bit	(bĭt)	o͝o	put	(po͝ot)
ā	bait	(bāt)	o͞o	boot	(bo͞ot)
ĕ	bet	(bĕt)	oi	boil	(boil)
ă	bat	(băt)	ou	pout	(pout)
ī	bite	(bīt)	î	peer	(pîr)
ŏ	pot	(pŏt)	â	bear	(bâr)
ô	bought	(bôt)	ä	par	(pär)
ŭ	but	(bŭt)	ô	bore	(bôr)
ə	rabbit	(răʹ bət)	û	pearl	(pûrl)

Word List

Essential Words

gone, look, most, people, see, water

Unit Words

Syllabication

above	blanket	commend	finish	melon	salad
across	blossom	commit	gallon	method	second
adapt	bonnet	common	gallop	minutes	select
adult	bottom	connect	happen	panel	seven
album	bucket	consent	hundred	planet	status
along	button	consist	husband	pocket	sudden
amend	cannon	constant	intense	prison	suspend
append	channel	cotton	involve	problem	ticket
assess	chicken	cricket	jacket	radish	vanish
assist	children	dentist	kitten	random	visit
atlas	collect	dozen	lemon	rascal	wagon
attach	comma	dragon	linen	ribbon	woman
basket	command	expand	magnet	rocket	

Shifting Stress

affect	conduct	consult	contrast	present
compact	conflict	contact	extract	subject
complex	construct	content	object	suspect

Words with Prefixes

disrupt	instruct	nonfat	unlock
distinct	invent	nonstop	unplug

Spelling Lists

Lessons 1–5

across	cotton	look	
most	ribbon	water	
atlas	gone	magnet	
people	rocket		
command	invent		
problem	see		

Lessons 6–10

blanket	I'm	nonstop
method	suspect	object
bottom	infant	present
nonstop	ticket	suspect
common	it's	ticket
object	upset	upset
disrupt	kitten	
present	method	

Word List

Essential Words

day, little, may, new, say, way

Unit Words

r-controlled syllables

after	correct	forget	mark	part	start
are	current	forgive	market	partner	starve
art	dark	form	matter	pattern	store
bar	desert	garden	member	pepper	storm
better	dirt	girl	modern	per	summer
bird	distort	govern	more	perhaps	target
born	doctor	hard	morning	permit	third
burn	during	harvest	never	person	turn
car	enter	her	nor	plural	under
carpet	ever	herd	north	rather	verb
carve	expert	horn	northern	remorse	verse
chapter	explore	horse	number	river	western
chart	far	hunger	observe	score	whether
church	farm	hurt	occur	serve	winter
color	fern	infer	or	sharp	yard
core	first	jar	orbit	short	
corn	for	letter	order	sir	
corner	forest	march	park	sister	

o = / ŭ / + er

another	brother	cover	mother	other	wonder

Words with Prefixes

interact	interest	interpret	underbrush	underpass	understand

Spelling Lists

Lessons 1–5

art	little	say
chart	may	shorter
day	mother	turn
first	new	verb
girl	north	way

Lessons 6–10

another	harvesting	they're
cover	interact	understand
darkest	letter	we're
doctor	numbers	wonder
garden	order	you're

Word List

Essential Words
good, great, right, though, through, year

Unit Words

a	detect	he	memo	pilot	so
acorn	diet	hello	menu	poem	spider
ago	diverse	hero	minor	prior	thesis
apron	elastic	hi fi	moment	program	tiger
be	electric	hotel	motel	prohibit	tornado
become	equal	human	motive	project	torpedo
before	equip	I	motor	protect	total
began	even	idea	music	pupil	undergo
begin	evil	item	no	quiet	unit
being	evolve	later	ongoing	reserve	video
belong	favor	legal	open	reverse	we
broken	fever	liar	over	resolve	zero
defend	flavor	lion	overlap	secret	
deliver	focus	major	paper	she	
depress	go	me	pecan	silent	

Words with Prefixes

predict	preset	prevent	record	relax	report
present	preshrunk	react	reject	remember	represent

Spelling Lists

Lessons 1–5

across	great	right
before	human	though
desert	music	through
equals	opening	year
even	paper	
good	report	

Lessons 6–10

diet	menu	remember
elastic	poem	return
heroes	predict	superstar
I've	quiet	video
memo	reacted	you've

Word List

Essential Words

again, sound, today, tomorrow, want, work

Unit Words

admire	create	equate	incline	parade	repetitive
arrive	debate	erode	include	passive	require
athlete	decline	escape	injure	pasture	revise
awhile	define	evaluate	inside	polite	secure
became	demote	exclude	intervene	positive	statement
beside	derive	expose	invite	presume	suppose
candidate	describe	extreme	invoke	primitive	surprise
climate	devote	figure	likewise	promise	trombone
compile	discrete	finite	locate	promote	underline
complete	dispose	handshake	migrate	provide	volume
comprise	divided	hurricane	minute	purchase	
compute	entire	impose	negate	refine	

Words with Prefixes

antilock	subject	subset	suburb
antitoxin	antitheft	submit	subtract

Spelling Lists

Lessons 1–5			Lessons 6–10		
again	divided	tomorrow	admired	described	secured
became	figure	want	antitoxin	handshake	subject
beside	polite	work	athlete	he's	subtracting
complete	provide		climate	invite	they'd
create	sound		compute	promise	you'd
define	today				

Word List

Essential Words
answer, certain, engine, laugh, oil, poor

Unit Words
Syllabication

army	dynamic	hobby	myself	rely	taffy
baby	Egypt	hurry	navy	shy	thirty
belly	empty	imply	nobody	silly	tiny
body	eye	jolly	party	sixty	try
buggy	firefly	lady	penny	sky	twenty
by	fly	lazy	pony	story	type
candy	forty	levy	poppy	study	ugly
copy	fry	lily	pretty	style	unify
cry	glory	military	priority	supply	why
deny	grizzly	mummy	property	symbol	
dry	happy	my	pyramid	system	

Words with Prefixes

conduct	construct	contrast	transmit
conflict	contract	transfer	transplant

Words with Suffixes

dryly	happily	lazily	quickly
exactly	hurriedly	prettily	suddenly

Spelling Lists

Lessons 1–5

answer	laugh	poor	
baby	mummy	property	
certain	oil	quickly	
engine	party	sky	
exactly	penny	why	

Lessons 6–10

contrast	eye	rely	
copy	firefly	style	
deny	funnier	system	
Egypt	happiest	transfer	
empty	hurried	trying	

Word List

Essential Word Review

again, answer, certain, gone, laugh, people, poor, their, there, they, though, through, to, today, tomorrow, too, two, want, what, who

Unit Words

after	deliver	first	market	polite	stampede
alone	diet	flavor	members	primary	students
arrived	direct	gases	menu	problem	summer
body	discovered	govern	merchants	products	supplies
brother	divine	gravel	migrate	remote	symbols
burning	entered	hammer	minutes	report	thinning
canine	explode	happened	mother	river	tornado
canyon	exploring	harvest	music	second	traffic
carpet	extreme	inflate	nickel	secrets	trapped
contact	factors	insects	normal	sharp	tried
continent	farmers	interesting	number	shipped	western
corner	feline	letter	only	sister	winter
covered	fever	linked	perfume	smart	wonder
create	fingers	living	planets	spotted	
cried	finished	located	plaster	squirrel	

Spelling Lists

Lessons 1–5

answer	their	want
hammer	there	what
open	to	who
people	too	
remote	two	
symbols	upset	

Lessons 6–10

antilock	outside	tried
brother	pathway	relocated
exploring	pipeline	report
maybe	problem	translate
music	tornado	understand

Unit 13

addend	combat	expend	obstruct	discuss	instep
addict	compress	extend	offense	disgust	insult
adding	congress	extent	pallet	disinfect	intact
aspect	conquest	fantastic	pelvis	dismiss	intend
ballot	constrict	fishnet	pilgrim	dispel	intent
bankrupt	contempt	fossil	ransom	distrust	invest
blacktop	contest	gasket	salesman	indent	nonskid
blemish	contract	hamlet	splendid	infect	unbend
bullet	convent	helmet	strengthen	inflect	unbent
cabstand	convict	infant	stressful	inflict	unclad
cactus	craftsmen	instinct	tablet	inhabit	unclasp
campus	denim	laptop	upset	inject	undress
camshaft	dropkick	limit	velvet	inland	unfit
casket	droplet	locket		input	unhand
catnap	enlist	magnetic	**Words**	inrush	unmask
checklist	enrich	matchbox	**with**	insect	unpack
clamshell	entrap	medic	**Prefixes**	inset	unrest
closet	exempt	nonsense	discredit	inspect	unwell

Unit 14

anger	cord	furthermore	observer	shore	**Words**
arm	darling	girth	offer	silver	**with**
bark	differ	hamburger	organ	smart	**Prefixes**
barn	dockyard	hammer	organic	sore	discard
birth	enterprise	harbor	perfect	sort	distort
border	explorer	harsh	plaster	spark	disturb
bore	export	horseback	platform	sport	intercom
burst	factor	ladder	popcorn	star	interject
butter	farmer	lantern	porch	starch	interlock
canter	farmland	lumber	pore	survive	Internet
cart	farther	membership	port	tender	interrupt
cartel	finger	minister	printer	term	intersect
charm	fir	monster	purse	thunder	underarm
charter	firm	mortar	record	transport	undercut
clerk	forgot	murder	rubber	trigger	undergo
cluster	fork	nerve	rural	urban	undershirt
collar	former	nevermore	server	whatever	undersized
conquer	fur	normal	shark	yarn	
convert	further	nurse	shirt		

Unit 15

banjo	dictator	indigo	overcome	rodeo	prehistoric
basic	dictatorship	indirect	overhang	ruin	pretend
basin	dissect	iris	overrun	sandpaper	reborn
beforehand	divert	judo	paperback	solo	recall
beginner	driver	jumbo	polo	student	recover
begun	eclipse	kimono	poster	subtotal	redo
bronco	ego	labor	pro	super	reflect
cargo	elect	lasso	protest	tempo	reform
china	embargo	leftover	refer	veto	refund
clover	equator	local	relapse	volcano	regard
crater	erupt	locust	reporter		reorder
crisis	event	meter	republic	**Words**	reprint
cubic	fiber	migrant	request	**with**	rerun
data	final	modem	respond	**Prefixes**	respect
defense	flu	moreover	revive	disfavor	revamp
depart	fro	motto	riot	disregard	reword
deserve	fuel	oasis	river	disrespect	superego
detector	halo	omit	robot	prefab	superman
diameter	hi	overcast	rodent	prefix	superscript

Bonus Words

Unit 16

advertise	dilate	homemade	overtime	transitive	interstate
alive	dilute	homesick	oxide	translate	prescribe
altitude	dioxide	inhale	ozone	tribute	refine
awake	dispute	insane	palate	turbine	relate
backbone	divine	invade	pancake	umpire	remote
baseline	dominate	lifelike	pavement	unite	subarctic
bedside	educate	lifetime	pensive	unlike	subcompact
behave	elope	limestone	permissive	unwise	subnormal
blockade	empire	livestock	pollute	uppercase	subplot
campfire	episode	mandate	predicate	useless	refund
cascade	erase	maritime	premise	valuate	regard
classmate	estate	missive	private	vibrate	reorder
compose	evade	mistake	purpose	vindictive	reprint
concave	exhale	multitude	sandstone	windpipe	rerun
concrete	exile	nitrate	shoreline		respect
decade	explode	obese	sunrise	**Words**	revamp
decode	framework	obtuse	sunshine	**with**	reword
delete	franchise	oppose	tadpole	**Prefixes**	superego
despite	grapevine	otherwise	template	antimatter	superman
dictate	hillside	overdose	termite	antiseptic	superscript
diffuse	homeland	overtake	transcribe	dislike	

Bonus Words

Unit 17

angry	fifty	misty	satisfy	**Words**	grimly
buddy	frosty	myth	shortly	**with**	lately
bumpy	funny	nasty	simply	**Prefixes**	lively
bypass	gabby	ninety	sly	confess	madly
crazy	glossy	nobility	somebody	connect	monthly
crypt	granny	nylon	sorry	consult	oddly
crystal	gravity	pantry	spy	content	promptly
curly	handy	pastry	stormy	convict	richly
daddy	hardy	plenty	storyteller	transact	sadly
density	hasty	polygon	sunny	translate	softly
derby	holly	poverty	symptom		solely
difficulty	hungry	puppy	syntax	**Words**	stiffly
dignity	hybrid	quantity	synthetic	**with**	strictly
dolly	ivy	rarely	syrup	**Suffixes**	strongly
dusty	jelly	reply	varsity	badly	swiftly
duty	jellyfish	rusty	vinyl	briskly	thickly
dye	jury	rye	windy	disturbingly	under-
entry	liberty	safety		frankly	standingly
envy	lofty	sandy		freshly	vastly
enzyme	lucky	sanitary		gladly	

Unit 18

archway	driveway	gateway	lifeline	parkway	super
clockwork	ego	hatchway	likewise	pathway	tiresome
command	entryway	hereby	limestone	pigpen	underwater
define	flyer	homework	namesake	stalemate	
discover	gangway	hotel	oneself	strengthen	

Text Selections

"I'm proud that I'm pushing myself to be better. I love learning and I don't ever want to stop improving."

– Fabiola da Silva (1979-)

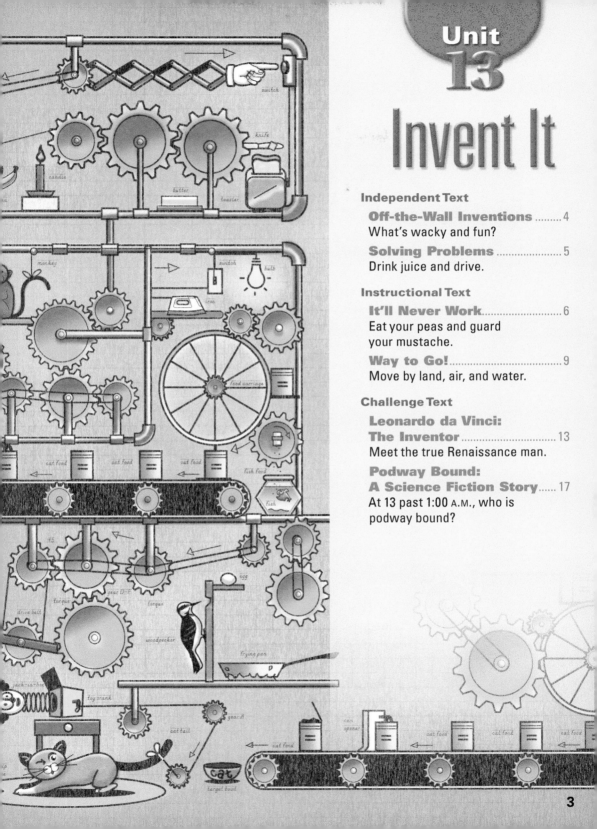

Invent It

off-the-wall INVENTIONS

Some inventions are made just for fun. Some of them are odd, and many of them have odd names. What do we call inventions like these? They are "off-the-wall." They are just not useful, so not many of them will sell. They
5 will not have any impact, but they are not supposed to! Many "off-the-wall" inventions have become fads. A fad is a quick craze. Fads become the rage, and people like them. Fads are fun, but not for long.

Here's the King

Do you know someone who comes up with "off-the-
10 wall" inventions? Meet Mr. Robinson. He has thought of lots of nutty things. One of his crazy inventions stretches pasta! Another one puts a square peg in a round hole! How useful is that? Are you impressed? No, but you are amused. That's why Mr. Robinson invents this nutty
15 stuff. He just loves tinkering, and he loves odd things. Mr. Robinson is the king of "off-the-wall" inventions!

Drive the C5

Step back in time to 1985. In England, a man is making a small three-wheeled bike. This bike isn't ridden, it's driven! It's called the C5, and it runs on batteries, not
20 gas. It emits no gas fumes. Some ships have used the C5 because the small C5s can drive across the decks of big ships. A C5 helps move things on a ship. But there is a problem. If you drive the C5 in traffic, you'll find that it's too small and sluggish. The driver is too exposed. Passing
25 cars emit gas fumes, and drivers inhale the fumes!

C5 3-wheeled bike.

SOLVING PR♻BLEMS

What makes an inventor? Inventors have quick minds. They think about problems, and they come up with solutions. Many inventions impact our lives by making our lives better. Lots of us have ideas and think
5 about things. If you have an invention, you should get a patent, which says that your invention belongs to you. It stops others from robbing your idea.

Plastic: A Problem Solver

Inventors begin with a problem and think about it. They think of possible solutions. This is how they may
10 think about cars. For example, most cars use too much gas. The gas makes fumes and pollution. Think about these problems. What if you could make a car that pollutes less? Is it possible that a car can use less gas? It is, and here is one solution.
15 Make a car of plastic; that could solve it. The car wouldn't be as heavy, so it would use less gas. It would pollute less, too. Plastic lasts and doesn't rust, and the color doesn't fade. There would be a bonus, as well, since plastic is manmade, and it can be reused.
20 Think of all the juice we drink that comes in plastic jugs. We could use the same plastic to make more cars. Is plastic the answer to making better cars?
25 Many think so.

It'll Never Work

Some inventions are wacky! Some are so preposterous that they're funny. Here are a few that really missed the boat!

How do you feel when peas fall off your fork? Are you as **annoyed** about this as Heath Robinson was? Robinson invented a machine to remedy the problem and gave it a compelling name. He called it the Interesting and Elegant Apparatus Designed To Overcome Once And For All The Difficulties Of **Conveying** Green Peas To The Mouth. It was just one of his innovations.

Robinson is the king of silly inventions in England. Most of his whimsical designs never made it past the drawing board. They weren't meant to be serious products, but that's a shame in a way. Maybe someone really yearned for his spaghetti stretcher. And what about his machine that put square pegs into round holes? That might have been useful!

Some Inventions That Never Took Off

One example of an unsuccessful invention was the Sinclair C5. This vehicle was supposed to solve the traffic problems in **Britain**. It could travel, but it went only about 15 miles per hour. What was it? Actually, it was a battery—and pedal-powered—tricycle. And it sold—but not well, or for long. Within 10 months, the C5 was **defunct**!

annoyed
irritated; upset

conveying
carrying

Britain
a western European island nation, comprising England, Scotland, Wales, and Northern Ireland

defunct
no longer in existence or working

A second unsuccessful invention was a machine with
25 many functions. This multipurpose contraption was
a strange-looking vehicle. It was designed to combine
several transportation modes. It was a car. It was a boat.
It was a plane. It purported to be all three. Too bad the
idea didn't take off. And neither did the machine.
30 Another strange invention was the Spring Walker.
This walking device promised to be fun—to put a spring
in your step. It was supposed to be just the thing for a
stroll around the park. But running for the bus could
have disastrous results! A person could trip and fall!
35 Then there was Piggles Takes to the Air. Intended
to be another transportation sensation, it was pieced
together from scrap metal and an old motorcycle engine.
It was created to raise money for charity. Did it work?
Sure. It worked about as well as pigs fly!
40 A final example of an unsuccessful invention was the
Dynasphere. Invented in 1932, this creation moved by
means of a giant wheel that turned around the driver. It
sped along at nearly 30 miles per hour. To its credit, a
version of the Dynasphere was powered by electricity.
45 It polluted less than a gas-powered car. Even so, it
didn't exactly roll off the production line.

Strange but True: Other Unbelievable Inventions

First, there was the Mustache Guard,
invented in 1885 by Thomas Ferry. This gadget
prevented food or drinks from getting trapped
50 in a man's mustache.
Next, there was the chocolate medicine
spoon, created in 1937. This wasn't an
overwhelming success, either. Sure, a chocolate
spoon encouraged kids to take their medicine.
55 But, then they ate the spoon!
Another odd invention was a hat that blew
soap bubbles. This bit of tomfoolery was created
by American inventor Alden L. McMurty in 1910.
He said it made quite a sight.

Dynasphere and its inventor.

patented

obtained the right to make, use, or sell an invention

Sahara Desert

a large North African desert

Corrine Catapano, engineering student, competes in the national finals of the Rube Goldberg Machine Contest.

60 Then there was an airplane security device. An inventor is said to have **patented** this idea in 1976 to keep planes from being hijacked. A large metal ball was strapped into all the passengers' hands. This prevented them from holding a gun.

65 Last, consider the very long water pipeline. Englishman Arthur Pedrick conceived this idea for providing water to the **Sahara Desert**. He dreamed up a plan to lay a long pipeline that originated in the Amazon and ran under the Atlantic Ocean to bring water to the

70 parched Sahara Desert. Needless to say, Pedrick's idea never took hold.

Today, Purdue University's famous college of engineering sponsors a Rube Goldberg contest for student engineers. People in the United States

75 refer to strange contraptions or inventions as Rube Goldberg arrangements. Go to the Web, and do a little investigating of your own to find out what this means. Where did the expression come from?

Adapted with permission from "It'll Never Work!" by Nick Griffiths

Answer It

1. Choose one of the inventions from **"It'll Never Work."** Infer something about its inventor.

2. What can you generalize about the types of inventions described in the section of text titled "Some Inventions That Never Took Off"?

3. Illustrate one of the inventions in the section of text titled "Strange but True: Other Unbelievable Inventions."

4. What can you infer about the reasons inventors created products in the section "Strange but True"?

5. What can you infer about who Rube Goldberg was from the last paragraph of this selection?

Way to Go!

Dodge Intrepid ESX2.

Drink Juice and Drive

Pour a glass of juice. Empty the container. Where does it go when you finish the juice? It goes into the recycling bin. But then what? Someday, you could be driving those empty containers. An auto show in Detroit
5 exhibited a car made of the same plastic as juice cartons. The car was just a **prototype**, but someday, cars may be made of recycled plastic rather than metal. Steel is much heavier than plastic, so a plastic car would use less gas. It would get about 70 miles to the gallon and produce
10 less exhaust. Still, the plastic would be strong enough to protect passengers in a crash. It never rusts. It never needs painting. So drink your juice! And don't forget to recycle your containers. They might become your *way to go.*

prototype
an original model used for testing before producing the final version

The Ultimate Bike

Now, here's a bicycle! It's made of the same carbon-
15 fiber materials that are used on modern fighter jets and uses solid instead of spoked wheels. Its tires are made of silk and **Kevlar®** fiber. But don't fill them with air. Use **helium**! The bike weighs about 11 pounds, and is it ever fast! Its designer set the world **solo** cycle speed
20 record when he rode it at more than 200 miles per hour. Engineers are using the technology from this model to improve bicycles. They're also using what they've learned to improve wheelchairs. *Way to go!*

Kevlar®
a brand of a special type of strong fiber

helium
a gas present in the Earth's atmosphere

solo
alone

Now That's a Big Balloon!

Can you imagine a dirigible that can carry big loads
25 of **cargo** and passengers? A dirigible is sometimes called
an airship, but actually it is a huge helium balloon.
Propellers move it. It's similar to the kinds of blimps
you've seen on TV carrying television crews over sports
fields. But there's a difference between a dirigible and a
30 blimp. A dirigible has a rigid inside frame. It can be much
bigger than a blimp. The best-known dirigible was the
Hindenburg. In 1937 it caught fire, killing 37 passengers
and the crew. In those days, helium was not available,
so **flammable** hydrogen was used to lift the vessel. The
35 fabric for the outer skin also was flammable. After the
Hindenburg crash, this type of airship was rarely used.

Now, engineers are proposing new kinds of dirigibles.
If approved, these will use high-strength, low-weight
fibers and be filled with nonflammable helium. Solar-
40 power cells will replace gasoline engines. The propellers
would run on clean, inexpensive electricity. Some design
ideas call for airships a mile long! Dirigibles are definitely
coming back. There are plans for bigger ones. One
company has designs for a version over 500 yards long.
45 Soon you may be able to look up and see a balloon longer
than the tallest skyscraper. You'll watch it gently floating
by. Now *that's a way to go!*

cargo

products carried
by ship, plane, or
other vehicle

flammable

able to catch fire
easily

Skimming the Water

Is it an airplane that doesn't quite fly? Is it a boat that doesn't quite float? It's neither. It is a ground-effect plane,
50 zooming along about three feet above the water. But it can't fly higher than about six feet above the water. It doesn't touch the water until it lands. Technically, it's not an airplane, so you don't need a pilot's license to operate it. A ground-effect plane can go much faster than most
55 boats—up to 100 miles per hour. And it uses only half as much fuel as a plane. In years to come, we may see it more often in places where there is lots of travel between islands. That'll be *a great way to go.*

Now for Something Really Fast

Do you like speed? Here's how to go really fast. Take a
60 big jet engine (or two). Attach some sturdy wheels. Strap on your helmet, and fire up. Not long ago, a challenge race was held in the Nevada desert. A British car (if you can call a rocket on wheels a car) sailed along at about 700 miles per hour, powered by two engines similar to
65 those used in fighter jets. That's a lot of power! Designing a car like that takes careful planning. One small error could spell disaster. Your jet engines could carry you toward the sky, instead of down the road. On second thought, a pickup truck might be *your best way to go!*

A ground-effect plane can zip along above water at 100 miles per hour.

Wheeling Down the Mountain

70   Riding on mountain trails is not only for bicyclists. Make way for the off-road wheelchair. That's right. A wheelchair has been created for mountain-trail racing. The designer, Michael Whiting, dreamed he'd lost the use of his legs and couldn't get out into the wilderness.

75 He woke up the next morning and realized that for some people, this is reality. So he designed a mountain wheelchair using the best bicycle technology. The machine allows riders to move along wilderness trails and race down mountains. They can go as fast as 50 miles per

80 hour. Michael has given lots of people the opportunity to live fuller lives. *Way to go!*

Michael Whiting's off-road wheelchair.

Adapted from "Way to Go" by Steve Miller
© by Carus Publishing Company.
Reproduced with permission.

Answer It

1. Plastic could be used to produce machines besides cars. Generalize what other types of inventions could be made with recycled plastic.

2. Different types of gas have been used to fill dirigibles. What can you infer about the safety of helium as opposed to hydrogen?

3. Explain why a person does not need a pilot's license to operate a ground-effect plane.

4. What can you generalize about the speed of the inventions in **"Way to Go!"**?

5. What can you infer about the impact of new materials on the inventions described in **"Way to Go!"**?

Leonardo da Vinci

THE INVENTOR

Artists have often found it difficult to make a living. Even a master painter like Leonardo da Vinci needed to take on other work to support himself. So, he **adapted** his drawing skills to other
5 fields. He worked as an architect, a military engineer, and a canal builder. He was also a weapons designer.

Most of Leonardo da Vinci's inventions were not built during his lifetime. Still, he may have been the greatest inventor who ever lived. The chain and gear system that
10 powers bicycles was first designed in 1490 by Leonardo. It was Leonardo who invented the first **rotisserie** oven and the first diving suit. He was also the first person to have the idea of making contact lenses. He even developed a form of air-conditioning—500 years ago!

15 His notebooks are amazing. They show his futuristic devices, all centuries ahead of their time. Some of his ideas still look modern today. Once, Leonardo was asked to prepare a peace offering. It was for a meeting between the pope and the King of France. His creation may have been
20 the first robot. Shaped like a lion, it walked on its own into the room. The robot then opened its breast, showing a heart full of lilies, the emblem of the French king.

Leonardo thought war was madness. But he also thought it necessary "to preserve the chief gift of Nature, which is Liberty." Although a peace lover at heart,
25 Leonardo once got a job working for the Duke of Milan.

adapted
changed to meet a new situation

rotisserie
a cooking device that turns meat while it cooks

In this role of military engineer, he outlined some ideas for weapons and **fortifications**. In those days, armies still used **catapults**. But Leonardo invented a rapid-fire
30 canon, perhaps the first machine gun. He also envisioned a rocket that could travel three miles into the sky. And he developed the idea for a submarine. He also designed diving suits for the ship's crew.

He dreamed up brilliant ideas throughout his life,
35 and some were used during his time. Leonardo worked another stint as a military engineer and architect for the infamous military leader, Cesare Borgia. Leonardo proposed creation of a dry route across the Gulf of Istanbul. It would consist of a bridge to span the Golden
40 Horn. Like many great ideas, his bridge plan was rejected. Ordinary engineers laughed when they found out how big the bridge would have to be. Leonardo's supporters get the last laugh, though. Modern engineers have concluded that the bridge would have been completely safe, and its
45 construction entirely **feasible**. Once again, Leonardo proved himself to be one of the smartest men ever.

Leonardo da Vinci was intrigued by mechanics. In particular, mechanical gears fascinated him. He studied them with enthusiasm. This fascination resulted in
50 many different conceptions. He envisioned the bicycle, a helicopter, an "auto-mobile," and some gruesome weapons.

Some of his greatest mechanical ideas made use of water. Nobody had yet harnessed electricity. In his time, water was the ultimate source of power. Leonardo
55 studied water in all its forms, including liquid, steam, and ice. Among his ideas were a device to measure humidity, a steam-powered cannon, various waterwheels, and assorted other machines powered by flowing water. He also created an ambitious plan to **revitalize** Milan
60 with canals. He wanted to put the canals into operation using equally ambitious construction machines. Once Leonardo got started on the subject of water, it was hard

Leonardo da Vinci's sketch of a helicopter.

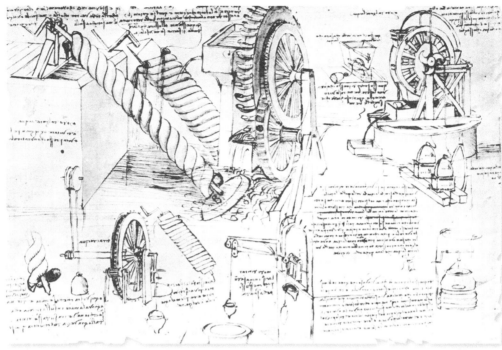

Leonardo da Vinci's sketches of some of his inventions.

for him to stop. He was forever imagining things like floating snowshoes for walking on water, underwater

65 breathing devices (including a diving hood), and webbed gloves to explore below the surface. He designed a life preserver, devices to attack and sink ships from underwater, an "unsinkable" double-hulled ship, and dredges for clearing harbors and channels.

70 　How did Leonardo dream up so many great ideas? He was a true Renaissance man. He was interested in everything! Many of his ideas were intertwined with others. Just studying the petals of a flower was enough to inspire him. In his mind's eye, he conceived a new type of

75 gear—a multi-blade shield to protect soldiers—and even a system of radiating highways.

　Leonardo filled notebooks with thousands of sketches. Often, he crowded many ideas onto the same page as he

jumped from one concept to another. His notes are written
80 mostly from right to left. The reason for this is unclear.
Perhaps he wished to keep his ideas secret. He was left-
handed, so some believe writing from right to left was more
natural for him. His notebooks document a lifetime of
natural world study. They also reflect how his mind worked.
85 Leonardo was able to draw exactly what he imagined as well
or better than the greatest artists in history.

Today, we remember Leonardo da Vinci as one of
the first modern engineers. He emphasized the role of
experimental models to test out his ideas. The drawings
90 he made were so detailed that modern craftsmen can
build replicas of his remarkable machines and watch
them work. Leonardo da Vinci is acknowledged as one of
the greatest inventors of all time.

Adapted from "From the Notebooks of Leonardo"
by Nick D'Alto and "Leonardo's Notebooks"
by Milan Kralik, Jr. © by Carus Publishing Company.
Reproduced with permission.

*This model, based on
Leonardo's sketches, is a
precursor of the modern
car, as well as the world's
first self-propelled wagon.*

Think About It

1. This selection is a biography of Leonardo da Vinci.
   What aspect of his life does this selection discuss
   in detail?

2. List different types of work that Leonardo did to
   support himself.

3. Describe how Leonardo wrote in his notebooks.
   Explain possible reasons for this unique style
   of writing.

4. Name three things that Leonardo designed or
   invented that are widely used today.

5. List three questions you would ask Leonardo if he
   were alive today.

6. Explain why many people think Leonardo da Vinci
   was the greatest inventor of all time.

Podway Bound

A Science Fiction Story

Officer Lucas glanced impatiently at the digital readout implanted in her wrist. Where was Officer Carson, anyway? It was 10 minutes past the start of the new officer's shift. Lucas sighed and decided that she
5 would have to do the routine 1:00 A.M. check on the prisoners by herself. Only the control room separated the cellblock from the podway and the rest of the outside world. She was understandably a little uneasy.

She approached the digitized wall of the cellblock.
10 She put her thumb on the **sensor** panel and waited for it to read her print. The cellblock door flashed clearance and began to slide into the wall. Her eye caught a blur of movement. Before she could react, a man in prison uniform leaped out, knocked her down, and sprinted into
15 the control room with her. Reinforced with a grid of hair-fine Kevlar® strands, the **impenetrable** polymer wall of the control room—including the entrance panel—was now all that could prevent the convict from escaping to the city outside. Plus, of course, Lucas.

sensor

a mechanical device used for identifying something by heat, motion, light, or sound

impenetrable

incapable of being passed through

20   He won't get past the robots, Lucas thought, as she struggled to her feet. But then how did the man get out of his cell?

      Just then, to her horror, Lucas saw the outer entrance panel slide open. Carson stepped in. It was 13 minutes past
25 1:00 A.M. It had been a quiet night—until now. Lucas leaned on the emergency alarm, but she knew it was too late.

      "Carson!" she shouted. The relief guard froze at the sight of the prisoner bearing down on him at full speed. The man dived past him and through the narrowing
30 gap left by the closing entrance panel. The impenetrable shield slid silently shut between them.

      Lucas had never had much confidence in the robot guard system. A single human corrections officer in a high-security holding prison was risky business. Yes, the
35 prison commissioner guaranteed the new Robotic Guard System 2080 was fail-safe. But robo-systems had failed before, and where were the 'bots now?

      Lucas jumped to her feet and ran toward the outer door. There was a moment's pause while the panel's
40 computer read her fingerprint. The door slid open. Outside was a narrow platform. Beside it ran a large, **translucent** tube. The ground lay hundreds of meters below. Towering buildings rose all about them, connected by the translucent tubing running in dizzying loops
45 and snarls in every direction. Visible through the walls

translucent

allowing light to pass through; almost transparent

of the tubing were countless moving lights. These were attached to pods that carried passengers through the city at hundreds of kilometers per hour. But there was no sign of the former prisoner.

50   "Maybe next time you'll get here on time," Lucas said accusingly to Carson. She turned back inside and ran to the control panel. Sure enough, every guard-bot inside and out had been **deactivated**. Lucas quickly reset them. Next, she hit a button. A three-dimensional video
55 screen came to life. A picture of what looked like badly tangled spaghetti appeared, hovering above the surface of the panel. White, yellow, and orange dots zipped along **intertwined** green strands.

deactivated
turned off

intertwined
twisted around
something

      "What's that?" Carson asked in surprise.
60   "Don't tell me you've never seen a traffic computer," answered Lucas. "What are they teaching you these days in basic training?" Her fingers flew over the keyboard. "This is a map of the podway that connects everything in the city. The gray lines are the tubes the pods travel
65 through. The dots are the pods themselves. White stands for public pods. The yellow ones are private. The orange ones are government-owned—construction, maintenance, and so on."

      "How's that going to help?" Carson whined. "We're
70 never going to catch that prisoner now. There are hundreds of thousands of pods he could be in. He could be heading anywhere!"

      "Watch and learn," Lucas grinned. "We're going to narrow down the possibilities. To start with, we know
75 the top speed of the pods. We know about how long it's been since he escaped—so that tells us how far he could have gotten." She hit a few more keys and the screen went dark, except for a small sphere near the center. "He can't be outside that radius. But we have to work fast. The
80 longer we take, the farther he can get."

"There are still hundreds of pods there," Carson objected.

"We can probably assume he's heading away from the prison," said Lucas, continuing to type. More than half
85 the dots winked out, leaving only those traveling outward from the center of the screen. "And when you get into a pod, it reads your thumbprint and checks your identity. It starts up only if you're authorized to use it. He wouldn't be authorized to operate a government pod." The orange
90 dots vanished.

"Now, could he be in a private pod? There are . . ." — green lettering appeared on the screen as she continued to type furiously—"two pods he's registered to use." Two red dots appeared on the screen, both well outside the
95 lighted sphere. "And both are farther away than he could have gotten in the time he's been on the loose.

"Which means he must be in a public pod. Anyone's allowed to use them, but they still read the fingerprints of their passengers and record their identities. This means
100 we'll know in a minute which one he's in." Lucas hit a final key and leaned back. White dots began disappearing from the screen. Within a minute, all of them had vanished. Lucas' mouth opened and closed, but no sound came out.

105 "He must have had a partner," Carson said, "someone who was waiting outside in a private pod sped off with him as soon as he jumped in."

Lucas pounded the desk in frustration. "Then we'll never find him!" She paused a moment in thought. "The
110 tube system automatically measures the weight of each pod to control its power and acceleration correctly. We can look at just the pods that weigh at least as much as the pod itself, its driver, and the prisoner put together. That'll tell us which ones *could* be carrying him. Then,
115 if we check that list of drivers to see which ones knew the prisoner or have a criminal record, we might be able

to tell which pods he's likely to be in. But we still won't be certain. Anyway, it'll take us forever to finish all that. He might leave whatever pod he's in and disappear into
120 the city any minute. There's got to be another way to find him!"

Lucas stared off into the distance for a minute. Suddenly she sat up
125 straight, glanced at Carson, and mumbled, "Here's an idea. . . ." She started typing again. The orange
130 dots reappeared on the screen, and a moment later all but one of them went out.

135   Carson, who had been edging toward the exit, made a sudden lunge for it. But Lucas had already
140 made certain the panel would no longer open in response to Carson's fingerprint. A guard-bot whirred into
145 view (the commissioner *said* the system wouldn't fail!) and handcuffed the rogue guard.

"You were right about the prisoner having a partner," Lucas explained. "You must have applied to work here at the prison intending to help him escape. You authorized
150 him to operate one of our pods. Then, last night you deactivated the guard-bots and let him out of his cell.

You timed your late arrival this morning so the outer panel would be open when he made his escape."

"You may have caught me," Carson snarled, "but
155 you'll never get him back. He'll be long gone by the time you can catch up with him."

"That's the best part," Lucas smiled. "In case something happens in the line of duty, pods driven by police, firefighters, and rescue workers can be remotely controlled
160 from their station. I can lock the doors of his pod and bring him right back to this prison in air-conditioned comfort." She hit a few keys and the orange dot slowed, reversed direction, and began retracing its path.

Ten minutes later, the two conspirators were
165 reunited—in **adjoining** cells.

adjoining
next to; bordering

Adapted from "Podway Bound" by Justin Werfel
© by Carus Publishing Company. Reproduced with permission.

Think About It

1. Why did the guards put their thumbs on the sensor panel?

2. Name the type of work that Carson did at the prison.

3. Explain what the prison commissioner meant when he said the new Robotic Guard System 2080 was fail-safe.

4. Cite evidence the author provides to indicate Carson was involved in the escape plot.

5. In the story, everyone uses pods that look the same for transportation. Tell the advantages and disadvantages of having the same type of vehicle as everyone else.

6. Draw a map of the setting. Create a map key to show the podways, the pods, and the other places mentioned in the story.

Unit
14
Make Art

23

MAKING ART

Sketching

What do you do when you're bored? Some of us just sit and think, while others pick up a pen. If you have a pen, you might sketch. It feels natural, so almost everybody likes to sketch. Sketching is a basic form of
5   art where lines can turn into shapes. Some shapes are so abstract that you may not know what they are. Other shapes can remind you of familiar things, and you can turn them into objects. Your pad gets filled with art. When you sketch, you're getting absorbed in art.
10 You're expressing yourself by making art.

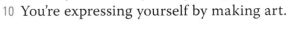

Distracted with Art

The bell rings, and class begins. Everyone is sitting at a desk, and some begin to take notes. You begin to sketch, and your lines become art. Your name becomes art. The sun comes up—on your paper—and stars appear, too.

15 But, what happens when it's time for the test? Where are your notes? Notes will help you pass the test, but sketches won't. It's hard to sketch and take notes at the same time!

And Sew On

Meet Michael A. Cummings. He was born in Los Angeles. Now he lives in a 100-year old brownstone in
20 Harlem. Since he was a child, he liked to draw and paint. He always knew he wanted to be an artist. Then one day, he made a banner. He said to himself, I don't need pens and brushes. I can sew my art. He expresses himself with a sewing machine. His canvas is fabric.

25 What different things could you use to express yourself in art?

ART AT HOME
and
ART IN CAVES

Elisa Kleven

Art From Scraps

Fame was in store for Elisa
Kleven. She made a name for herself.
It began when she was a little girl.
Common scraps fascinated her,
5 so she used scraps to make art.
Nutshells became beds. Caps
from drinks became small baking
pans. She loved to make little settings. Elisa's settings
inspired her. She began to tell little tales. Her tales led
10 to books for children. Next, Elisa's scraps became 3-D
art in her books. Yarn made a horse's mane, and twine
made a first-rate bird's nest. Bits of colored rags made a
dozen different shapes. Elisa had discovered something.
Common scraps can make fantastic art.

Where Did Art Start?

15   The first form of art was cave art. Cave artists made lots of sketches inside caves. Caves protected the art. Wind didn't hurt it, and water didn't wash it off. The sun didn't fade it. A hundred tales are told in cave art. Cave art tells the tales of the lives of cave people. The cave dwellers hunted
20 and fished. They sketched crude maps and made messages for each other. The art they made is still there. The messages they left us tell us much. From cave art, we learn history and about the lives of some of the first humans. We learn something even more important. We learn that humans
25 have always been engaged with making art.

Adapted from "Elisa Kleven: From Scraps to Magic," by Patricia M. Newman © by Carus Publishing Company. Reproduced with permission.

From The Lion and the Little Red Bird, *by Elisa Kleven (Dutton, 1992).*

From Rock Art
to Graffiti

Art has form and beauty. One unusual art form is rock art. Thousands of years of art exist on rocks and cave walls. This art can be found around the world.
5 People still make rock art. Murals and urban graffiti are two examples of this style. All rock art reflects the times when it was made.

What Is Rock Art?

From the beginning, humans have created rock art. What is this artistic style? Primarily, it is the art
10 of making marks on rock. The marks may be cut, carved, etched, or drawn. People have made this art

Cave painting from Altamira Cave in Spain.

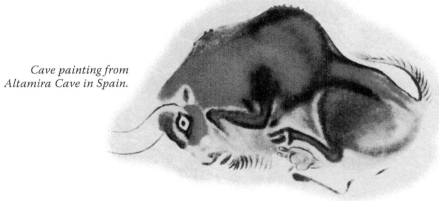

since **prehistoric** times, so there are millions of images recorded on stone.

There are different kinds of rock art. Early styles, called pictographs, are drawings or rock paintings
15 that are made by using a brush, or just the fingers. Engravings are another form of rock art. In this style, the rock surface is cut, leaving a picture. Petroglyphs are yet another early type of rock art. Material is removed from the rock's surface, and the rock is hammered to
20 produce images. Sculptures are rock carvings. Many are freestanding. Others are made in the form of reliefs, or sculptures that only partially stand out from the front surface of a rock wall.

Ancient rock art had different purposes. Some held
25 messages. We don't understand the meanings of all these marks. The people of the time did, though. Maybe the art recorded events from the past, or served as **boundary** lines. Maybe it marked astronomical time. Rock art might have recorded laws. Some of it probably told stories.
30 Some may have represented myths or revealed secrets. Rock art could have been used to play games. Some of it was intended simply for decoration—or to celebrate life.

prehistoric
belonging to a time period before written history

boundary
a border or edge that marks a specific area

Adapted with permission from "The Start of Art" by Paul Bahn © by Carus Publishing Company.

Diego Rivera in his studio.

Mexican Murals: Rock Art Finds Walls

During the nineteenth century, artists in Mexico painted murals. They painted them in village churches.
35 They painted on the outside walls of shops, taverns, and hotels. All over Mexico, walls are covered with these beautiful mural paintings.

Many of the Mexican murals had a purpose. In the early 1900s, several Mexican artists were caught up in a
40 revolution. The murals they created showed their hopes for the Mexican people. They painted murals on outside walls for all eyes to see. Their murals celebrated the triumph of the revolution. They also celebrated the rich cultural heritage of Mexico.

45 Three of Mexico's most famous muralists were Diego Rivera, Jose Clemente Orozco, and David Siqueiros—all trained artists. During the early 1900s, they renewed Mexico's great mural-making tradition by using bold colors and creating striking images. They painted Indian
50 ancestors, Spanish conquistadors, heroic peasant leaders, and even hated dictators. Their murals had many themes. Many represented **controversial** ideas. But the quality of art was not controversial. The world recognizes these muralists as great artists.

controversial

causing arguments or disagreements

Adapted from "The Murals of Aztlán" by Craig Gingold
© by Carus Publishing Company. Reproduced with permission.

Detail of David Siqueiros' Women in Procession (*Mural, 1952–54*).

American Graffiti Artist: Modern Rock Art

55   Today, graffiti has become a modern form of rock art. In the 1980s, many young people went to New York City to study art. Keith Haring was one of them. Haring was an art student who **immersed** himself in graffiti. As in many cities, graffiti appeared on the walls and in
60 the subways of New York. It was rendered with dazzling colors and shapes.

    "The kids who were doing graffiti were young," Haring said. "They were from the streets. But they had this incredible mastery of drawing. It totally blew
65 me away. I mean, just the technique is amazing. It's incredibly difficult to do."

    In 1980, Haring began drawing his own graffiti on the streets. Like other graffiti artists, he
70 invented his own tag, or signature. His first tag was a picture of an animal. Then, he drew a little person crawling on all fours. Eventually, it became known as
75 "The Baby."

    One day, he was waiting on a subway platform. He noticed some empty black paper panels leaning against the platform walls. They covered some old advertisements. Haring thought, "These panels
80 are just dying to be drawn on!" Then and there, he rushed out of the subway. Haring bought some white chalk and returned to draw on the black panels. His drawings were simple. He drew pyramids and flying saucers. He drew humans and winged figures. He drew
85 television sets, animals, and babies. New York subway riders began recognizing Haring's drawings. But they had no idea who created them.

    "Actually, my drawing on those black panels made me more **vulnerable** to being caught," he said. "I started
90 spending more time in the subways. I developed a route where I would go from station to station to do *just* those drawings."

immersed
became completely involved

D.J. Dog *by Keith Haring.*

vulnerable
unprotected; open to harm

Haring started to become famous. People on the subway saw his work. It was on TV and in the newspaper.

95 Soon, New Yorkers began to seek out his art. His first exhibition was a huge success, with more than 4,000 people in attendance. The exhibit showed Haring's amazing art. It showed the electricity of his work and reflected every **facet** of his style. The pieces featured

100 pictures of break dancing, rap music, and other scenes. Critics called the exhibition dazzling and applauded its rich inventiveness. They loved its energy. Suddenly, the name Keith Haring was part of New York's art scene.

facet

one part

Adapted with permission from "Keith Haring" by John Gruen

Answer It

1. There are many types of rock art. What can you infer about the types of tools used to create engravings, petroglyphs, and sculptures?

2. Define **muralist** in your own words.

3. Using a timeline, show the progression of rock art from prehistoric cave paintings to modern graffiti.

4. The text describes how rock art has changed throughout history. Predict what art form will be most popular in 10 years.

5. A metaphor is a figure of speech that compares people, places, things, or feelings without using the words **like** or **as**. The phrase "the electricity of his work" (line 98) is a metaphor. Explain what this metaphor tells you about Haring's art.

Becoming an Artist

Seeing the World in New Ways

Even at a very young age, Pablo Picasso knew he was an artist. He had amazing drawing talent. His father, an art teacher, encouraged the young Pablo. Some people today look at Picasso's art and think it's simple. But
5 simplicity was Picasso's **genius**. He looked at the world in new ways. Once, Picasso noted that all children are artists because they can see the world with new eyes. The problem, he said, lies in how one manages to remain an artist after growing up. Can adults continue to view the
10 world in a unique way? Picasso himself grew up to be one of the greatest artists of all time.

genius
an exceptional ability

Adapted from "Famous Artists' Beginnings" by Patricia Wild
© by Carus Publishing Company. Reproduced with permission.

Artist and Teacher

Augusta Savage was 17 when she knew she first wanted to be an artist. In 1919, her sculptures
15 won an award. That event inspired her. In 1921, she moved to New York, where many African Americans were relocating. There, artists had a chance. In
20 Harlem, Augusta began her career as an artist and a teacher.

Savage's art was unique. Some of it focused on facial features of her subjects that suggested character. Often, her sculptures reflected
25 African American culture. Some of her pieces illustrated old Negro spiritual songs. One sculpture is called *The Harp*. It symbolizes pride and was inspired by the song, "Lift Every Voice and Sing."

In 1929, Savage won a fellowship. She studied in
30 Paris for a year. On her return, she taught others and eventually became the first director of the Harlem Community Arts Center. African Americans studied fine arts there. In her later years, Savage continued teaching sculpture to children and adults. She inspired some of
35 them to become artists and teachers.

Carl Van Vechten

Augusta Savage's sculpture, The Harp (Lift Every Voice and Sing), *illustrates pride.*

Source: "Augusta Savage" http://northbysouth.kenyon.edu/ 1998/art/pages/savage.htm

Action Artist

Like Picasso and Savage, Alexander Calder began making art as a child. He loved making things move. "I was respected by my playmates for what I could make out of wood and leather with my tools and hands," he
40 said. Calder's art is known for its **motion**. For ideas, he watched machines. "I was always delighted by the cable car. . . . The machinery and movement interested me." He studied to be a mechanical engineer and studied how to make structures and machines. Calder also imagined

Calder's sculptures play with color and motion.

motion
motion

45 "moving" art. So he invented the mobile—a form of dangling art that swings in the air. His art is playful, and some of his biggest fans are kids. After an exhibit of his work in New York, he joked, "My fan mail is **enormous** —everyone is under 6."

enormous
huge

Adapted from "Action Artist" by Louise L. Greene
© by Carus Publishing Company. Reproduced with permission.

A Way with Fabric

50   Like other artists, Michael A. Cummings was developing his talents at a young age. "Whenever I gained consciousness as a child," he said, "that is when I knew I wanted to be an artist." First he tried painting. Then, almost by accident, he discovered his art form. He was
55 asked to make a banner using fabric, and the possibilities for creating quilts came to him. He didn't know how to sew, so he had to teach himself. It took **persistence** . He bought a sewing machine, and it has been his companion for working on quilts.

persistence
trying hard without giving up

60   What kinds of images does Cummings sew into his quilts? "It is just a matter of reaching into your mind for ideas," he says. He draws inspiration from his life experiences as well as from jazz, different **species** of butterflies, Africa, and African American art.

species
a group of individuals with common characteristics

65   Cummings says that it is **rare** for a man to be a quilter because most quilters are women. However, he likes his unique role. "It forces people to reassess what they think men can and cannot do," he says. "And if you dig a little deeper, you'll learn that in Africa and other
70 non-Western places, men have been the ones who have created and worked with fabric—for centuries."

rare
not often found or seen

Source: "Michael A. Cummings"
http://www.michaelcummings.com

Answer It

1. What can you generalize about the artists described in this selection from reading the first sentence under each section's heading?

2. Explain the meaning of Augusta Savage's sculpture titled *The Harp*.

3. Explain what Alexander Calder meant when he said, "My fan mail is enormous—everyone is under 6."

4. Use a Venn diagram to show the differences between the art of Alexander Calder and Michael A. Cummings.

5. Classify the artists in **Becoming an Artist** by the type of art they created— painting, sculpture, or quilts.

Painting	Sculpture	Quilts

Harriet Tubman Leading a Family to Freedom. Commissioned for the new National Underground Railroad Museum in Ohio. 6 feet by 10 feet, 2003.

Leonardo the Artist

What if you were as smart
as Einstein, as artistic as Picasso,
and as musical as Beethoven?
Do you think that you'd have a
5 pretty good shot at getting your
dream job? In Italy, at age 26,
Leonardo da Vinci was all of the
above. But when he tried to get
a job painting for the Duke of
10 Florence, the duke wouldn't
hire him.

It may have been because
Leonardo da Vinci seldom finished a painting. He also
had trouble painting how he was told to paint. "To give
15 orders is a gentleman's work," he said. "To carry them
out is the act of a servant." Instead, he followed his
inspiration.

inspiration
motivation to take
action

Leonardo's rebelliousness began with an **unconventional** childhood. He was born in 1452 to
20 unmarried parents. Until he was about 4, his mother raised him. Then he went to live in Vinci with his well-to-do father and his family. Because his parents were unmarried, Leonardo could not attend the university. He couldn't become a lawyer, like his father, or a doctor or a
25 professor. Part of his education was at home. It's not hard to see why he hated society's rules.

A Marvelous Beast

Leonardo da Vinci's mind was busy with questions. He grew restless. He had so many questions that no one could answer. He would run to the woods to examine
30 glowworms, lizards, or the structure of a lily stalk. He often kept an animal to observe its behavior. Then, he would draw it for future reference. His learning method combined art with science, and this probably helped him gain entrance into the workshop of Andrea del
35 Verrocchio, a successful artist in Florence.

There is a story about one of Leonardo's early attempts at art that goes like this: his father gave him a round panel of wood to decorate. Like many teenagers, Leonardo thought it would be cool to paint a really
40 creepy head. So he brought home all sorts of vermin, including lizards, bats, and maggots. He painted a disgusting monster exhaling smoke and poison gas. When Leonardo had finished, he propped the wood panel up on his easel. Light was shining onto the panel when
45 his father opened the door. Leonardo's father gasped! He was startled by the painting of a realistic-looking beast with fiery breath that looked ready to **pounce**. "This work has served its purpose," the young Leonardo said matter-of-factly. That work of art convinced his father
50 that Leonardo had a future in painting.

Leonardo Leaves Home to Begin Apprenticeship

When he was about 15, Leonardo da Vinci left his father's home for Florence, where he entered Verrocchio's workshop. Here, Leonardo could work with scholars who could answer his questions. In fact, Florence had become the center of an explosion of knowledge—a time now known as the **Renaissance** .

As an apprentice, Leonardo plunged into work. He learned how to mix paint, bronze statues, and even play the lyre. It is said he invented perfumes to mask the bad odors of the plague and taught his friends magic tricks.

Physically, he became quite the man. He was tall, with a handsome, well-proportioned face. Legend has it that Leonardo was so strong he could bend a horseshoe with his bare hands.

At 20, he graduated from Verrocchio's workshop and joined the ranks of professional painters. Verrocchio was working on a painting. He asked Leonardo to add an angel next to the one he had painted. Leonardo's angel was magnificent. Verrocchio exclaimed that he had been outdone by his own student! During the next 10 years, Leonardo da Vinci gained a reputation as a groundbreaking artist. Still, the Duke of Florence would not hire him.

Super-Vision and Virtual Reality

Leonardo's notebooks show that he wanted to know not only how something worked, but why. Born with a gift, he was able to see and portray images in two ways—through memory and imagination.

Renaissance

the time of a revival of art, literature, and learning that began in Europe in the 14th century and lasted into the 17th century

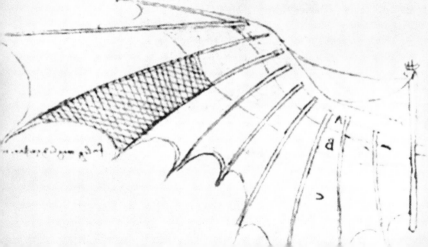

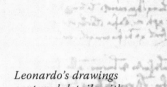

Leonardo's drawings captured details with great accuracy.

Leonardo da Vinci had a highly developed visual imagination.

Through *visual memory*, he could freeze a bird's wing movements in his mind. He could remember
80 them distinctly and then draw them. This scientifically accurate visual representation of wing movements was never copied until the camera was invented.

Through visual imagination, Leonardo could draw what he did not see, but calculated must be there. This
85 ability helped him to render highly accurate maps without the aid of satellite imagery. He drew the first detailed images of human organs, muscles, and bones long before the CAT scan was invented. Leonardo drew 360-degree cross-sectional views of body parts that were so good,
90 they could qualify as the first virtual-reality images.

In addition to observation, Leonardo da Vinci had a passion for experimentation. He always wrote down his findings. He repeated his experiments and recorded them in detail. This scientific approach was just
95 developing at the time. It helped him make extraordinary discoveries. Leonardo studied the processes governing plant growth. He developed the rules of perspective for such masterpieces as *The Last Supper*. He also created techniques for casting the largest horse statue in the world.
100

A Painter in Great Demand

prolific

very productive

Around 1500 in Florence, he began a **prolific** period of painting. Three of his great works—*The Last Supper*, *Mona Lisa*, and *Battle of Anghiari*—were all produced within a period of about 10 years. Of them, only *Mona Lisa* remains in reasonably good condition. *The Last*

105 *Supper* is but a shadow of its former self. *The Battle of Anghiari* has almost completely disappeared and is known only through copies.

The earliest of these works is *The Last Supper*. It is in the monastery of Santa Maria delle Grazie in Milan.
110 Leonardo completed it around 1498. Monasteries and convents often had this scene painted on a wall in their dining halls. Leonardo shows 13 figures seated on one side of a long table. He studied the faces of real people to create his figures. He also finished many drawings before
115 he began painting. Legend has it that the prior (the head of the monastery) was annoyed with Leonardo because he was not working quickly enough.

The painting is now in very poor condition. Leonardo seems to be at least partly to blame. He did not paint
120 in fresco, the traditional method for wall painting. This technique calls for the artist to apply a thin layer of plaster over masonry and then paint on the wet surface. As the plaster dries, the paint is absorbed. It becomes part of the wall. If the building is not exposed
125 to excessive moisture, fresco can last for centuries. Leonardo was a **perfectionist**, and he did not like to paint as quickly as this technique demanded. Instead, he invented his own method for painting on a drier base so he could work at his own pace. But the results of
130 this experiment were disastrous. Just 20 years later, the picture was ruined.

Another wall painting by Leonardo da Vinci, *Battle of Anghiari*, suffered a worse fate. Asked to produce a battle scene, he painted it in a large hall at the Palazzo Vecchio
135 government palace. Leonardo was supposed to paint the battle in which Florence defeated Milan in 1440. But the great Florentine artist Michelangelo was hired to paint another scene in the same room. These two great painters apparently disliked each other. They were
140 competing side by side.

Leonardo again experimented with his technique. This time, he used heat to bind the paint to the wall.

perfectionist
a person who tries to do things without making any mistakes

The effort was unsuccessful. Leonardo left Florence without completing the work. Michelangelo left his piece
145 unfinished as well and departed for Rome. Had they been completed, both of these paintings might have ranked among the greatest artistic masterpieces of Renaissance Italy. Sadly, all traces of both these works are gone.

The last of Leonardo da Vinci's three great works is
150 *Mona Lisa*. It is probably the most famous image in the world. Apparently, he never gave it to the person who ordered it. Leonardo took it with him when he moved to France near the end of his life. Some think the portrait is actually a self-portrait! X-rays of the painting and close
155 comparison with other of Leonardo da Vinci's drawings suggest that this may be true. But others believe the lady in the painting was the wife of a Florentine merchant named Francesco del Giocondo.

Leonardo da Vinci's Mona Lisa *is one of the most famous paintings in the world.*

Leonardo did not paint a lot. But he is considered to
160 be one of the greatest artists who ever lived. Every year,
millions of people go to the Louvre Museum in Paris to
see *Mona Lisa*. They line up outside of Santa Maria delle
Grazie to see *The Last Supper*. People visit the Palazzo
Vecchio, where his *Battle of Anghiari* was, wondering if
165 there is any of Leonardo's painting left inside the wall.

Five centuries have passed since Leonardo lived.
Someone who can compare with him has yet to be born.
There may never be another man with the artistic and
scientific genius, and the talent, of Leonardo da Vinci.

Adapted from "Leonardo: Engineer, Anatomist, Painter…Magician?"
by Katherine S. Balch; and "The Master Works" by Denise Budd
© by Carus Publishing Company. Reproduced with permission.

Think About It

1. Explain why the Duke of Florence would not hire Leonardo da Vinci.

2. Explain why two of Leonardo's greatest works, *The Last Supper* and *Battle of Anghiari*, deteriorated.

3. List Leonardo's three great paintings and their current locations.

4. Leonardo was rebellious. He was not afraid to try new painting techniques. What would happen if nobody ever tried new things or demanded perfection?

5. Based on this article, what can you infer about the author's opinion of Leonardo?

6. Leonardo did not like to paint in fresco. Tell about a time when someone did not follow a recommended method for doing something. What were the results?

Art in Space

Turn your imagination around. Turn it upside down and inside out. See floating dancers. Imagine **galactic** art galleries with paint balls bouncing in the air. Artists often have been among the first explorers of new places, and space is no exception. Already, artists are planting the seeds for tomorrow's culture there. The setting for their work is zero gravity.

Dancing on the Ceiling: Kitsou Dubois, Space Dancer

Kitsou Dubois thought about dancing in space. What dancer doesn't dream of overcoming gravity? She dreamt about lifting above the floor and floating through the air. Dubois, a French dancer and **choreographer**, has worked with astronauts and **cosmonauts** for several years. She teaches them fluid dance steps. Dubois discovered that many dance steps help astronauts work effectively in the weightlessness of space. Many astronauts are not well

With some dance training, astronauts adapt more rapidly to living in space.

trained in the control of their bodies. Certainly, they are not as well trained as dancers. But with some dance training, they can adapt more rapidly to life in space.

Dubois flew in planes for space training and acquired
20 experience dancing in zero gravity. She found it liberating and exciting. In zero gravity, dancers can express themselves not only on the floor, but on the walls and ceiling. They can even dance in the middle of the room, between the floor and ceiling. Floating upside down for a
25 dancer isn't as odd as it may seem to the rest of us.

From this experience, Dubois became fascinated that most of us see the world in only one **orientation**. The average person becomes confused when seeing things in different orientations in space. After all, in space, two
30 people can walk into a room through a door, one person with their feet on the ceiling and the other with their feet on the floor. Try looking at a picture of yourself or a friend upside down. Do the faces still look familiar?

orientation
location or position

Drift Painting: Frank Pietronigro, Space Painter

Like Dubois, Frank Pietronigro brought
35 new ideas to art. He thought about how to make paintings that float. Imagine free-flowing liquid paint. Picture moving circles of color colliding in space and making new colors. Pietronigro thought painting in space
40 was an intriguing concept.

NASA's astronaut training plane.

He took his paints aboard NASA's astronaut training plane. (The plane is known as the "Vomit Comet," because its up-and-down motions make many people feel sick.) Pietronigro had long wanted to experiment with
45 his paints in zero gravity and was thrilled when NASA officials gave him the go-ahead.

Liquids act differently in zero gravity than they do on Earth. This makes for some interesting changes in painting technique. Pietronigro set up a large plastic tent
50 as a studio in the plane and squeezed rainbow colors of paint out around himself. He floated in the tent and mixed **pigments** by pushing globs of paint together. The paint drifted around in the space surrounding him. He had created a "drift painting."

pigments

powders or pastes mixed with liquid to make colors

Celestial Sculptures: Arthur Woods, Space Sculptor

55 Arthur Woods also created a new art form for space. Woods grew up near Cape Canaveral, Florida. This is close to the Kennedy Space Center where the original launch pad for the space shuttle is located. So it's not surprising that space became the setting for his art.
60 For the last 10 years, Woods has developed space-art projects. One was a proposal for a large inflatable space sculpture. The piece would have been visible from Earth and acknowledged as a symbol of global unity. The project never took place, but Woods did organize the
65 first art exhibit in space. It was held onboard the Russian *Mir* space station. For this showing, Woods organized an

Frank Pietronigro painting in his plastic "studio," aboard NASA's astronaut training plane.

exhibition of 15 paintings inside the space station. The cosmonauts selected their favorite work to take home.

70 Space sculptures often are moving objects that can be viewed from any direction. After the success of the art exhibition, Woods convinced the cosmonauts to take *Cosmic Dancer*, one of his space sculptures, aboard the space station. *Cosmic Dancer* is a small, geometric sculpture made from aluminum. It floated in the middle
75 of the cabin, and the cosmonauts took turns spinning it.

Destination—Earth, ETA—52000: Jean-Marc Philippe, Space Media Artist

Jean-Marc Philippe is yet another space artist. The Milky Way is the medium against which he composes his artistic messages. Throughout his career, he has tackled projects with an eye toward **jettisoning** them
80 into space. His first successful project made use of a large radio telescope to broadcast messages. Philippe sent into space poems, questions, and texts written by thousands of French residents. He is building a floating time capsule called *Keo*. He has invited people from around the world
85 to submit artwork, text, and sounds to travel aboard *Keo* on a 50,000-year voyage.

Philippe also has been working to place the first sculpture on Mars. His idea is to have one of the space probes position it on the planet. The sculpture is made
90 from an extraordinary "shape-memory" metal alloy. It changes into different shapes, depending on the temperature. Philippe designed the sculpture so it will have a different shape during the Martian sunrise, when

jettisoning
throwing off

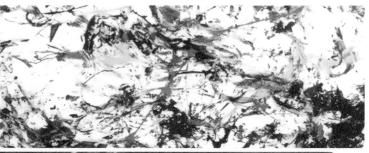

A "drift painting" created by Frank Pietronigro.

it is coolest, than it does during the Martian afternoon,
95 when it is warmest.

Art in Tomorrow's Space

The work of today's artists is setting the stage for a new space culture. Several hundred years from now, humans may be living in colonies within our own solar system. These colonies will include artists. Today's space
100 artists will be remembered as the first to include the new space frontier in our expanding view of the universe.

Artists traveled to the Americas with early explorers. Now, the work of artists is accompanying astronauts into space. Humans will continue to travel into space, and
105 space artists will be there too, exploring new worlds with their art.

Adapted from "Space(y) Art" by Roger Malina
© by Carus Publishing Company. Reproduced with permission.

Think About It

1. Kitsou Dubois taught dance to an unexpected professional group for several years. Who were her students, what did she teach them, and why?

2. Describe what it is like to dance in zero gravity.

3. Define Frank Pietronigro's style of art known as "drift painting."

4. Describe Arthur Woods' art exhibition in space.

5. Jean-Marc Philippe relays his artistic messages into space. What can you infer about his audience?

6. Name a specific kind of art that you predict will develop through the space age, and tell why you think this art form will continue to grow.

Be a Hero

Mythical Heroes

Superheroes

They fill comic strips and have superhuman skills. They're strong, quick, talented, and wise. They ensure that good wins over evil. Who are these superhumans? Superheroes! We all love heroes, as heroes can inspire us
5 and give us hope.

What Is a Myth?

Humans wanted to make sense of their world. They wanted to understand its order and its origin. They strived to understand its conflicts, so they made up tales to explain their world. These tales are called myths.
10 Myths are just made-up tales, but people have believed them. People have lived their lives as if myths were based in fact. In these tales, different gods ruled over the world.

Statue of Jupiter.

Roman Gods

Long ago, the Romans told about the gods in their myths. Saturn was one of their gods, the god of time.
15 Saturn had three sons: Jupiter, Neptune, and Pluto. Jupiter ruled the air and was the king of the gods. He was the strongest god. Juno was Jupiter's wife, and the goddess of husbands and wives. Neptune ruled the seas. He gave the waves white caps and made the waters still.
20 He held the fate of ships in his hands, so a trip could be safe or unsafe. It was Neptune's choice. His brother, Pluto, ruled over the dead. His kingdom was a dark and gloomy land. Pluto ruled over all who entered his kingdom. Once the dead entered Pluto's underworld, they could never
25 leave. These myths are still told. Ancient myths are intriguing. They give us insight into how the people who lived before us explained what happened in the world.

Unsung HEROES

Everyday Heroes

Not every hero is a superhero. For some, spending their lives helping others is a job. Think of firefighters, soldiers, and police. Often, these are the unsung heroes, as they risk their lives.

Fires

5   No matter where you live, fire can be a big problem. Firefighters save lives when a home catches fire. A call to 911 is a call to save lives. It's your direct line to the unsung heroes. What happens when a forest catches fire? Fires burn huge plots of land, and they kill birds and
10 plants. Enter the unsung heroes, as they put out the fires.

Serving with Pride

When men and women join the military, they put their lives on the line. They protect us and watch over the homelands. Sometimes, war breaks out, so they are called to protect and defend. No matter what the issue,
15 some people support it, and others reject it. It is hard to do your job when many people do not support you. Yet our soldiers do their jobs and expect little in return. We should be proud of them. They deserve their country's thanks. They, too, are unsung heroes.

Stopping Crime

20   Crime is a big problem. Some people shoplift or use drugs. Some are reckless drivers, and some harm others. The police are there to help and bring back order. They help solve crimes and work to make our lives safer. Like soldiers and firefighters, they are unsung heroes.

LEGENDARY SUPER HEROES

wits

powers of understanding; intelligence

villain

a bad or wicked person

Some people are born with special powers. Others have only their quick **wits** to rely on. But everybody has what it takes to be a hero!

Picture this scene. Terrible danger is threatening
5   the world. We're all at the hands of some dastardly **villain**. Time is running out. Can anyone save the day? We need someone strong, someone fearless—we need a hero!

This isn't just the plot of an action-packed film. It's a
10   story that's been told again and again. It's been told since people first began to entertain each other by making up stories. The stories became legends. They started as tales about real people. But as the stories were passed on for many years, they became more and more exaggerated. A
15   fight against three people turned into a battle against ten. Eventually, there were 100 fearsome enemies! A favorite weapon became an **invincible** magic tool. The superheroes described in these stories can be identified by a variety of traits.

invincible

unbeatable; unstoppable

Superstrength

20   First of all, most legendary heroes have some kind of
superhuman power. The heroes of ancient Greek legends
were usually related to the gods. This meant that they
would be extra strong, extra **clever**, and always have luck
on their side. The best known of the Greek superheroes,
25 Hercules, was only a baby when he strangled two snakes
that had been sent to kill him!

Magic Powers

Also, some superheroes use magic. One example is
Odin. He was the most important Norse god. He had an
invincible spear called *Gungnir*. He also had two ravens.
30 They would perch on his shoulders and fly off to spy on
his enemies. His son, Thor, had a hammer called *Mjolnir*
("the destroyer"). The hammer returned like a boomerang
whenever he threw it. Thor also had a magic belt. This
belt doubled his strength.

35   In contrast, some superheroes
have had to rely on their own
smarts. Not all superheroes
have superhuman skills
or magic powers. Take
40 Odysseus, for example. He
captured the city of Troy
by hiding his army inside
a huge wooden horse.
The Trojans thought it
45 was a gift from the
Greeks. But they got
an unpleasant surprise
when Odysseus' men
jumped out!

clever
smart;
quick-thinking

*Odin, the most
important Norse god.*

Fatal Flaw

50   In addition, some superheroes have a fatal flaw. Few heroes are totally invincible. Most have one weakness that can destroy them. With Superman, it was a mineral, kryptonite. In the case of Achilles, the great Greek warrior of the Trojan War, it was his heel. When Achilles
55 was a baby, his mother dipped him in the magic river Styx. This made his whole body **invulnerable** —except for the heel by which he was held. He finally died when a poisoned arrow struck him on the heel. (Today, we still say a person's weak point is an Achilles' heel.)

Taste for Adventure

60   Finally, some superheroes participate in quests. When they're not saving the world, many superheroes go on quests.
65 These are long, dangerous journeys. The objective of a quest is to search for a special place or object. King Arthur's knights, for
70 example, went on a quest to find the Holy Grail, a sacred cup. In a quest, a hero faces many **perils** and challenges. These test strength, courage,
75 and honor to the very limits. But for a hero, that's all in a day's work!

The marriage of King Arthur and Guinevere.

Profiles: Famous Heroes and Heroines

    Hercules—Hercules was famous for the 12 tasks, or labors, set for him by King Eurystheus of Tiryns. These
80 tasks included killing monsters, cleaning a stable by diverting a river, and taming a herd of man-eating horses. He proved his amazing strength many times. Once, he even held up the sky in place of the giant named Atlas.

Scheherazade—Scheherazade is a Persian heroine, a
85 female hero, whose husband had been married many times
before. He always killed his wives the morning after he
married them. But Scheherazade was clever. Each night,
she told him a story. But she always stopped at such an
exciting point that he would let her live to finish it.
90 After 1,001 nights, the king found he was too much
in love with Scheherazade to kill her.

Odin—Odin was the Norse god of war and
wisdom. He rode upon an eight-footed steed, Sleipnir.
Odin had only one eye. He loved learning so much
95 that he traded one of his eyes for a drink from the
well of wisdom. This drink gave him knowledge.

Thor—Thor, Odin's son, was the Norse god of
thunder. He was large and powerful. He had a red
beard and eyes of lightning. Despite his threatening
100 appearance, he was very popular. He protected both the
gods and humans from the forces of evil. Thor got into
frequent fights with giants. One of them was Skrymir, a huge
frost giant. The giant was so big that Thor slept in the thumb
of his empty glove—thinking he was inside a house!

The Persian heroine, Scheherazade.

Adapted from "Super Powers" by Claire Watts
and Robert Nicholson from *Super Heroes*.
Reprinted by permission of Cooper Square Publishing.

Answer It

1. Infer what happened when Odysseus' men jumped out from hiding in the wooden horse.

2. Identify the fatal flaw of two superheroes.

3. List the characteristics of superheroes. State whether you think everyone has what it takes to be a hero.

4. Use ideas in this text selection to create a superhero of your own. Be sure to include a name, superpowers, examples of heroic deeds, and one weakness.

5. The stories of some of these legendary superheroes come from myths. Name the mythical Greek heroes mentioned in this article. Discuss whether any of the heroes were real people.

by Gary Soto

Preface:

Often, we think of a hero or heroine as a person who does something to save the day. But a true hero is a person who shows strength of character. There are heroes all around us. As you read this play and act it out, think about the qualities that make a person a real hero.

CHARACTERS	PROPS
Manuel	A sewing machine
Mother	A clunky pair of boy's shoes
Angel, the school bully	A new pair of penny loafers
Elena, Manuel's sister	A letter
Manuel's relatives	A wrapped birthday present
Tío José, Manuel's uncle	Two cots with pillows
Ceci, the girl whom Manuel likes	
Partygoers	
SETS	**COSTUMES**
Living room of Manuel's house	Everyday clothes
A street in the neighborhood	
Bedroom of Manuel's house	

(Manuel paces back and forth in big clunky shoes while his mother sits at a table sewing patches onto a pair of pants.)

MANUEL: *(indicating his shoes)*: Look at them!

MOTHER: They're nice, *mi'jo.*

MANUEL: Nice! They're too big! They're old! They're ugly. *(Stomps his feet.)* And can you hear them?

MOTHER: They're like drums.

(Manuel stomps louder.)

MOTHER: No, like congas.

MANUEL: Everyone will hear me. They'll laugh and say, "Here comes Manuel in his big ugly shoes."

MOTHER: *Mi'jo,* it will be like music from your feet.

MANUEL: *(kicking up a shoe)*: And look. There's a start of a hole on the bottom. Rain will get in. *(Desperately)* And they're from the thrift store.

MOTHER: Sure, they're a little bit used, but these shoes are new for you.

MANUEL: Mom!

MOTHER: Manuel, new things cost money.

(Manuel's sister enters stage left, balancing three boxes of shoes and slowly walking across the stage.)

MANUEL: But look at Elena! She's got new shoes. Lots of them!

MOTHER: She saved her money for them. And what did you do with your money?

*(Manuel forces a **moody** face.)*

MOTHER: Come on. *Dime.* Tell me.

MANUEL: *(low voice)*: I bought a hundred ice creams.

moody

temperamental; sulky

MOTHER: Louder!

MANUEL: I bought a hundred ice creams for my friends. *(Pause)* I should have bought a bicycle. Then I could ride by real fast and no one would see that I have ugly shoes.

(Telephone rings, and the mother gets up to answer it. Her face brightens as she hears a relative's voice.)

MOTHER: *¿Quien es? ¿Pablo? ¿Dónde está? En Chula Vista. Pues, Fresno no es muy lejos. Por Greyhound dos días, no más.*

(Her voice fades, but she keeps talking into the telephone.)

mocking

making fun of; imitating

MANUEL: *(to audience)*: Mom's always helping relatives from Mexico. (**mocking**) "Please, stay with us. Don't worry. We have room for you." And me? I get stuck with old shoes or . . . *(looking at the table piled with sewing, among it a patched-up pair of old pants)* or jeans like these.

(Lights fade, then come up on Manuel and his mother. Manuel holds up a pair of brand-new loafers.)

MOTHER: Take care of them. They're for your birthday, except early.

MANUEL: Thanks, Mom! They're really nice.

(He hugs his mother, kicks off his old shoes, and starts to put on the new loafers.)

MOTHER: They're called loafers. *Mira,* you can put pennies in them.

MANUEL: Where?

MOTHER: Here. In these slots. *(Bends to put in pennies.)* That's why they're called penny loafers.

(Manuel clicks the heels of his penny loafers; Mother leaves stage.)

MANUEL: But why should I put pennies in? I'd rather have dimes!

(Manuel bends to insert two shiny dimes in the slots. He walks around the stage, admiring his shoes. **Transfixed** *by the shoes, he doesn't notice Angel, the school bully, who has come onstage, "tagging" walls.)*

transfixed
held motionless in amazement

ANGEL: What's wrong with you, homes. You loco?

MANUEL: Oh, hi, Angel!

ANGEL: There's something different about you. . . . *(circles Manuel)* How come you're wearing those kind of shoes? You look like a nerd, homes.

MANUEL: They're penny loafers. Stylish, huh?

ANGEL: *(pointing)*: What's that?

MANUEL: What's what?

ANGEL: That shine! Looks like dimes. Give 'em up!

MANUEL: *(whining)*: Angel.

ANGEL: Come on! Give 'em up. I could use a soda. Yeah, a root beer would make me feel real happy.

(Manuel squeezes the dimes from his shoes. He hands the dimes over to Angel, who leaves, flipping the coins. Manuel walks **dejectedly** *back to his house. He takes the shoes off and throws them into a box.)*

dejectedly
in a low-spirited or depressed way

MANUEL: *(to audience)*: Months pass. My mom keeps taking in relatives from Mexico, and I keep on wearing my old shoes.

(Relatives march in a line across the stage; then his mother appears holding a letter. She sniffs the letter.)

MANUEL: *(to audience)*: And you know what else happens? I grow two inches. I get big. I can feel my shoulders rise like mountains . . . well, more like hills. But still, they get bigger. . . . Then, I get an invitation.

MOTHER: Manuel, here's a letter . . . from a girl.

MANUEL: A girl wrote to me?

MOTHER: *(holding it under the light)*: Yeah, it says—

MANUEL: Mom! It's personal!

(Manuel takes the letter from his mother, who leaves stage.)

MANUEL: Wow! An invitation to Ceci's birthday party. "Games and dancing" and "Dress to impress."

(Manuel runs offstage. Mother and Tío José, a Mexican immigrant, enter.)

MOTHER: Let me show you your room. You'll share it with Manuel.

TÍO JOSÉ: *(looking about)*: Nice place, ¡Y qué grande!

(The two exit; Manuel enters, wearing a tie and holding a wrapped gift. He looks down at his old shoes.)

MANUEL: I can't wear these shoes.

(He turns to the box holding his loafers. He takes out the loafers, fits in two dimes, and then struggles to put them on.)

MANUEL: Hmmm, kind of tight. Guess my feet were growing with the rest of me.

(Manuel walks around stage, taking hurtful steps.)

MANUEL: But I got to go to the party! It's going to be a good one.

(Manuel walks painfully, crawls, swims, and then gets back to his feet.)

MANUEL: Maybe if I walk backward, my toes won't feel so jammed.

(Manuel begins to walk backward, sighing with **relief***.)*

relief
an easing of distress or pain

MANUEL: Wow, the world looks different. The birds look different, and the cars, and those kids over there on their bikes.

(As Manuel absorbs the world in his backward walk, Ceci and partygoers come onstage. Manuel bumps into Ceci.)

MANUEL: Sorry, Ceci.

CECI: That's okay. How come you're walking backward?

MANUEL: Oh, you know, to see how the world looks from the other direction. *(Pause)* Also, I'm inventing a dance.

CECI: You're what?

MANUEL: A new dance. It's called . . . the Backward Caterpillar.

(Manuel demonstrates by cha-chaing backward. Ceci and partygoers fall in line and cha-cha backward, too.)

CECI: Look at Manuel slide in his new shoes!

(Partygoers ad-lib "Cool shoes," "Look at the dude slide," "Manuel's the best!" Partygoers cha-cha off the stage. Lights dim, then come up on Manuel and Tío José in their beds, ready to go to sleep, their hands folded behind their heads.)

MANUEL: Doesn't that crack on the ceiling look like lightning?

TÍO JOSÉ: *(getting up):* Wish me luck tomorrow. I'm going to Modesto. I think I got a job in a restaurant there.

MANUEL: How will you get there?

(Tío José sits up.)

TÍO JOSÉ: *(hooking thumb into a "hitchhiking" manner): Un poquito de éste* and lots of walking. *Pero mira, mis huaraches son rasquachis. (Laughing)* I hope they can make it to Modesto.

MOTHER: *(offstage): José ¡Teléfono!*

(When Tío José leaves, Manuel examines his uncle's worn sandals. Manuel scribbles a note as lights dim.)
(Lights come up on Tío José and Manuel asleep: Tío José rises, sleepily rubbing his face. A rooster crows offstage.)

TÍO JOSÉ: These shoes? For me? They're too nice for a worker like me.

MANUEL: You have a long way to go, Tío, and you need good shoes.

(Tío José is touched by this **gesture** *. He puts on shoes and walks a few steps as he tries them out.)*

gesture
an action that is meant to show feeling or thought

TÍO JOSÉ: They're perfect. *Adiós,* Manuel. These shoes will take me a long ways, and by the time they are worn out, you'll be as tall as your parents. They'll be looking up to you.

(Tío José walks offstage, and Manuel lowers his head back onto the pillow.)

Answer It

1. Use drawings to show the expression of Manuel's mood change from the beginning to the end of the story. Then explain the mood change in words.

2. Describe Manuel's feeling for his mother.

3. Discuss whether Manuel is a hero at the end of the story.

4. Infer what Manuel learned by giving his shoes to his uncle.

5. **"These Shoes of Mine"** is a drama. Explain how this type of writing is different from a story such as **"Podway Bound"** in Unit 13. Explain whether a play is easier or harder to read.

NAVAJO CODE TALKERS

Navajo radio operators.

A Marine officer questioned Private Samuel Billison at basic training camp. "Are you Indian?" he asked.

"No, sir, I'm Navajo," Sam answered.

"Can you speak Navajo?"

5 "Yes, sir," Sam replied.

"Can you speak English?"

"A little, sir," he said.

"Then we have a special training program for you. Get your duffel bag."

10 Sam didn't know it was just the start of a great adventure.

Bullets and shells tore through the air as U.S. Marines hit the beach. On the sands of Iwo Jima island, any other World War II code machine would have been 15 too slow to use in the heat of battle. But the Marines had highly mobile cryptographs, each with two arms, two legs, and an unbreakable code.

From the first day's invasion to the final battle a month later, the human code machines kept messages 20 crackling over military radios. *Gini,* the code said.

Behnaalitsosie. Neasjah. Lotso. Throughout the mortal combat, more mysterious words filled the airwaves. Finally, as a photographer took the famous picture of the American flag flying over Mt. Suribachi, the news went
25 out in Navajo.

Naastosi Thanzie Dibeh Shida Dahnestsa Tkin Shush Wollachee Moasi Lin Achi. Ordinary Marines listening to this babble were as confused as Japanese soldiers **intercepting** the messages. Had they spoken Navajo,
30 they would have recognized the words—"Mouse Turkey Sheep Uncle Ram Ice Bear Ant Cat Horse Intestines."

But what could such nonsense mean? To the Navajo Code Talkers, the first letter of each word spelled out Mt. Suribachi. Other code filled in the announcement: Iwo
35 Jima was under American control.

The Navajo Code Talkers were unique in cryptographic history. From 1942 to 1945, more than 400 Code Talkers stormed the beaches of Pacific islands. Instantly **encoding** and **decoding** messages, they
40 helped Marines win the war in the Pacific. Even today, their code remains one of the few in history that was never broken.

In Navajo, Memory Is Everything

When World War II began, hundreds of Navajo men volunteered to fight. Many of them had never been off
45 their reservation, a high, arid plain that included parts of Arizona, Utah, and New Mexico. The reservation had no electricity or indoor plumbing, and only a few schools. There they lived as a separate nation, as many still do today. Many Navajo herded sheep and bought
50 from government trading posts what little they needed and could not make. They spoke some English, but the business of their daily lives was conducted in the language of their ancestors—Navajo.

Among languages spoken by only tens of thousands of
55 Americans, Navajo was the one least likely to be known to foreigners. The language was entirely oral. There was

intercepting
stopping or interrupting the progress of something

encoding
writing in code

decoding
translating a code into its original language

no written language. Not a single book had ever been written in Navajo.

Unlike English, Navajo is a tonal language. Its vowels
60 rise and fall depending on the situation. Change the pitch or accent of a Navajo word, and you change its meaning. Each Navajo verb contains its own subjects, objects, and adverbs. A single verb can translate into an entire sentence. In Navajo, one native speaker said, words "paint
65 a picture in your mind."

A non-Navajo proposed the Navajo code. Philip Johnston was the son of missionaries. He grew up on the reservation. Marine officers were **skeptical** at first. American armies had used other Indian languages to
70 send messages during World War I. Because the ancient languages had no words for machine gun or tank, the experiment failed. Johnston had a better idea—a language combined with a code.

At Camp Elliott, north of San Diego, California,
75 Johnston arranged a test. "Translate some messages from Navajo to English and back again," he told some old friends. As iron-jawed Marines listened in, their faces went slack. The words were not encoded, yet top cryptographers had no hope of **deciphering** them.
80 Navajo itself was a mystery, even without a code. Soon, the Marines went looking for what they now call "a few good men." These good men had to be fluent in English and Navajo.

Making a Code

The Navajo language contained no words for the
85 horrors of war. "Bomber," "battleship," "grenade"—all were terms foreign to the Navajo. But the Navajo soldiers based their code on things in nature. They named military planes after birds. *Gini*, Navajo for "chicken hawk," became "dive bomber." *Neasjah*, meaning "owl,"
90 meant "observation plane." They named ships after fish. *Lotso*, meaning "whale," was the code word for "battleship," and *Beshlo*—"iron fish"—meant "submarine."

skeptical

doubtful; uncertain

deciphering

understanding; converting a code to known language

To spell out proper names, the Code Talkers encoded a Navajo zoo. Soldiers spell out abbreviations with their
95 own alphabet, which begins Able, Baker, Charlie. The Navajo version began *Wollachee, Shush, Moasi,* meaning Ant, Bear, Cat.

Finally, Code Talkers created clever terms for friends and enemies. "Lieutenant" was translated as "One Silver
100 Bar." Mussolini, Italy's fascist dictator, was *Adee'yaats' iin Tsoh*—"Big Gourd Chin." Hitler became *Daghailchiih*—"Moustache Smeller."

Test Time

With just 400 words encoded, the Navajo put their cryptology to the test. They handed a message to Navy
105 intelligence officers. The experts spent three weeks trying to decipher it. The experts failed. Then, armed with a code and M-1 rifles, a few dozen Code Talkers shipped out to the Pacific. Two remained behind to teach the code to other Navajo recruits.
110 On Guadalcanal, Code Talkers had to prove themselves again. In other fields of battle, machines encoded messages. How could simple soldiers do

BREAKING THE CODE

Gini – Navajo for "chicken hawk," became "dive bomber."

Neasjah – meaning "owl," meant "observation plane."

Lotso – meaning "whale," meant "battleship."

Beshlo – meaning "iron fish," meant "submarine."

intelligence work? And how could they do it without codebooks, at that!

115   Officers staged a race. They set up Code Talkers against a mechanical cryptograph. They sent a message through the jungle. But they forgot to tell other radio operators. The Navajo Code Talkers sent their messages. Seconds later, frantic messages poured into headquarters.

120 "They're jamming our frequencies!" the radiomen reported. Told that the strange words came from fellow Marines, one radioman asked, "What's going on over there? You guys crazy?"

    The Code Talkers won the race handily. The Navajo
125 code, officers said, proved "**indispensable** for the rapid transmission" of secret messages. The Code Talkers went into battle.

    On the island of Saipan, an advancing American battalion was shelled from behind by its own troops.
130 Desperate messages called, "Hold your fire!" But the enemy could imitate Marine broadcasts. Nobody knew whether the cry was real. Then headquarters asked, "Do you have a Navajo?" A Navajo sent the same message just once. The shelling stopped.

indispensable

necessary; needed

Congressional Medal honoring Navajo code talkers.

135   Between invasions, the Code Talkers met to encode new battle terms. They transmitted thousands of messages without error. Before the war ended, several were killed in action. Marine Major Howard Connor assessed their contribution. "Without the Navajos," Connor said, "the
140 Marines would never have taken Iwo Jima."

Adapted from "Top Secret: An Interview with Sam Billison, Navajo Code Talker," by Nancy E. Cluff, and from "Human Code Machine," by Bruce Watson © by Carus Publishing Company. Reproduced with permission.

Think About It

1. What can you infer about the requirements for attending the special training camp mentioned in the dialog at the beginning of the article?

2. Most of the Navajo Code Talkers came from their reservation. In which three states is the Navajo Reservation located?

3. What happened the first time Navajo Code Talkers put their cryptology to the test?

4. American armies had used other Indian languages during World War I, but the experiment failed. How did the Navajo Code solve the problem?

5. Explain the inability of the enemy to decipher the Navajo code.

6. Howard Conner said, "Without the Navajos, the Marines would never have taken Iwo Jima." How do you think the Navajo Code Talkers felt about their contribution? Discuss people you know who have made contributions to your school or community.

The Ride of Her Life

Imagine jumping onto a horse and riding 40 miles alone on rocky dirt roads on a stormy night. Imagine taking your dangerous ride at a time when you are more frightened than you have ever been, and still remaining

5 **focused** . Now, think about doing this in the middle of a war! What if your ride had to do with a secret war mission, when enemies and robbers were roaming the countryside, and nobody would think twice about killing you?

10 More than 200 years ago, in 1777, Sybil Ludington, a girl from New York state, faced this dangerous adventure head-on. On her horse Star, Sybil rode 40 miles to warn the **local** citizens of approaching enemy danger.

During this time in American history, the people

15 were fighting for their freedom. From the early 1600s, the American colonies were not a free nation. They paid taxes to England and were ruled by the king of England.

focused

to be concentrated on a goal without distraction

local

having to do with a particular place, like a neighborhood or town

But they were not represented in the English government, and they longed to be free. The American colonists had
20 declared their independence in 1776. They fought the American Revolutionary War for eight years to win that independence. During the war, Sybil Ludington's ride helped the Americans win a battle in her community.

Late in the evening of April 26, 1777, a messenger
25 appeared at the Ludington farm in Fredericksburg, New York. (Today, that area is called Ludingtonville, in honor of Sybil!) Sybil's father, Henry Ludington, commanded a militia. This was a local group of farmers and merchants who would be called upon to defend their community as
30 soldiers in times of danger.

The messenger, **anxious** and exhausted, informed Colonel Ludington of bad news. About 2,000 British troops had landed on the Connecticut coastline. They had marched to the nearby town of Danbury. There,
35 they'd immediately begun setting fire to houses and American army supplies. Colonel Ludington knew that his militia was the closest group of soldiers who could hold off the British. There was grave danger, and he knew what he had to do. He had to call his men together
40 quickly; he had to gather his militia.

anxious

nervous; worried

Historians aren't sure how Sybil was chosen to saddle up for her famous ride. At 16, she was the oldest of the eight Ludington children. She was probably a good rider. Some people think that Star was Sybil's horse, and that
45 her father thought she'd handle the horse better than anyone else.

How Sybil was selected didn't matter at that moment, anyway. Her orders were to ride Star through the countryside, stopping very briefly at every farm or
50 inn along the way to shout: "The British have burned Danbury! Muster at Ludington's!"

Sybil and her parents must have felt frightened as she rode off. The dangers were very real. If the British saw Sybil riding, they would have stopped her, perhaps

55 suspecting her to be a spy. Criminals, whom the people called "skinners," roamed the countryside looking for people to rob. Star would have been an attractive horse to steal. Thieves wouldn't have cared that Star's rider was a young girl.

60 Today, it would take about an hour to drive this 40-mile route. But on horseback—with the old road conditions, in a storm, in the dark—it probably would have taken Sybil most of the night. When she returned home in the wee hours of the morning, the militia was 65 getting prepared at her family's home.

Colonel Ludington's militia marched 20 miles that night. The young Americans won the battle. The attacking soldiers retreated to their ships.

In spite of Sybil's incredible feat of bravery, no 70 historical documents mention her ride. But that wasn't unusual for the times. The activities of women weren't written about or discussed much. What we've learned about Sybil came from records of the community itself and from the Ludington family's **descendants** .

descendants

people who come from the same family

75 She may not have received any military honors, but New York state took notice of Sybil's courage in the 1900s. In 1935, a series of roadside markers went up along Sybil's route. In 1961, a famous artist created a huge bronze statue of Sybil riding Star. And in 1975, the U.S. Postal 80 Service issued a stamp as a tribute to Sybil.

Sybil Ludington postage stamp.

It's never easy to **venture** into the unknown and do what you must when danger **lurks**. But Sybil Ludington did just that. We don't know what she looked like, what she said, or how she felt as she galloped across the countryside. But we know what she did. And because of courageous people like Sybil, the United States became "the land of the free and the home of the brave." And brave people from around the world still come to the United States, to share in its precious freedoms.

85

venture
to do something dangerous

lurks
hides; sneaks

Think About It

1. Explain the purpose of Sybil Ludington's ride.

2. Explain why civilians in the American colonies were willing to risk their lives to fight professional soldiers.

3. Describe the emotions Sybil's parents felt as they watched their daughter ride into the night.

4. Explain why early history books made no mention of Sybil Ludington's famous ride.

5. Use a timeline to show how Sybil Ludington has been memorialized in the last several decades.

6. Sybil had to ride a horse 40 miles to get a message to the local citizens. This took her approximately three hours. List other methods of communication that would be used to spread the message today.

Cheer an Athlete

The Complete Athlete

The Motto

"Let me win. But if I cannot win, let me be brave in the attempt." Special Olympics athletes think like this, as this is their motto.

Uncommon Athletes

Take Steven Walker, who competes in Special
5 Olympics. He is a runner who runs marathons and wins gold.

Getting Started

One person can make things happen, as Eunice Kennedy Shriver did. She began a summer day camp in 1962. She held the camp at her home and invited athletes
10 like Steven. She watched them compete in sports and saw their desire to work hard and win. She planned games such as swimming and track. Competing was a thrill, and they loved it! They were happy. Shriver saw them smile, and she made up her mind. In 1968, her camp became
15 *Special Olympics*, and the games grew. More people came, and by 1970, all 50 states sent athletes. Now, Special Olympics is important in the lives of many people. Today, there are 27 official sports, including summer sports and winter sports. From all over the world, athletes come
20 to take part in the games. These athletes compete at no cost. How are the games funded? Shriver has used grants, and many have donated money. Many others have made money by holding events. You can help, too, so get started and help fund Special Olympics!

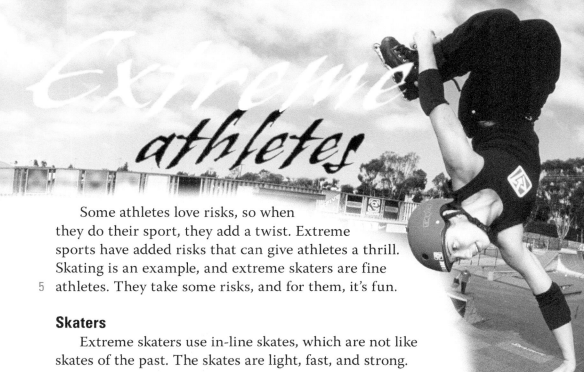

Extreme athletes

Some athletes love risks, so when they do their sport, they add a twist. Extreme sports have added risks that can give athletes a thrill. Skating is an example, and extreme skaters are fine
5 athletes. They take some risks, and for them, it's fun.

Skaters

Extreme skaters use in-line skates, which are not like skates of the past. The skates are light, fast, and strong. Skaters don't use skating rinks; they use skate parks that have ramps. Skaters even have a jargon, or their own
10 words. Take the metal bar at the top of the ramp where they do tricks. It has a name. It's the "coping." The skaters twist, turn, and do amazing jumps. They spend lots of time practicing. They start with easy in-line tricks. First, there's the "crossover," where they just cross one skate over
15 the other. Then they practice harder tricks, but learning them takes time. For example, they try "bashing," or going down steps. Sometimes, there's no skate park, so they go somewhere else. They use steps, parking lots, and even curbs. They really take skating to the next level!

Professional in-line skater Fabiola Oliveira Samoes da Silva competes and wins against the best men and women skaters in the world.

Safe Athletes

20 Extreme athletes protect themselves by using helmets and pads, but they still can be injured. Without protection, skaters can get hurt even more. They can miss a landing or lose control. Extreme athletes are risk-takers, and they love to compete and take their sport to a new level. But they
25 think of safety, too. They have to. They have fun, but they need to always take care. They need to be safe athletes.

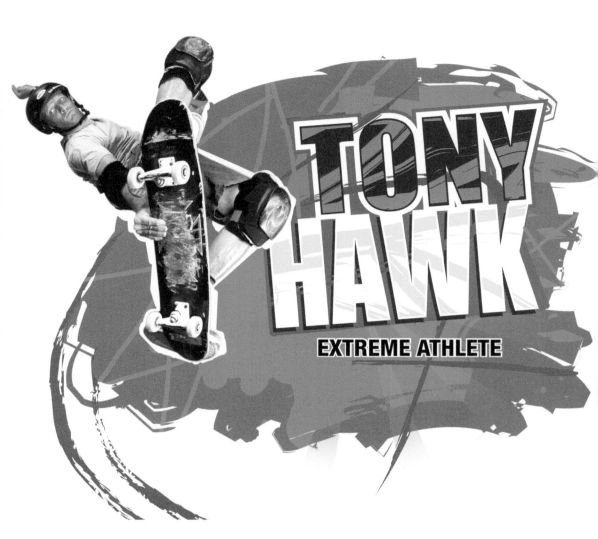

TONY HAWK
EXTREME ATHLETE

When Tony Hawk was 6 years old, his mom took him to an Olympic-sized pool. "He decided that he had to swim the length of it without a breath," his
5 mom remembers. He couldn't do it. "He was so hard on himself," his mom recalls about how frustrated he was when he could not accomplish his goals. Two years later, Tony's brother changed his life.
10 Tony's big brother, Steve, found the answer to Tony's **dilemma**. It was a skateboard. Tony started playing on the bright blue board. Crash! Bang! Slam! His thin

dilemma
a difficult problem

body finally started to catch up with his brain. "When he started getting good at skating, it changed his

15 personality," Steve said. "Finally, he was doing something that he was satisfied with. He became a different guy. He was calm. He started thinking about other people and became more generous. He wasn't so worried about losing at other things."

20 But Tony was still beating himself up. What happened if he didn't skate his best in a contest? Even if he won, he would be silent. He'd go home and take his trusty cat, Zorro, up to his room. He had to be by himself. "If I don't do my best, it kills me," he said.

25 Even so, Tony's skateboarding success continued. By 12, Tony had a skateboard company as a sponsor. By 14, he was pro. By 16, Tony was the best skateboarder in the world. Over the next 17 years, he entered about 100 contests. He won 73 and placed second in 19. His record

30 is by far the best in skateboarding history.

There was one problem. Success in skateboarding did not guarantee **financial** security. Skateboarding popularity went up and down. Tony had great financial success early in his career. For example, he was able to

35 buy his own house when he was a 17-year-old high school senior. Two years later, he bought another house. This time, Tony built a monster skate ramp at the top of a hill. He wedged a smaller ramp between his house and pool. Tony traveled worldwide for demonstrations and contests.

40 He made enough money to buy trips to Hawaii for his friends. Everyone could vacation together. In addition, Tony was an electronics nut. He was always updating his computers, stereo systems, video cameras, and cars.

This financial success did not last forever. In 1991,

45 it all came to an end. When Tony looked up, it was too late; the sky was falling. People lost interest in skateboarding. Skating died. As a result, Tony's income shrank **drastically**. He didn't see it coming. He did not plan ahead.

50 During this time, Tony lived in a blur of financial uncertainty. He sold one house. He refinanced the

financial
having to do with money

drastically
suddenly; severely

other. He started a skateboard company with a fellow skateboarder. The company didn't make money. Tony's future was unclear. "I thought skating was over for me," he said. He realized that he might not be able to earn a living skating. He thought of options. He could edit video. He could get a computer job.

Instead, skateboarding came back. It became cool again. And the Hawk became the " **Phoenix** ." Tony's success rose again. His company began to succeed. It is now one of the largest skateboarding companies in the world. In addition, Tony signed six-figure **endorsement** deals. In 1999 Tony hooked up with an electronics company. Together, they created a skateboarding video game. It became a best-seller. Tony's success overflowed into the non-athletic world as well. His autobiography, *HAWK—Occupation: Skateboarder* was a *New York Times* best-seller. A final example of Tony's success is the Tony Hawk Foundation. It promotes and helps finance public skate parks in low-income neighborhoods across America. Tony feels that it is important to give back to the sport that has given him so much.

At times, Tony's days **adhere** to a strange dichotomy. He divides his time between skateboarding and fatherhood. One day, he slit his shins open while shooting a TV commercial. He couldn't go to the hospital; there was no time. He had to pick up his son, Riley, from school.

Tony retired from professional skateboarding when he was 31. But in skateboarding, the word "retire" doesn't mean he stopped skating. It just means he's stopped competitive skating. He still skates almost every day. He learns new tricks. He does several public demonstrations a year.

"I'm pretty happy with the way things turned out," Tony says. "I mean, I never thought that I could make a career out of skateboarding." Tony Hawk is an example of a truly extreme athlete.

Adapted with permission from the biography page of the Tony Hawk Official Web site

phoenix
a mythical bird that lived for 500 years, set itself on fire, and was born again from the ashes; a thing or person who makes a remarkable comeback after difficulty

endorsement
a legal agreement that allows companies to use the name of a famous person to sell their products

adhere
to stick closely to

Answer It

1. Describe Tony Hawk as an athlete. Use examples from the selection.

2. What can you infer about the goals Tony set for himself as a child?

3. Read this quote from the selection: "Tony started playing on the bright blue board. Crash! Bang! Slam!" The words **crash**, **bang**, and **slam** are examples of onomatopoeia. Explain the effect this type of word has on the reader.

4. Select two of Hawk's accomplishments that you think are the most amazing. Explain why.

5. The sport of skateboarding and Tony Hawk's career declined but later became successful again. The author describes Hawk's rising success with the statement, "And the Hawk became the 'Phoenix.'" Explain what the author meant by this statement.

A Special Kind of Athlete

The Special Olympics Games are unique sporting events. What's different about them? All the athletes have intellectual disabilities. The coaches, the trainers, and even the officials are **volunteers**. Special Olympics

5 **achieves** at least three goals. First, the games provide experience. Second, they boost athletes' self-confidence. Last, they give athletes the joy of competition. Every athlete benefits from the positive experience of competing in a sport. But winning is not the sole focus.

10 In fact, the Special Olympics Athlete Oath reads: "Let me win. But if I cannot win, let me be brave in the attempt."

Special Olympics has grown over the years. It began as a day camp and rapidly evolved into an **international** event. The first International Special Olympics Games

15 took place in 1968. Chicago was the first host for this hugely successful event. Later, many different communities began to host the games. Today, the Special Olympics Games include 27 official sports. There are individual events like gymnastics and swimming, and

20 there are team sports, such as basketball and softball. More than two million athletes participate around the world, and there are more than 700,000 volunteers.

Athletes' families play a key role in Special Olympics. Former board chair Sargent Shriver explains: "Families are the backbone of the Special Olympics. They
25 help to coach and train their athletes. They provide transportation. They sit on the board of directors. They raise money."

George Ashley was a coach. He coached his stepdaughter, Shannon. Ashley is an **amateur** athlete
30 himself, and through Special Olympics he learned that everybody wins. The games taught him the true meaning of sport. "It was really the most rewarding thing I have ever done," he said. "I went into it thinking I was this big, tough guy. I found out that there are many things we take
35 for granted. To be at the finish line when a **competitor** comes in and see the sense of accomplishment is worth whatever work goes into it. I think anyone who plays a sport should take some time and volunteer for Special Olympics."
40   Special Olympics is organized with fairness in mind. People compete in divisions, with each division including competitors of about the same age and ability. Team sports are divided into three age divisions to help participants build self-esteem and develop physically.
45 This system boosts self-confidence. It's a design that gives everyone a chance to win.

Special Olympics is different from the actual Olympic Games. In the Olympic Games, much time, money, and effort are **invested** in winning. The number of gold
50 medals won becomes an emblem of national pride. In contrast, Special Olympics emphasizes the participation and training of individuals. Winning is not as important, and all competitors are honored whether they win or not.

amateur
unpaid; not professional

competitor
a person who participates in a sport

invested
put time, effort, or money into something

Adapted from "The Special Olympics" by Gary Crooker
© by Carus Publishing Company. Reproduced with permission.

A Gold Medal for Running

One Special Olympics athlete is Steven Walker. He
55 is from Kansas City, Missouri. In the summer of 2003,
he traveled to Ireland to compete in the games and won
gold!

Walker loves to run, and he is good at it. He placed
22nd in the Chicago Marathon, finishing the 26.2-mile
60 race in 3 hours and 17 minutes. He was then invited
to run at the Special Olympics Games and ran the
marathon in 3 hours and 38 minutes to win the gold
medal. However, running is not the only sport Walker
enjoys. He plays softball, volleyball, and basketball, and
65 also does some bowling.

Walker likes hearing the shouts and cheers of his
fans during races. He has a good time meeting the other
competitors who come from all over the globe. "I have
enjoyed World Games because I have met people from
70 other countries," Walker said. "I enjoyed being able to
race with all of them."

Adapted from "Marathon Madness" by A.J. Hellickson from
Scholastic News Online, June 2003. Reprinted by permission.

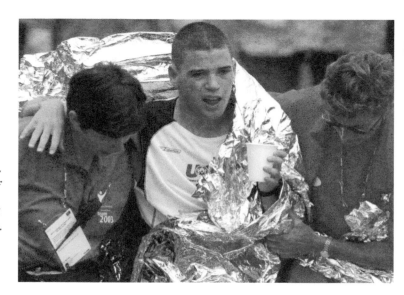

Steven Walker finishes the half marathon in the 2003 Special Olympics.

Answer It

1. Distinguish Special Olympics from the Olympic Games.

2. What can you infer from the Special Olympics Oath about what is important in Special Olympics?

3. Select two events included in Special Olympics that you would like to coach. Tell why you made your selections.

4. Distinguish whether the following statements about Special Olympics are facts or opinions:
   a. Special Olympics began as a day camp.
   b. Special Olympics is a great event.
   c. Today Special Olympics has 27 official sports.
   d. Special Olympics athletes are determined.
   e. Special Olympics is different from the Olympic Games.

5. What can you infer about Steven Walker's personality?

SWIFTER, HIGHER, STRONGER

motto
a short saying that explains a basic belief or goal

striving
trying very hard

The Latin **motto** for the Olympic Games is "Citius, Altius, Fortius." It means "Swifter, Higher, Stronger." Athletes have been **striving** to improve their athletic skills since ancient times. The ancient Greeks held
5 athletic contests. They held dance contests. They held horse, boat, and torch races all over their country. Greek literature tells of the many sports that were popular in ancient times. Murals and statues show discus throwers, wrestlers, and charioteers.
10 Organized games in Greece began about 3,500 years ago. By 500 BC, there were several Greek sporting festivals. The most important one took place in Olympia every fourth summer. The Olympic Games honored Zeus, the father of the Greek gods. Only citizens of Greek
15 city-states could participate. The only race then, a sprint, was run over a distance of about 200 yards. Coroebus, a cook who won the race in 776 BC, was the first recorded champion.
Gradually, other running events were added. They
20 also had horse racing, chariot racing, wrestling, and boxing. The pentathlon (pronounced *pĕn-tăth'lŏn*) was a track-and-field event. In this event, athletes competed in five contests. The contests usually included sprinting, hurdling, long jump, and discus and javelin throwing.

25   There were parts of the ancient Olympic Games that made them different from modern events. First, all athletes competed in the nude. They thought it helped them do their best. In addition, women could not participate, and married women could not watch. Olympia was considered
30 sacred for men. Finally, the champions received olive wreaths as awards.

    When Rome conquered Greece in the second century BC, the games continued. In AD 394, the Roman emperor Theodosius, a Christian, banned all festivals that honored
35 Olympic gods. The Olympic Games ended. It wasn't until 1,500 years later, in 1887, that the Frenchman Baron Pierre de Coubertin (pronounced *kōō-bare-tĕn'*) revived interest in the games.

    The modern Olympic Games were organized as a way
40 of **promoting** peace, friendship, and healthy sporting competition among the youth of the world. Athens, Greece, was the site of the first modern Olympics. Held in April 1896, these games involved 14 nations. There were 311 male athletes who participated in 42 events and
45 nine sports. (Women were not allowed to participate until 1912.) The United States won nine of the track-and-field events. Greece won the most medals with 46.

promoting
contributing to; supporting

peasant

a poor farmer

"Victory!"

(thud!)

ceased

stopped

ultimate

greatest possible

The highlight of the 1896 games was the victory of a Greek **peasant**, Spyridon Loues, in the first-
50 ever marathon. The course was the same 26.2-mile route Greek hero Pheidippedes covered in 490 BC. Pheidippedes had carried news of a Greek victory over the invading Persian army in the Battle of Marathon. He was so exhausted when he reached Athens, he
55 shouted one word: "Victory!" Immediately after his announcement, he dropped dead.

Today's Olympic Games happen in a different country every four years. At the opening ceremonies, the Greek team always leads the parade of athletes. The Olympic
60 flame is still lit in Olympia, Greece. It is carried to the site of the games by a series of torchbearers. This tradition began in Germany in 1936 when 3,000 runners crossed seven countries on their journey from Greece. The passage of the Olympic torch captures the imagination of the world,
65 reminding people of the original focus of the games—world peace and sportsmanship.

In ancient Greece, all wars **ceased** for as long as the games lasted. Unfortunately, that has not been the case in modern times. The 1916 games were canceled because
70 of World War I. World War II caused the cancellation of the 1940 and 1944 games.

Winning an Olympic medal is the **ultimate** goal for many athletes around the world. The pursuit of this goal allows athletes from all over the world to put aside
75 national interests and come to the Olympic grounds. There they compete with athletes from many other nations. These Olympic athletes help all of us focus on a loftier goal. During the Olympic Games, they model how to live and work together as citizens of Planet Earth.

Adapted from "Swifter, Higher, Stronger" by Ann Stalcup,
© by Carus Publishing Company. Reproduced with permission.

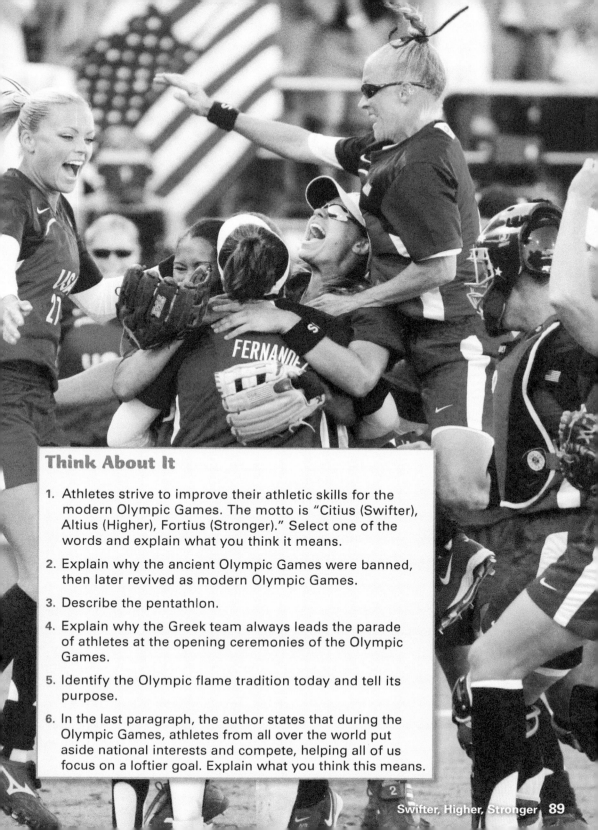

Think About It

1. Athletes strive to improve their athletic skills for the modern Olympic Games. The motto is "Citius (Swifter), Altius (Higher), Fortius (Stronger)." Select one of the words and explain what you think it means.

2. Explain why the ancient Olympic Games were banned, then later revived as modern Olympic Games.

3. Describe the pentathlon.

4. Explain why the Greek team always leads the parade of athletes at the opening ceremonies of the Olympic Games.

5. Identify the Olympic flame tradition today and tell its purpose.

6. In the last paragraph, the author states that during the Olympic Games, athletes from all over the world put aside national interests and compete, helping all of us focus on a loftier goal. Explain what you think this means.

ROBERTO CLEMENTE:
The Heart of the Diamond

ROBERTO CLEMENTE

"Any time you have an opportunity to make things better and you don't, then you are wasting your time on this earth." —Roberto Clemente

The boy wound the string carefully around the scuffed golf ball, neatly tucking in the ends of each short piece. He did not hear his mother until she was right beside him.

5 "Roberto," she said, shaking her head. "Did you take more string from the rice bags?"

The boy held up the half-finished ball. "We need a new baseball," he answered. "We're going to play tomorrow."

makeshift

temporary substitute

10 His mother looked at the **makeshift** ball and then at the hope in her son's eyes. Giving him a quick hug, she said, "Just make sure you don't forget your chores."

The boy went back to his work on the ball, winding more string and then sealing it tightly with strong white 15 tape.

The boy's name was Roberto Clemente, and one day he would sign new baseballs to give away to his fans. But

Puerto Rico

a self-governing island of the U.S. in the Caribbean Sea

when he was a young boy in Carolina, **Puerto Rico**, in the early 1940s, there was never enough money for 20 baseballs. Most of the people in Carolina worked in the sugar-cane fields, and they earned barely enough for food and clothing. Clemente often had to work in the fields with his father and brother, but he always found time for baseball.

25   As Clemente grew older, he realized that many people on the island were poor and discouraged. He also saw how much they loved the baseball heroes from the United States. "We should have a hero of our own," he thought, "someone like Babe Ruth, but Puerto Rican, so
30 our people can be proud and look up to him." He did not know if he could be that hero, but he was determined to become the best baseball player he could be and make his people proud of him and of their country.

    Clemente had to work hard to make his dream come
35 true. Throughout high school, he played on a regular team with good equipment, and coaches helped him develop his natural abilities. To improve his athletic skills, he joined the track team. He ran races and threw the javelin. These events helped his performance in baseball.
40 After graduation, a professional team in a nearby town selected Clemente, and people began to notice his skill on the diamond.

    A year later, when Clemente was 19 years old, a scout from the Brooklyn Dodgers noticed him, too. The
45 scout watched this young player of medium height and weight with an awkward batting **stance** and an equally awkward throwing motion—who nevertheless hit, ran, caught, and threw better than anyone else on the team. The scout offered Clemente a chance to play with the
50 Dodgers' farm team in Montreal. Clemente accepted with excitement and anticipation; he had a chance to play in the major leagues!

stance
a position of the body when standing

    Clemente was often confused and discouraged in Montreal; he didn't always understand what was
55 happening. The Dodgers were trying to hide Clemente's talents from other teams, so the coaches would take him out if he was playing well; they'd leave him in if he was having just an ordinary day. Clemente missed the warmth and friendliness of his native island, but his
60 dream of being a major-league baseball player kept him from giving up and going home.

The Dodgers were not able to keep Clemente's talents hidden for very long. He was traded to the Pittsburgh Pirates the next year. In Pittsburgh, Clemente found fans
65 who loved him and managers who let him play the way he wanted. He was soon setting records in hitting and fielding. Opposing pitchers searched unsuccessfully for a pitch he could not hit. Clemente's spectacular catches in the outfield had fans and players gasping in astonishment.
70 In 1961, Roberto Clemente became the first Hispanic to win the National League batting championship. He went on to win this award three more times during his fantastic career in the majors. He won 12 Gold Glove awards for fielding. He played in 12 all-star games and led
75 the Pittsburgh Pirates to two world championships.

Clemente became famous for something else, too. He wasn't just a part of the baseball diamond; he was the *heart* of the diamond. Throughout his career, he never lost his love for playing or his **gratitude** to his fans. He
80 always felt a responsibility to play his best because he thought he owed it to the people who paid to see him.

gratitude

thankfulness; appreciation

Throughout his career, Clemente never lost his love for playing or his gratitude to his fans.

Every winter, Clemente returned to Puerto Rico. There, he married a woman from Carolina and they lived with their three sons in Rio Piedras, a nearby town. Clemente
85 said that he wanted his sons to be strong and be able to accept hardship. He thought accepting and learning to overcome difficulties gave children the strength they needed to succeed in the world.

Clemente never forgot the hardships he had overcome
90 growing up in Puerto Rico. He loved playing baseball because it **enabled** him to help the people on the island. He managed the San Juan baseball team, teaching the young players all he knew, and he planned a sports center where young people could play their games with the
95 best equipment and surroundings. When he played in the United States, Clemente always had a kind word and helping hand for young Hispanic players when they found themselves homesick and discouraged in their first years away from home.

enabled
made possible

100 Because he was a celebrity, Clemente was asked to help in many **charitable** efforts. When an earthquake struck Managua, Nicaragua, in December 1972, he felt personally involved. He had taken his San Juan team there to play, and he knew many of the people. Clemente
105 insisted on going to Managua to make sure that donated food and medicine were given to the neediest people. He boarded the plane that carried all of the volunteers. Shortly after takeoff, the plane crashed into the ocean and all onboard died.

charitable
generous to speople who need some help

110 People around the world mourned the death of this athlete, this outstanding human being who had not only opened the doors of professional sports for his people, but also became an inspiration to all people to strive to do their best. After all, it had been Clemente who had
115 said, "Any time you have an opportunity to make things better and you don't, then you are wasting your time on this earth." Baseball managers and players, along with government leaders and ordinary citizens, joined in paying tribute to the man from Carolina, Puerto Rico,
120 who died as he had lived, helping those who needed it. In

1973, Roberto Clemente was the first player elected to the Baseball Hall of Fame before the required five-year waiting period. His memory lives on in the many Hispanic players who are filling the ranks of professional sports.

125   In his 38 years on this earth, Roberto Walker Clemente accomplished what many people are never able to do. He had a dream, and he worked hard to make that dream come true. Roberto fulfilled two goals: he did become "the Babe Ruth of Puerto Rico," and his selfless
130 devotion to others provided the example of a lifetime commitment for all of us.

Adapted from "The Heart of the Diamond" by Joanne Loftus, © by Carus Publishing Company. Reproduced with permission.

Think About It

1. Distinguish fact from opinion, after reading these two statements:
   a) Clemente worked in the sugar-cane fields as a young boy.
   b) Many people in Clemente's hometown were discouraged.

2. List the reasons why Clemente's dream to become a great baseball player came true.

3. Compare the differences between Clemente's experiences playing for the Dodgers and the Pirates.

4. Infer why Clemente was elected as a member of the Baseball Hall of Fame without having to wait the required five-year waiting period.

5. Roberto Clemente was an extremely talented athlete. The author states that Clemente was never just part of the diamond; he was the *heart* of the diamond. Discuss what you think this means.

6. Discuss lessons that we can learn from the way Roberto Clemente lived and the way he died.

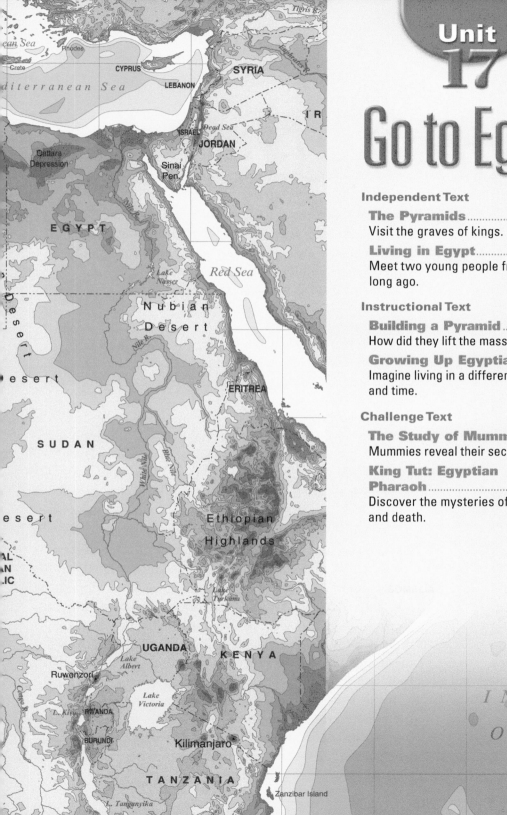

Go to Egypt

THE PYRAMIDS

BASICS

Solve this puzzle: Its huge base is flat and has four corners and four sides. The sides slope up, but the top isn't flat. It has a sharp tip and was made long ago in Egypt, where about 90 of them remain. You figured it
5 out. It's a pyramid, and it's amazing!

USES

Pyramids were constructed for two basic uses. First, they were sacred sites where rites were performed. Second, they were designed as final resting sites, the graves of kings.

CONSTRUCTION

The pyramids were constructed long ago, when there
10 were no motors. There were probably no cranes, and workers may not have even had wheels. It seems like an impossible task. The stones the workers moved were huge, and they made millions of stone blocks. One base block was so big, it weighed 70 tons. How did they do it? Their
15 method involved steps. First, they dug the stone, and then it was put on a raft. The raft drifted down the Nile River. At the site, the stone was taken off, and workers chipped and shaped it. They sculpted and carved a channel into the stone. Next, they drove a wooden wedge into it. They
20 drenched the wedge in water, and it expanded. They added more water, so the wedge expanded more. At last, the stone split, and they cut it. They used chisels and stone hammers to make it the desired shape. Up the ramps it went, and the pyramid rose. So did the ramps. Stones were dragged
25 into place as block stacked upon block. Finally, the workers reached the top where they put on a capstone, and it was finished. One more amazing pyramid!

Workers used copper chisels and stone hammers to construct the pyramids.

LIVING IN EGYPT

Visualize yourself living in a different place and time—how about ancient Egypt? What would be different about your life and what would be the same as your life now? Let's travel back in time where we'll meet two
5 young people living in ancient Egypt.

Moses

First, meet Moses, a farmer's son. In Egypt, people depend on farmers because they supply all the crops. During the growing season from November to February, Moses helps his dad plant the crops. They work to plow
10 the rich, black soil that has been brought by the Nile. They work to make certain the crops will be plentiful. By June, the crops need to be harvested and stored. Moses' dad cannot farm the land from June to September because the Nile River floods in these months. It floods
15 their fields and brings new, rich soil to cover the land. When the river floods, they work elsewhere. Moses and his Dad work on the pyramids. When the river subsides, they return home, and life on the farm begins again.

Hebeny

Hebeny studies hard because she wants to be a scribe.
20 She studies at home because only boys can go to school. Her father is a scribe, and his job is highly valued in Egypt. It is one of the few jobs that requires a formal education. The writing is done with a code. The code doesn't have letters as we know them. It uses symbols to represent
25 ideas. Most scribes are men, but Hebeny wants to master the skill. She wants to work as a scribe like her dad.

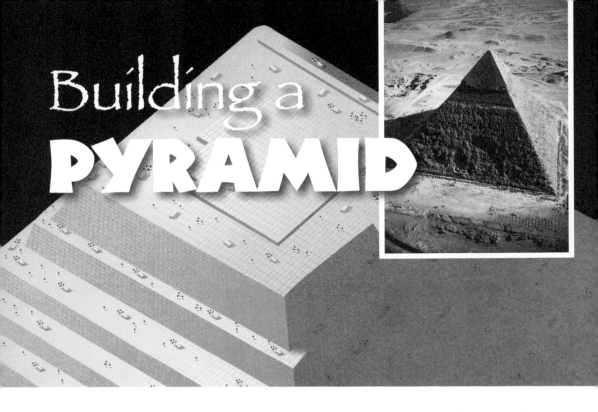

Building a PYRAMID

When building the pyramids, workers used ramps to move stones into place. This view is looking down on a pyramid.

Egypt's pyramids are true engineering feats. In other words, they are amazing accomplishments. They are also mysterious and intriguing. Pyramids served as tombs for the mummified bodies of dead pharaohs who once
5 ruled Egypt. The Great Pyramid is the biggest of them. Of the Seven Wonders of the Ancient World, it is the lone survivor. It was built by King Khufu. Its builders were great mathematicians. The base of the Great Pyramid is 13.5 acres. That's bigger than 10 football fields—but its
10 geometry is perfectly square. No written records survive to explain how the pyramids were built. Yet archaeologists have found valuable clues to the Egyptians' methods.

First, Egyptians identified a site for the pyramid. They built their tombs west of the Nile because this region was
15 thought to be the **realm** of the dead. It was also the place of the setting sun. Egyptians called this area *Imentet*. Builders wanted the pyramids to be close to the stone quarries from which they extracted blocks that weighed as much as 70 tons. Proximity to the construction zone
20 was important because there were no wagons, trucks, or

realm

a region, often a kingdom

trains to transport the blocks. All of them were moved by workers. Finally, the pyramid had to be near a waterway because boats were used to deliver some **imported** rock that was used in the construction. This included
25 limestone, granite, and alabaster. We know they used boats because a docking harbor has been uncovered near the Great Pyramid.

Next, the ground and building materials were prepared. The ground had to be leveled before any stones
30 could be placed. To do this, workers may have dug a series of trenches into the land and flooded them with water. The water acted like a level. Workers dug earthen "islands" between the trenches to match the level of the water. Next, they quarried giant
35 stone blocks to build the actual pyramid. Quarry laborers drew square outlines onto stone surfaces, drove wooden wedges into the rock, and soaked the wedges with water until they expanded and split the stone. The workers then cut the rough blocks into
40 the desired shape. They used copper chisels and stone hammers to make these cuts.

As pyramid construction began, the ancient Egyptians worked hard to achieve **precision**. It is amazing how they did such precise work with such simple tools. The
45 builders had to be sure the stones for the base of the pyramid were placed in a straight line. It is thought that they accomplished this by drilling holes in the stones at regular **intervals**. These went all around the base. They put a stake into each hole to make **reference** lines. Traces
50 of these markings remain visible on some of the blocks. Builders also used the reference lines to mark midpoints on the base. This helped them place the stones.

As the pyramid rose, the Egyptians had to create ways to lift the huge stones. Each stone had to be moved
55 from the quarry to the construction site. At the pyramid, the stone had to be lifted into place. The Egyptians used ramps to move the stone. A huge ramp extended from the quarry to about 100 feet above the pyramid's base. This ramp may have spiraled around the pyramid as it

imported
brought in from another country

Ancient Egyptians used copper chisels to build the pyramids.

precision
exactness; accuracy

intervals
amounts of space or time between two things or events

reference
a source of information

encased

covered up or wrapped up completely

60 rose until eventually it **encased** the entire structure. Remains of a ramp have been identified. The ramp was made of rubble (limestone chips) and *tafla* (chalky clay) and designed so that the huge stone blocks did not press against the pyramid. To position the blocks, many

65 workers would have dragged them up the ramps without the aid of wheels. The workers probably pushed the blocks on special platforms called *sledges*.

A full funeral complex also included a mortuary, temple, causeway, and often a second, smaller pyramid.

70 As burial places, the shape of the pyramids may have had many meanings. The capstone at the top of each pyramid was connected with the sun. It was covered in gold. Some think the building symbolized the sun's slanting rays. Another theory proposed that the pyramid was a

75 stairway to heaven. The pharaoh could climb it to the sky when he died. There, he would become a star in the heavens. Whatever their meaning, the pyramids and their construction remain fascinating to many.

Workers pushed the stone blocks on sledges.

Adapted from "Building a Pyramid" by Mariam Ayad, © by Carus Publishing Company. Reproduced with permission.

Answer It

1. List three major tasks involved in building a pyramid and organize them in the proper sequence. Use transition words to make the order of the tasks clear.

2. Before building a pyramid, workers used a series of steps to level the ground before any stones were placed. Organize the following steps into the correct sequence.
   a. dug the earth between trenches to match the level of the water
   b. flooded ditches with water
   c. dug a series of trenches

3. Throughout the article, the author states several intriguing, or mysterious, facts about the Egyptian pyramids. Select one intriguing fact. Explain why that fact is intriguing to you.

4. The shape of a pyramid may have had different meanings to the ancient Egyptians. Describe the possible meanings of the pyramid shape mentioned in the article.

5. What can you infer about the people who built the pyramids?

Growing Up EGYPTIAN

Read these clues. Can you guess the time and place?
- Kids liked listening to music.
- They liked sports and games, including street hockey, handball, and board games.
- They liked spending time with friends and family.
5 - Their families had cats, dogs, and other pets.

   Do all these things sound familiar? They describe kids who lived some 4,500 years ago in ancient Egypt. You might notice that you and your friends have a lot in common with them.
10   There were differences, too, of course. Read about this powerful kingdom on Africa's **Nile River**. Then compare how your world is similar to—and different from—life in ancient Egypt.

Nile River
a river in northeast Africa

Home and Work

   The size of Egyptian homes depended on the father's
15 job. Was he the pharaoh? Then his family's home would be a **palace** made up of buildings with many rooms. Was he a **nobleman** or a scribe—one of the few people who could write or read? If so, his large house may have had a private courtyard with flowers and a fishpond. Perhaps
20 he lived in one of ancient Egypt's great cities—Memphis or Thebes. The families of artisans and craftsmen lived

palace
the official home of a king, queen, or other royal person

nobleman
a man of high rank or title

in smaller homes. A weaver or baker would have had a small house, close to others like it. Its doors would have opened onto a dusty, narrow street. A rich farm family would have lived on a huge farm along the Nile. A poor farmer would have settled in a tiny town near the fields.

Houses in ancient Egypt were built of mud bricks and stood one to three stories tall. They had flat roofs. Because of the hot weather, these roofs were popular spots for families to sit and cool off in the evenings. Families often slept there on hot nights. The homes were built on the sand. Except for a narrow strip of fertile soil along the Nile, almost every place in Egypt is sand.

Education

In ancient Egypt, only boys went to school where they studied to become scribes. Scribes were very important people in ancient Egypt; their ability to read and write earned them special status. Although records tell us there were a few female scribes, most were men. Boys entered scribal school when they were quite young. They had to study hard for about 10 to 12 years.

Learning the ancient Egyptian language was difficult. Ancient Egyptians did not use an alphabet. Instead, they used hundreds of picture symbols to represent words. These symbols, called *hieroglyphs*, were complicated.

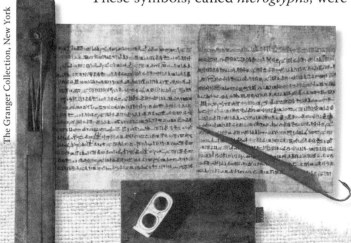

Scribes used tools such as these for writing. The wood palette at left holds reeds, which were used as pens. The container below holds cakes of red and black ink.

45 Young scribes spent years learning the hieroglyphic writing system. Scribes also had to learn how to write *hieratic*. This was a shorthand script they used for everyday writing.

Students learned about more than just language in
50 scribal school. They practiced writing by copying things they read: letters, literature, and religious records. They copied business and government **documents**. As they copied, they learned about the subjects of all these documents.

55 Students practiced the hieroglyphic signs on a variety of surfaces. They wrote them on pieces of stone, pottery, or wood. Students often practiced writing on flat pieces of **limestone** that were common in Egypt. Many school texts, or homework, have been found on these flakes
60 of stone. When a student or a scribe needed to write something very important, he wrote on *papyrus*. Papyrus was an early kind of paper made from the papyrus plant that grew in the **marshes** along the Nile.

A student who finished scribal school could usually
65 get a good job in ancient Egypt. He might have become a doctor or a priest. He might have worked as the secretary to a noble family, or as the manager of a group of workers. Jobs that required the ability to read and write were desired, and young scribes worked hard. They knew
70 that a good education meant a good life.

Child to Adult

While childhood in Egypt could be carefree and happy, a person's life was often very short. There were no special teen years, so most youth were married by 13 or 14 years old. By that age, they were prepared to take on
75 most adult responsibilities. As a rule, children were also expected to follow in their parents' footsteps in work and life.

The word "Egypt" written as hieroglyphs.

documents
written or printed papers that contain information or proof of something

limestone
a kind of rock formed mostly from shells and other animal remains

marshes
swamps; bogs

Adapted from "Growing Up in Another Time, Another Place" by Peggy Wilgus Wymore, and from "School Days" by Joyce Haynes, © by Carus Publishing Company. Reproduced with permission.

Answer It

1. List four things that children in ancient Egypt did which children today still do.

2. Refer to lines 14–26 in "**Growing Up Egyptian**," and select the type of house that you would like to own if you lived in ancient Egypt. Tell what you would have to do in order to own that type of house.

3. Tell why it was difficult to learn the ancient Egyptian language.

4. Reread lines 41–63. Outline the way that students learned to become scribes. Be sure to provide main ideas and supporting details in your outline.

5. Distinguish between the career choices that teenagers in the United States have today and the career choices that teenagers had in ancient Egypt.

THE STUDY OF MUMMIES

The ancient Egyptians believed that within everyone were spirits that lived on after death. They believed that the spirits needed to be able to recognize the body so they could use
5 it as a dwelling place forever. For them, it was important that a body be preserved after death. To keep the body from decaying, they developed the process of mummification.

To start, the ancient Egyptians removed
10 organs that would be hard to dry out. The first was the brain. They believed the brain was the " **marrow** of the skull." They threw away the brain. Then they took out the liver, stomach, lungs, and intestines, dried them separately, and placed them in
15 protective containers called canopic jars.

Next, the Egyptians removed all the moisture from the body. They packed it in a blend of salts called *natron*; these salts were sacred. At last, the body was completely dry, like leather. They added oil, spices, jewelry, and
20 finally the linen wrappings.

Last, the Egyptians protected the mummy and made it waterproof. To do this, they spread layers of rubbery tree gums or resins over layers of linen bandages. These resins turned black over time. They still can be seen on
25 most mummies. In fact, the word "mummy" comes from the Arabic word *mumia*, meaning "tar" or "bitumen."

marrow

the soft tissue that fills the hollow center of most bones

Painted wooden canopic jar.

Later generations incorrectly associated these resins with the black tar that comes from petroleum.

WHY STUDY MUMMIES?

Mummies can tell scientists much about the people
30 who once lived in ancient Egypt. With careful study, scientists can **reconstruct** details about a person's life.

reconstruct
to rebuild or recreate

The style of mummification usually identifies the time period in which the person lived. For instance, a mummy made in the Old Kingdom (around 2500 BC)
35 looks much different from one made in Greek and Roman times (332 BC–AD 395).

In addition, mummies provide clues about the wealth of the person. One of these clues is the style of mask on the mummy. Is the mask simple? Is it elaborate? Another
40 clue is the kind of jewelry the mummy is wearing. Is the jewelry ordinary? Is it fancy?

Egyptologists
people who study ancient Egypt

Sometimes, **Egyptologists** are able to learn the approximate age of the person when he or she died. The teeth are a good clue to a person's age at death. Does the
45 person have a juvenile set of teeth or those of a mature adult? Egyptians' teeth wore down as they grew older. This was primarily due to the sand that was accidentally blended into the flour used to make bread. As a result, someone whose teeth are heavily ground down was likely
50 to have been older than someone whose teeth are not.

Physicians who study the skeleton of a mummy can even learn whether a person was sickly or healthy during life. Scientists can detect the diseases or injuries a person might have suffered by examining the mummified organs

diagnosis
a medical opinion about what is wrong with someone

55 and bones. X-rays help the doctors make a **diagnosis**. They also use an instrument called an endoscope. They insert a tiny tube with a light attached into the mummy and examine it from the inside. This tells doctors if the person had parasites, arthritis, polio, or even a lung disease. CAT
60 scans and other modern scientific tools allow scientists to study every inch of the inside of the mummy.

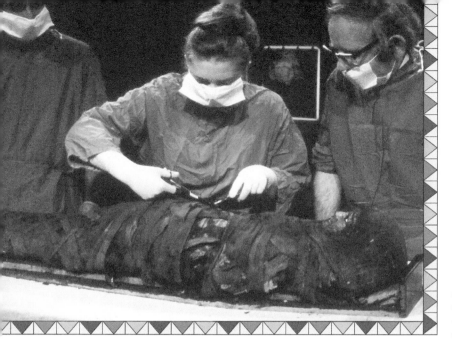

Dr. A. Rosalie David led the group that unwrapped Mummy #1770.

UNWRAPPING MUMMY #1770 ON JUNE 10, 1975

In 1975, a team of scientists and Egyptologists in Manchester, England, performed the first scientific unwrapping of a group of mummies. Dr. A. Rosalie
65 David, an Egyptologist at the Manchester Museum, led the group. She was assisted by doctors and scientists. There were specialists in anatomy, blood, X-rays, teeth, and fingerprints. They studied 24 human and 34 animal mummies. They had two goals. They wanted to gather
70 information about the diseases and causes of death of the mummies. They also wanted to create a system for examining mummies.

Over a two-week period, team members unwrapped and examined a mummy of special interest, #1770. They
75 kept a detailed record on every fragment of bone, blood, skin, tissue, and bandage they examined. By the time they completed their study, they had learned a great deal about the woman and her medical history. They also learned what she looked like! They knew that she had
80 lived to be about 14 years old. She was probably from a fairly wealthy family. They knew this because she had a **gilded** mask and gold-painted caps on her fingers. Her lower legs had been amputated about two weeks before

gilded
covered in gold

her death. Wooden legs and feet formed of mud and
85 reeds had been placed in the coffin to make her body
complete for her afterlife.

The scientists also made another interesting
discovery—the body had been buried twice. They dated
the wrappings and the bones with a technique called
90 *radio carbon* dating. They discovered that her bones were
at least 800 years older than the linen wrappings. This
meant that her body had been moved from its original
burial site and rewrapped centuries later.

The final work done on Mummy #1770 was a
95 reconstruction of how the young woman might have
looked in her lifetime. A plaster cast was made of the
skull. The depth of the soft tissue was estimated over
the entire surface. Then, soft tissue was sculpted onto
the skull. Glass eyes were fitted into her head, which
100 was painted and covered with a wig. The final result was
like gazing into
the face of a very
realistic-looking
young woman of
105 ancient Egypt.

*A reconstruction of
Mummy #1770, showing
how she might have
looked in her lifetime.*

INTERNATIONAL MUMMY TISSUE BANK

Because of the work done at the Manchester Museum, scientists formed the International Ancient Egyptian Mummy Tissue Bank there. Scientists from around the world now send their research on mummies
110 to the Manchester Museum. There, it is collected, computerized, studied, and made available to **scholars** everywhere. The information in the computer database can be accessed under a variety of topics. For example: where the mummy was found; when the person lived;
115 whether it was male or female; what X-rays are available; and what types of diseases were discovered. With the tissue bank and new technology, it is no longer necessary to unwrap or destroy mummies in order to learn the stories of their lives or the secrets of their deaths.

scholars

people who study things; students

Adapted from "The Story of the Manchester Museum Mummies"
by Joyce Haynes, © by Carus Publishing Company.
Reproduced with permission.

Think About It

1. Explain why the ancient Egyptians developed the process of mummification.

2. Outline the steps of Egyptian mummification.

3. State at least two reasons that scientists study mummies.

4. Explain why mummy #1770 was unwrapped in 1975.

5. Describe the International Ancient Egyptian Mummy Tissue Bank and its value to Egyptologists.

6. Egyptologists study artifacts from a culture that existed thousands of years ago. Why is it important to study artifacts from the past, such as mummies, arrowheads, fossils, ect.?

King Tut:
Egyptian Pharaoh

by Jane Sherer and Susan Washburn

Tut, the Boy King

In 1922, British Egyptologist Howard Carter discovered the tomb of King Tutankhamen. The tomb, **virtually** intact, gave the world an incredible view of Egyptian history.

virtually
for the most part

5

Buried in his tomb were many objects that provided information about the life of this pharaoh. There were golden statues, cases of jewels, models of boats to carry the pharaoh along the Nile, and models of servants to assist him in the afterlife.

10

Ruler of all Egypt, the Pharaoh Tutankhamen (pronounced *tōō-tăng-ka'-mən*) wore a tall crown with a figure of a cobra in the front. A bull's tail on his belt was a symbol of his strength. He wore a false beard to symbolize power. The word of Tutankhamen was law; yet he was only 9 years old when he **ascended** to the position of pharaoh!

ascended
climbed; advanced

15

Young Tutankhamen—sometimes called King Tut—became pharaoh of all of Egypt when the **preceding**

preceding
coming before

pharaoh died. The **legacy** of Tutanhkamen's father and
20 grandfather was enormous. Because King Tut was so
young, many advisers helped him rule; these advisers
held great power. A general, Horemheb, was probably
the one who ran the country. Nevertheless, young
Tutankhamen was pharaoh, so his word was final.

25   When he died nine years after he became pharaoh,
Tutankhamen was only 18 years old. Egyptologists have
good reason to suspect that the young pharaoh may have
been murdered.

When ancient Egyptians died, their bodies were
30 preserved in a unique manner. Their bodies were
preserved as mummies. The mummy of a pharaoh or a
queen went into a special tomb. Because the Egyptians
believed in life after death, they placed in the tomb
things that the dead person would need in the next life.

35   In Tutankhamen's tomb there was a **considerable**
amount of information about his life. Many objects were
from Tutankhamen's childhood: small gloves that he
probably wore as a child, brightly colored balls, and a
wooden cat with a jaw that moved and a tail that wagged.
40 Tutankhamen must have liked to play games, because
four senet boards were buried with him. He must have
liked to hunt, because bows and arrows were buried with
him.

Tutankhamen lived and died more than 3,300 years
45 ago. People can only wonder what it would have been like
to rule over all of Egypt as a boy king, just 9 years old.
The **contents** of his tomb provide some answers to these
questions.

Adapted from "The Boy King," by Jane Sherer and Susan Washburn
© by Carus Publishing Company. Reproduced with permission.

legacy
money, property, or power passed down from someone who came before

considerable
large in size or amount

contents
something contained within something else

Exterior view of the entrance to King Tut's tomb (bottom right) in the Valley of the Kings.

Tut's Tomb

Interior view of King Tut's tomb.

A. H. Gardiner's Account

This text is based on a letter of nine pages that was
50 *found in the papers of Sir Alan Gardiner. Gardiner was one of the top Egyptologists of the early twentieth century.*

Gurneh, 17 Feb. 23, 1923

Early in the morning I had climbed over the hill, and soon was at work with Breasted (pronounced *brĕs-tēd'*) on the **seals** of the closed door. Behind all that sealed
55 plaster lay—who knew what? Perhaps nothing, perhaps Tutankhamun himself. At all events we had to work hard. The countless seals which covered the plaster had indeed been photographed and rephotographed, and Breasted had spent two days on them. But in three hours
60 they were to be hacked away, and it would be possible only to preserve a few fragments intact. So the historical **evidence** which the seals might contain had to be studied now or never.

seals

designs or raised emblems showing that something is official

evidence

valuable information; proof

. . . It was the first chamber which had contained all
65 the marvellous furniture and treasures. Nothing now
remains of all these except the two vast black statues
of the king standing on each side of the famous closed
door as though to guard it from intruders. The little
room called the annex is still full of marvels, but in poor
70 condition mostly and at all events demanding years of
restoring work. The door to it originally bore seals, and
many are still left for us to study. The small hole which
had been made and which enabled us to peep into the
annex has now been closed up once more, and will not be
75 reopened for study perhaps for several years to come.

Yesterday it was the sealed door to the right of the
first chamber which commanded our interest, and here,
as I have said, we were working all the morning. Carter
had built a wooden framework all round the statues and
80 a small platform on which he could stand to cut down
the wall. . . . But we had to wait fully an hour more before
the great shrine or catafalque was revealed in all its
magnificence. It . . . measured at
least 24 x 16 x 10 feet. All the sides
85 were of gold plate, the interstices
between the ornamental symbols
being of deep blue faience. A
marvel of marvels, such as we
never dreamt of. The side—for it
90 was the side, not the front, which
was turned to us as we looked,
was hardly more than a couple
of feet behind the plastered door
where we had been studying the
95 seals, and the whole catafalque, or
shrine, very nearly filled the room
enclosing it. It was not without
much difficulty that one could
squeeze by to the right of the
100 shrine.

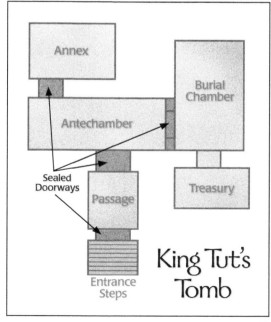

The floor plan of King Tut's tomb.

. . . At last my turn came to be allowed to pass into the new rooms, and with a little difficulty I squeezed along its front side. . . . The great heavy door of the catafalque had been forced open by Carter, and we

105 could just peep into it. Inside was yet another golden shrine of just the same kind, and only a little smaller! The inner shrine is sealed and intact. How many more similar catafalques will be found before the sarcophagus of the king (and queen) are found? It looks as though

110 the mummies had been cased in as by a series of those Chinese boxes you have often seen, each smaller than the last. We shall not know the answer to this riddle for another year at least.

In the tiny space between the outer and inner golden

115 shrine we could just discern marvellous things. Most delightful alabasters, one with a wonderful carved cat upon it, and another with a charming Nile-god. Over the inner shrine hung a pall of leather, tattered and torn. Had the robbers ceased their plundering just at this point,

120 dismayed by the obstacle of a series of inner shrines? In the right-hand corner were a number of sticks and staves of office, all ornamented with gold.

But we had more yet to see, so as our visit was to be a short one, Breasted and I pushed on to the inner

125 room. Here the sight was still more miraculous. Boxes everywhere, boxes of inlaid ivory, of ebony, of white wood—all deliciously carved. At the back of the room was a large golden shrine, somewhat after the style of the golden catafalque, and doubtless including the canopic

130 jars—the jars holding the viscera of the dead king. But the strangest and most novel feature of the golden canopic chest was that all around it were carved golden statues of goddesses, holding their arms out in the most graceful attitude, and . . . looking over their shoulders.

135 Never could we have imagined that Egyptians would have invented such figures!

Carter lifted the lid of one of the boxes, and there lay the Pharaoh's ivory fan, with marvellous ostrich feathers

in perfect preservation. Beside it stood a beautiful box
140 with a pattern of golden ankhs all over it. There may be
twenty-five boxes in all, and only two or three have been
opened. The doors of a shrine-like box stood open, and
within we saw two statuettes, about 20 inches high, of
Tutankhamun standing upon a puma. The king's face at
145 least was gold, and I am not sure that the puma was not
gold as well. Everywhere in this inner room there are boats,
model boats with elaborately painted cabins, boats with
sails up, boats with sails down, etc. In a corner I espied
a box with two strangely swatched figures. Were they
150 *ushabtis*? No one has been able to step across to them, and
that is one of twenty mysteries yet to be solved.

Reprinted with permission from the Griffith Institute,
University of Oxford

Glossary of common terms used in 1923

senet—an Egyptian board game, similar to backgammon

catafalque—a decorated platform or framework on which a coffin rests

interstices—narrow spaces between parts

faience—earthenware decorated with colorful glazes

sarcophagus—a carved stone coffin

pall—a heavy covering

staves—rods or poles

canopic jars—containers (usually numbering four) found in ancient
tombs that stored body organs, which were believed to be essential for
the dead person's existence in the afterlife

viscera—internal organs of a body

ankh—in Egyptian art, a cross with a loop at the top, symbolic of life

espied—caught sight of

ushabtis—statuettes used in tombs to carry out the farming duties for
the dead

Think About It

1. What can you generalize about the kinds of objects that were put into tombs?

2. What can you conclude about the statement: "Egyptologists have good reason to suspect that the young pharaoh may have been murdered"?

3. Gardiner referred to the seals on the doors of the tomb several times. What can you infer is the importance of these seals?

4. Using the graphic of King Tut's tomb and Gardiner's account, locate each part of the tomb where items were found.

5. Imagine you are standing in front of King Tut's tomb with Gardiner and Carter. Discuss the emotions you might be feeling as you enter this great tomb.

Explore a Continent

Life at the Pole

A Frozen Land

The temperature is below zero, and the wind gusts at more than 200 mph! The wind chill hits the danger zone, and the land is frozen. Welcome to the continent of Antarctica, home of the South Pole. It is very dry and
5 cold, yet life can still be found. Small plants live on the frozen shore, and krill thrive in the cold waters. Whales migrate to Antarctica just for krill. Other forms of life, such as seals and penguins, visit too.

A Mixed-Up Sky

In Antarctica, days are far from what we think of
10 as normal. In the summer, there is constant day, and it is never dark. Summer begins in October and ends in March, the fall and winter months in the U.S. When the southern hemisphere tilts toward the sun, Antarctica has constant sunshine. It is hard to go to bed when the sun
15 is still up, so dwellings in Antarctica have thick shades to make it dark inside.

When the southern hemisphere tilts away from the sun, it is winter in Antarctica. Then, it is dark all the time. It's hard to get up in the dark. An alarm clock
20 wakes you; not the rising sun. There is some light in

the sky that comes from gases. Swirling gases color the winter sky. To adjust to the constant darkness takes time!

Secrets in the Land

Many countries govern Antarctica, and people come from all over the world to study there. They set
25 up labs and work to understand the planet better. They study many things, like the thinning ozone and things preserved in the frozen land. Dark objects are quickly spotted, as they contrast with the land's white blanket. Even fossils and bits of Mars have been found! This land
30 was not always frozen. At one time, this land was part of a lush forest, filled with life. Life left its imprints, and these are trapped in fossils. Studying them helps us understand the past. A very long time ago, one landmass existed, and Antarctica was part of it. All the continents
35 were one, and fossils confirm these facts.

People do not make the Antarctic their home, so they come for a short time. They study, write, and uncover secrets from the past that unlock the future.

A panoramic view of the South Geographic Pole with South Pole station.

Mysteries of ANTARCTICA

longitude

imaginary vertical lines that are used to measure distance and divide the Earth into time zones

glaciers

enormous areas of ice that flow over land

windchill factor

the cold experienced by people and other living things, based on a combination of wind and cold

Antarctica is a mysterious continent. Some call it a penguin's playground, but others call it the end of the Earth. Antarctica is the home of the South Pole. Visit the South Pole and you'll find you can "walk around the
5 world" in just a few footsteps. You can step on every time zone and **longitude** in less than a minute. Check for yourself by looking at Antarctica on a globe.

In Antarctica, the seasons are opposite of what they are in the United States. Summer lasts from October
10 to March. Winter lasts from April to September. In the summer, daylight lasts 24 hours a day. During the winter, it remains dark all day. In the dark winter months, there is often an aurora display, characterized by green, orange, and red gas clouds flashing across the sky.

15 The weather in Antarctica is very dry, cold, and windy. Antarctica has the harshest climate of all the continents, even though only about three inches of snow fall each year. It has been called "the frozen frontier." In this frigid clime, the temperature hardly ever rises above freezing, and only
20 some of the land is free from ice. Antarctica's **glaciers** hold about three-fourths of the Earth's fresh water. Some of the icebergs breaking off from ice shelves are larger than the big island of Hawaii. Ferocious winds called *katabatics* blow at up to 200 miles per hour, driving the
25 **windchill factor** to extremely low levels.

Diane Di Massa, an Antarctic oceanographic engineer, says such weather "makes it difficult and dangerous to do research here."

Even with the harsh conditions, some plants and
30 animals can survive in Antarctica. It is home to some very small life-forms, including algae that live along the coastlines. These organisms live inside sea ice and can survive in salty brine channels during the dark winter. In springtime, when sea ice melts, they flow into the
35 ocean. Also called *phytoplankton*, they need sunlight and **carbon dioxide** to grow. Phytoplankton thrive at the low end of the food chain, below krill. Krill look like small red shrimp. They're a favorite food of Earth's largest mammal, the endangered blue whale. Blue whales migrate
40 to the southern oceans to eat this rich food. Other animals found in Antarctica include penguins, seabirds, seals, and additional species of whales.

carbon dioxide
an atmospheric gas

Each summer, about 4,000 scientists from many nations visit Antarctica to do research. Some live on ships
45 called icebreakers; others stay at land-based research stations. Their supplies and food must all be shipped or flown in. The scientists work hard to make sure that human visitors do not pollute this fragile place.

The Antarctic Search for **Meteorites** program has
50 been in operation since 1976. This program searches for clues about how and when our solar system formed. Team member Scott Sandford has been on three field trips to the Antarctic. "I've probably found over 300
55 meteorites," he says. "I get excited every time. One of our team's most

meteorites
natural objects that come from outer space and land on Earth

Researchers in Antarctica sometimes live on ships called icebreakers.

This meteorite, found on Antarctica, is about the size and weight of a car engine.

referred

known as

Leaf fossil found on Antarctica.

surprising discoveries was a meteorite that was a piece of Mars. Another was a piece of the moon." One reason so
60 many meteorites can be found on Antarctica is because its white and blue ice contrasts vividly with the uneven shape and dark, glossy surface of a meteorite.

Scientists have also found fossils in Antarctica. Fossils from dinosaurs and plants prove that millions of years ago,
65 Antarctica was not covered with glaciers. Instead, plants and trees grew in a warm rainforest, and the southern continents made up one big landmass. Scientists called this region *Gondwana*. It and another landmass known as *Laurasia* once comprised a super-landmass, **referred** to
70 as *Pangea*.

Antarctica is no longer connected to these other continents. However, we continue to study this mysterious, remote place because it has a lot to tell us about our atmosphere, our oceans, and our solar system. People have
75 explored the Earth for thousands of years, and yet there are still many mysteries to solve.

Adapted from "Mysteries of Antarctica" by Karen E. Lewis
© by Carus Publishing Company. Reproduced with permission.

Answer It

1. Explain why Antarctica is considered a mysterious continent.

2. Distinguish between the seasons in Antarctica and the seasons in your hometown.

3. Infer what would happen to the sea life in Antarctica if algae were no longer able to grow there.

4. Explain why scientists search for meteorites in Antarctica.

5. Was Antarctica ever connected to other continents? Explain. Is it connected now? Explain.

THE FIRST TRANSCONTINENTAL RAILROAD

Time: Just past noon, May 10, 1869.
Place: Promontory, a tiny town on the shore of the **Great Salt Lake** in Utah.

Event: A large crowd gathers to witness a very important
5 ceremony. Telegraph wires wait to carry the news across the nation. Two locomotives idle on their tracks, nose to nose. One comes from the east, the other from the west. Six Irish men lay down the last rail from the east. Eight Chinese men lay down the last rail from the west.

10 The president of the first **transcontinental** railroad steps forward. His job is to hammer in the last spike connecting the eastern and western halves of the railroad. He swings, and misses! The vice president of the Union Pacific Railroad misses, too—but the crowd

15 cheers anyway. Other important people take turns at hammering spikes of silver, iron, and gold into place. The first transcontinental railroad is complete!

A Transcontinental Railroad

Large groups of people were settling in California and in the western territories of the United States. A group of
20 businessmen had predicted that a railroad connecting the East and West Coasts would be a good idea. They said it would bring in profit from trade. They even talked about transporting goods brought to California from China.

At first, the task seemed impossible. But the Central
25 Pacific Railroad began construction in Sacramento, California, in 1863, and work commenced on the Union Pacific Railroad out of Omaha, Nebraska, in December of

the same year. In less than four years, workers would lay 1,776 miles of track across a vast wilderness.

30   Both companies had huge problems getting supplies to their workers. The Central Pacific had to ship construction equipment from the Atlantic coast. One way to do this was to transport the supplies via land over the **Isthmus** of Panama and then send them by ship to
35 San Francisco. The other way was to send the supplies by ship around **Cape** Horn on the southern tip of South America to San Francisco. Both methods of conveyance were expensive and time consuming.

    The Union Pacific had its own problems. At first, it
40 shipped supplies and equipment up the Missouri River by steamboat and then carried them overland by stagecoach and in wagons. Later, supplies went along tracks already laid. But the going was slow, and it took the labor of thousands to complete this incredible transcontinental task.

Who Built the Transcontinental Railroad?
From the East: The Workers of the Union Pacific Railroad

45   One group of workers was employed by the Union Pacific Railroad. This railroad company had already reached Omaha and was now moving west across the continent. It had all the workers it could use. Twelve thousand men had drifted there from the North and
50 South following the Civil War. Privates, sergeants, lieutenants, captains, and colonels signed on. Soldiers from both sides, former slaves, and ex-convicts all needed work. The biggest group of workers was the Irish, many of whom had fought in the war, or had just disembarked
55 from the boats that had carried them to America.

    Living conditions were difficult. The men lived in tents, converted boxcars, and in the portable towns that would spring up at the end of the line. After about 50 miles of new railroad had been laid, merchants and
60 townspeople would race down the track to set up a new town. They would disassemble their **flimsy** buildings—

isthmus

a narrow strip of land connecting two larger landmasses

cape

a point of land extending into a body of water

flimsy

not stable or strong

many of these had canvas roofs—and pile everything on wagons for the move.

From the West: The Workers of the Central Pacific Railroad

Thousands labored to complete the Transcontinental Railroad.

65 Another group of workers was employed by the Central Pacific Railroad. This company was laying track from Sacramento, California. Crews worked eastward toward the Union Pacific project. But the railroad bosses of the Central Pacific Railroad

70 had a harder time finding reliable workers. Many would work for just a week or two to earn a little money before quitting and returning to their gold prospecting efforts.

In 1849, some Chinese had come to California

75 looking for gold. But many of them wound up working for the railroad instead. Though they were smaller in stature, the other workers soon learned that their size didn't matter. The Chinese roadbed was straighter, smoother, and longer than that of any other crew. The

80 Chinese worked without stopping. Their cooks walked alongside them with steaming buckets of tea, hung from long rods across their shoulders. The tea kept these laborers working through the day.

The Chinese railroad workers became known for

85 their courage. Once, a railroad bed was needed halfway up a **precipice** overlooking the American River gorge. Construction seemed impossible. But the Chinese offered to try. Using reeds, they wove waist-high baskets with eyelets for inserting ropes. These baskets were lowered

precipice

a steep cliff or overhanging place

The reconstructed trains, named 119 and Jupiter, met in Promontory, Utah, at the Golden Spike Ceremony on May 10, 1994.

90 halfway down the cliff with one or two men in each. Then the men used tiny hand drills and inserted blasting powder into the side of the cliff to blast open the rock surface. The workers were pulled to safety before the explosion, but not always 95 quickly enough. Because of the bravery of these men, the railroad bed was completed.

When the two railroads finally met at Promontory, Utah, on May 10, 1869, a photograph was taken. But not one of the 13,000 Chinese 100 workers was in it. Had the western railroad been built by invisible men? The Central Pacific could not have been completed without the Chinese. The railroad itself is a testament to their bravery and perseverance.

Adapted from "The Builders of the First Transcontinental Railroad" by Charlotte Gemmell © by Carus Publishing Company. Reproduced with permission.

Answer It

1. Both the Central Pacific and the Union Pacific had problems getting supplies to workers. Distinguish between the ways the two companies shipped supplies to them.

2. Use a T-chart to show differences between the Union Pacific Railroad workers and the Central Pacific Railroad workers.

3. Describe the living conditions for the railroad workers.

4. What can you infer from the fact that no Chinese workers were included in the photograph taken at the completion of the railroad?

5. Contrast the mood conveyed by the author in the first two paragraphs of the selection with the mood conveyed in the last paragraph.

Continental Drift

Have you ever looked at a globe and asked why many of the continents look like pieces of a large jigsaw puzzle? Could you connect the east coast of South America with the west coast of Africa? Many serious thinkers before
5 you have asked those questions as well. The planet Earth once looked very different from the way it looks today.

Shifting Continents

Just below the surface of the Earth lie massive sheets of rock. We call these large pieces of rock "tectonic plates." They float on top of an almost liquid layer that
10 allows the plates to move around like very large, slow boats. Because of this, the surface of the Earth is often shifting. For example, India moved northward at about five centimeters a year until it eventually ran into Europe and Asia. This movement forced the ocean floor down
15 into the Earth's **mantle**. However, the **immense** pressure from India's land mass pushed up some of the ocean floor during the shift. It formed mountains like Mount Everest, which **looms** over Nepal and the **plateaus** of China. Before this movement of the tectonic
20 plates was understood, people were finding sea shells and fossils in the Himalayan Mountains and wondering how they got there. Eventually, scientists were able to study

mantle
a layer of the Earth between the crust and the core

immense
huge; extremely large

looms
appears very large

plateaus
high, flat areas of land

the Earth in new ways to discover why sea shells were
found on top of very high mountains when the ocean was
25 so far away.

Shells and Bones as Story Tellers

Scientists have learned much of what we know about
the history of our planet through studying fossils. These
fossils come from ancient animals and plants. Many
times these remains are preserved under many layers
30 of dirt and rock. Paleontologists may spend many years
carefully digging up these fossils and cleaning them so
that they can study them. After they study the fossils,
they often put them on display in museums for the public
to see.

35   As more people found seashells and fossils of strange
animals on mountaintops and in riverbeds, they began
to wonder what story these remains were trying to tell.
Sometimes people discovered the fossils of animals that
looked just like the fossils found thousands of miles
40 away on a different continent. This made scientists ask
important questions. Why were the fossils of similar
animals appearing around the world on different
continents?

*India crashes into Asia
in slow motion.*

Unlocking the Pangea Puzzle

One of the first scientists to offer a solution to the
45 question was not a paleontologist. He was a man who
studied the weather patterns on Earth. This German
meteorologist was Alfred Wegener. Wegener noticed
that many of the fossils found on a cold continent
like Antarctica could not have survived in such frigid
50 climates. These animals and plants, which would need
the warm climates found near the **equator**, could not
have traveled across so many thousands of miles of
ocean. Wegener knew there had to be a better reason.

In 1915, he claimed that over 300 million years
55 ago, all of Earth's continents were **fused** together. He
called this massive piece of land "Pangea." About 200
million years ago, the Earth's mantle started moving.
The supercontinent started to break apart, and smaller
continents began to drift.

60 He was the first person to make such a claim in a
book, and many people did not agree with him. Other
people believed that the continents were shifting, but for
different reasons. For example, some scientists believed
that the Earth was cooling down and that was causing
65 it to shrink. This, they said, would cause the land mass
to shift. However, as science progressed, more and more
people began to realize that Wegener's theory was true.
Scientists began to develop ways to support his theory.
One group of scientists discovered a way to take the
70 Earth's temperature. They proved that the Earth was
not cooling down. This put a rest to the claim that the
Earth was shrinking. Major technological developments
in the 1960s allowed scientists to do detailed mapping of
the ocean floor, which provided further evidence of the
75 movement of the tectonic plates.

Scientists now refer to this shifting of landmasses as
plate tectonics. Even today our land masses are moving.
The Pacific plate is moving away from North America at
a speed of about four centimeters a year. Australia (on the
80 Indian plate) is moving toward the Pacific plate at about
five centimeters a year. Modern scientists now measure

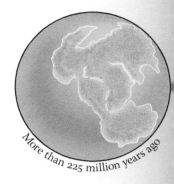

More than 225 million years ago

About 150 million years ago

Today

equator
an imaginary line
that divides the
Earth's northern
and southern
hemispheres

fused
joined together

this drifting with lasers and satellites. Can you imagine what the Earth will look like in another 200 million years? America could be a part of Asia. The Rocky
85 Mountains might be flat. The Atlantic Ocean could be twice as big and the Pacific Ocean might be gone.

Adapted from "Seashells on the Summit"
by Gretchen Noyes-Hull and "The Pangea Puzzle" by Mary Reina
© by Carus Publishing Company. Reproduced with permission.

Pangea consisted of all Earth's landmasses locked together.

Think About It

1. People who live atop the mountains of Nepal and the plateaus of Tibet collect seashells. Select possible explanations for the shells' presence.

2. The author writes that the shells and fossils found atop the Himalayas tell a story. Explain why this statement is an example of **personification** (a literary device).

3. Distinguish between Alfred Wegener's theory and the theories of those who thought differently.

4. List the ideas that seem to support Wegener's theory.

5. Discuss the possible reasons Alfred Wegener had the courage to announce his theory to the world. Discuss other ideas that take courage to share with others.

6. Use a globe or map to locate the following: Mt. Everest, the Himalayan Mountains, and the Indian Ocean. Distinguish these locations from where you live.

The Quest for a Continent

The flagship of Columbus' 1492 voyage—the Santa Maria.

Rodrigo de Triana, lookout on a small square-rigged sailing ship named the Pinta, shouted, "Tierra!" It was shortly after
5 midnight in October 1492, and these were welcome words. The boom of a cannon signaled the sighting to the Pinta's two companion ships. The three
10 vessels lowered their sails to wait for daylight; then, they would investigate the landfall. They had been sailing in search of land since early August.

15   The ships were Spanish, and they sailed under Captain General Cristóbal Colón. Historical evidence does not tell us much about this man or his journey. Colón called himself by different names during his lifetime; he was called Cristoforo Colombo,
20 Christobal Colom, and Xpoual de Colón (his signature in the journal he kept during his 1492 voyage). Today we know him as Christopher Columbus.

    Columbus was a sailor most of his life. He made many voyages on merchant ships, first in the **Mediterranean**,
25 and later along the Atlantic coasts of Europe and northern Africa. He became a skilled navigator. He read books that told of the journeys of Marco Polo and other explorers, books that revealed what was known about the lands and seas of the world at that time. In 1479, he

Mediterranean
an inland sea almost completely surrounded by Europe, Asia, and Africa

30 married Felipa Moniz Perestrella, and within a year or so, they had a son they named Diego.

Perhaps geography books inspired him. We don't know 35 for sure. But we do know that Columbus approached the King of Portugal in 1484 with an idea. He wished to sail in search of "islands and mainlands in the Ocean 40 Sea." He needed an investor to back what he called "the Enterprise of the Indies." The king's advisers rejected his request for ships and money.

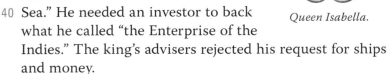
Queen Isabella.

Columbus' wife had died, so he took Diego and 45 traveled to Spain to try his luck there. Around 1486, he obtained an **audience** with Queen Isabella. She was intrigued, but her advisers were not convinced of the **feasibility** of Columbus' plan. She asked him to wait. In 1490, the queen turned down his proposal, but Columbus 50 kept waiting and trying. Finally, early in 1492, Isabella agreed to **finance** the plan.

Captain General Columbus was about 40 years old when his ships left the small Spanish port of Palos. Perhaps as a result of the books he had read and the 55 sailors he had met, he was convinced that the western shores of Asia, called the Indies (for India), could be reached by sailing west. Until then, the **profitable** trade with these foreign lands had gone east, a long and difficult journey.

60 Little evidence confirms that Asia was his goal. It may be that Columbus wanted an opportunity to search for fabled islands that sailors spoke of or other lands of great importance. Columbus sailed with a command from Isabella to "discover and **acquire** . . . 65 islands and mainlands in the Ocean Sea," and to call himself "Viceroy and Governor-General" of the lands he discovered.

audience
a formal meeting with a high-ranking person

feasibility
the likelihood of something being accomplished

finance
to pay for

profitable
beneficial; able to make money

acquire
to obtain; possess

Whatever he considered his destination, Columbus knew that if he succeeded, he would achieve glory. During his lifetime, trade with foreign lands was
70 growing, so discovery of new lands and markets brought wealth and fame to those who claimed them. They had no idea that two huge, unrecorded continents—North and South America—lay to the west.

So his journey began. After weeks of sailing on the
75 open sea, struggling to encourage his nervous crew and quiet their fears that they would never see land again, Columbus recorded in his journal signs of land—floating branches and flocks of birds. The next morning, Rodrigo de Triana saw the moon shining on the cliffs and sandy
80 beach of an island.

In truth, Columbus did not know exactly where he was, except in terms of the time he had traveled west from the Canary Islands off
85 the African continent. He called his landfall "the Indies" because he believed he was close to the Asian continent. Actually, several years passed
90 before navigators realized that he had reached a group of islands off the coast of two unrecorded continents.

Columbus was called
95 a discoverer of new lands, but he was not the first to discover them. The islands and continents he found were already inhabited by millions
100 of people. Many of them had societies at least as advanced as those in Europe. He was not even the first European

Columbus on the deck of the Santa Maria, *watching for land.*

to reach these lands. But he was the first to return there
105 more than once.

Even though he was not the first European to
discover the existence of the new continents, Columbus
is historically important. He began a process of change,
both for the people in these "new" lands and for the
110 people who lived on other continents. Why was that
important? For the first time, people of many different
continents were aware of each other and of the number of
continents in their world.

Adapted from "A Stranger to Foreign Shores" by Beth Weston
© by Carus Publishing Company. Reproduced with permission.

Think About It

1. What can you infer Rodrigo de Triana meant when he
   shouted, "Tierra!"?

2. Summarize the struggle Columbus endured to find
   an investor for his quest.

3. Explain why Columbus' voyage was such an
   important historical event.

4. It was very common for sailors to be at sea for
   months at a time. What do you think was difficult
   about spending so much time away from land?

5. Columbus was called a discoverer of new lands, yet
   these lands had been inhabited for many years. If
   you were one of the inhabitants, how would you feel
   knowing Columbus received credit for discovering
   your land? Why?

Resources

achieves (ə-chēvz') *verb*

accomplishes; completes successfully

The soccer team **achieves** victory when it scores more goals than the other team.

acquire (ə-kwīr') *verb*

to obtain; possess

Andre hoped to **acquire** a new bicycle before the start of the school year.

adapted (ə-dăpt'ĭd) *verb*

changed to meet a new situation

When we moved to the island, we **adapted** to a totally different way of life.

adhere (ăd-hîr') *verb*

to stick closely to

When you drive a car, you must **adhere** to certain traffic rules.

adjoining (ə-joi'nĭng) *adjective*

next to; bordering

The brothers built their houses next door to each other on **adjoining** lots.

again (ə-gĕn') *adverb*

once more

They liked the movie, so they decided to see it **again**.

amateur (ăm'ə-tûr') *adjective*

unpaid; not professional

The math teacher was also an **amateur** trumpet player.

annoyed (ə-noid') *adjective*

irritated; upset

The neighbors were **annoyed** when the dog kept barking.

answer (ăn'sər) *noun*

a reply to a question

Carla raised her hand because she knew the **answer**.

anxious (ăngk'shəs) *adjective*

nervous; worried

The new student was **anxious** about his first day of school.

ascended (ə-sĕnd'ĭd) *verb*

climbed; advanced

The visitors **ascended** the stairs to the museum's entrance.

audience (ô'dē-əns) *noun*

a formal meeting with a high-ranking person

The reporters were granted an **audience** with the king.

boundary (boun'drē) *noun*

a border or edge that marks a specific area

The **boundary** between the two properties was marked by a fence.

Britain (brĭt'n) *noun*

a western European island nation,
comprising England, Scotland,
Wales, and Northern Ireland

On their tour of **Britain**, the
students visited London, England.

cape (kāp) *noun*

a point of land extending into a body
of water

The ship rounded the **cape** and
sailed into the open ocean.

carbon dioxide
(kär'bən dī-ŏk'sīd) *noun*

an atmospheric gas

People breathe out **carbon dioxide**,
and plants absorb it from the air.

cargo (kär'gō) *noun*

products carried by ship, plane, or
other vehicle

The airport workers loaded the
cargo into the plane.

catapults (kăt'ə-pŭltz) *noun*

machines used for shooting rocks or
spears against an enemy

The soldiers positioned the **catapults**
close enough to hit the castle.

ceased (sēst) *verb*

stopped

When the teacher told the class to
quiet down, all the talking **ceased**.

certain (sûr'tn) *adjective*

sure about something

Han was **certain** that he would
graduate in May.

charitable (chăr'ĭ-tə-bəl) *adjective*

generous to people who need
some help

The volunteers helped raise money
for the food bank as well as other
charitable organizations.

choreographer (kô′rē-ŏg'rə-fər) *noun*

a person who plans the movements
of dancers

The dancers watched as the
choreographer showed them
the new routine.

clever (klĕv'ər) *adjective*

smart; quick-thinking

The **clever** fox found a way to open
the gate to the yard.

competitor (kəm-pĕt'ĭ-tər) *noun*

a person who participates in a sport

Kim was eager to be a **competitor** in
the bike race.

considerable (kən-sĭd'ər-ə-bəl) *adjective*

large in size or amount

During the zoo field trip, the class
saw a **considerable** number of
snakes in the Reptile House.

contents (kŏn'tĕnts') *noun*

something contained within something else

The **contents** of the treasure chest included gold coins, rubies, and diamonds.

controversial (kŏn'trə-vûr'shəl) *adjective*

causing arguments or disagreements

The most **controversial** suggestion was to disband the school's swim team.

conveying (kən-vā'ĭng) *verb*

carrying

The escalator was **conveying** shoppers to the second floor of the mall.

cosmonauts (kŏz'mə-nôts') *noun*

Russian astronauts

The **cosmonauts** and astronauts worked together to run the space station.

day (dā) *noun*

the time between sunrise and sunset

The class was going on a field trip the next **day**.

deactivated (dē-ăk'tə-vāt-ĭd) *verb*

turned off

The security guard **deactivated** the alarm every morning when he arrived at work.

deciphering (dĭ-sī'fər-ĭng) *verb*

understanding; converting a code to known language

The book was written in Greek, so we had little chance of **deciphering** it.

decoding (dē-kōd'ĭng) *verb*

translating a code into its original language

The radio operator was **decoding** the secret message so the general could read it.

defunct (dĭ-fŭngkt') *adjective*

no longer in existence or working

Terell couldn't order new parts for his computer because the manufacturer was **defunct**.

dejectedly (dĭ-jĕk'tĭd-lē) *adverb*

in a low-spirited or depressed way

When the team lost the game, they left the court **dejectedly**.

descendants (dĭ-sĕn'dənts) *noun*

people who come from the same family

At the family reunion, granddad was surrounded by his **descendants**.

diagnosis (dī-əg-nō'sĭs) *noun*

a medical opinion about what is wrong with someone

After running a few tests, the doctor's **diagnosis** was that Tina had an ear infection.

dilemma (dĭ-lĕm'ə) *noun*

a difficult problem

When Tuan graduated, his **dilemma** was choosing which college to attend.

documents (dŏk'yə-mənts) *noun*

written or printed papers that contain information or proof of something

The Declaration of Independence and the Constitution are the United States' most important **documents**.

drastically (drăs'tĭk-lē) *adverb*

suddenly; severely

The odds of a bike rider being hurt in an accident decrease **drastically** when the rider wears a helmet.

Egyptologists (ē'jĭp-tŏl'ə-jĭsts) *noun*

people who study ancient Egypt

The **Egyptologists** spent two weeks in the desert uncovering the hidden tomb.

enabled (ĕ-nā'bəld) *verb*

made possible

The ramp **enabled** people using wheelchairs to enter the building.

encased (ĕn-kāst') *verb*

covered up or wrapped up completely

When mud **encased** dinosaurs, many were preserved as fossils.

encoding (ĕn-kōd'ĭng) *verb*

writing in code

The spy was **encoding** his message so it could not be read by his enemies.

endorsement (ĕn-dôrs'mənt) *noun*

a legal agreement that allows companies to use the name of a famous person to sell their products

The football star's **endorsement** allowed his picture to be put on boxes of cereal.

engine (ĕn'jĭn) *noun*

a machine that makes power to produce force or motion

Lisa worked on the airplane **engine** to see if she could get it to start.

enormous (ĭ-nôr'məs) *adjective*

huge

The city library contains an **enormous** amount of books.

equator (ĭ-kwā'tər) *noun*

an imaginary line that divides the Earth's northern and southern hemispheres

Almost half of the Earth's rainforests are located along the **equator**.

evidence (ĕv'ĭ-dəns) *noun*

valuable information; proof

The detectives gathered **evidence** at the crime scene so they could find out what happened.

facet (făs'ĭt) *noun*

one part

One **facet** of being a good reader is having a large vocabulary.

feasibility (fē'zə-bĭl'ə-tē) *noun*

the likelihood of something being accomplished

The band members discussed the **feasibility** of raising enough money to make the trip to New York.

feasible (fē'zə-bəl) *adjective*

possible

The science project was not **feasible** because the students could not bring toxic chemicals into the school.

finance (fī'năns') *verb*

to pay for

The counselor helped Ana figure out how to **finance** her college education.

financial (fə-năn'shəl) *adjective*

having to do with money

Calvin had to make a **financial** decision between buying a new bicycle or saving money for a trip.

flammable (flăm'ə-bəl) *adjective*

able to catch fire easily

The dry forest was **flammable**, and when the lightning struck, it caught fire quickly.

flimsy (flĭm'zē) *adjective*

not stable or strong

The **flimsy** kite was torn apart by a sudden gust of strong wind.

focused (fō'kəst) *adjective*

to be concentrated on a goal without distraction

Efrain was **focused** on answering all the test questions correctly.

fortifications (fôr'tə-fĭ-kā'shənz) *noun*

walls or other structures used to protect soldiers

The soldiers were protected by their **fortifications** from the attacks of the opposing army.

fused (fyōozd) *verb*

joined together

Using a torch, the artist **fused** pieces of glass together to make jewelry.

galactic (gə-lăk'tĭk) *adjective*

having to do with galaxies in outer space

The scientists used a telescope to take measurements of **galactic** rotation.

genius (jēn'yəs) *noun*

an exceptional ability

Janice had a **genius** for solving difficult math problems.

gesture (jĕs'chər) *noun*

an action that is meant to show feeling or thought

The winning coach extended his hand to the losing coach as a **gesture** of good sportsmanship.

gilded (gĭld'ĭd) *adjective*

covered in gold

The art museum displayed the famous paintings in **gilded** picture frames.

glaciers (glā'shərz) *noun*

enormous areas of ice that flow over land

When Antarctic **glaciers** melt, huge blocks of ice can fall into the sea.

gone (gôn) *verb*

to have left a place

Erin looked everywhere for her brother, but he was **gone**.

good (go͝od) *adjective*

positive; desirable

It was a **good** day for taking a walk to the lake.

gratitude (grăt'ĭ-to͞od') *noun*

thankfulness; appreciation

When her parents gave her a dog for her birthday, Rita expressed her **gratitude** by giving them a big hug.

great (grāt) *adjective*

very good

The class thought the field trip to the science center was **great**.

Great Salt Lake (grāt sôlt lāk) *noun*

a large, shallow body of saltwater in northwest Utah

On their road trip through Utah, the family stopped to see the **Great Salt Lake**.

helium (hē'lē-əm) *noun*

a gas present in the Earth's atmosphere

They filled the balloons with **helium** so the balloons would float in the air.

immense (ĭ-mĕns') *adjective*

huge; extremely large

The **immense** Grand Canyon is 277 miles long, up to 18 miles wide, and over a mile deep.

immersed (ĭ-mûrst') *verb*

became completely involved

Omari **immersed** himself in his work and didn't hear the phone ring.

impenetrable (ĭm-pĕn'ĭ-trə-bəl) *adjective*

incapable of being passed through

The catapults threw rocks against the castle walls, but the thick walls were **impenetrable**.

imported (ĭm-pôrt'əd) *verb*

brought in from another country

Most of the cars in the parking lot had been **imported** from Japan.

indispensable (ĭn′dĭ-spən'sə-bəl) *adjective*

necessary; needed

Textbooks are an **indispensable** part of biology class.

inspiration (ĭn′spə-rā'shən) *noun*

motivation to take action

Watching the space shuttle launch was Jen's **inspiration** for wanting to be an astronaut.

intercepting (ĭn′tər-sĕpt'ĭng) *verb*

stopping or interrupting the progress of something

The police planned on **intercepting** the robbers when they left the bank.

international (ĭn′tər-năsh'ə-nəl) *adjective*

having to do with more than one country

The astronauts met the cosmonauts on the **international** space station.

intertwined (ĭn′tər-twīnd') *adjective*

twisted around something

The tomato vines were **intertwined** with the fence at the edge of the garden.

intervals (ĭn'tər-vəlz) *noun*

amounts of space or time between two things or events

The lines on the football field were painted at 10-yard **intervals**.

invested (ĭn-vĕst'ĭd) *verb*

put time, effort, or money into something

Jorge **invested** both time and money into making his business a success.

invincible (ĭn-vĭn'sə-bəl) *adjective*

unbeatable; unstoppable

Legend said the giant was **invincible**, but the knights rode off to fight it anyway.

invulnerable (ĭn-vŭl'nər-ə-bəl) *adjective*

unable to be hurt or damaged

Most viruses are **invulnerable** to treatment with antibiotics.

isthmus (ĭs'məs) *noun*

a narrow strip of land connecting two larger landmasses

Some scientists think the first ancient people to arrive in North America came across an **isthmus** from Siberia to Alaska.

jettisoning (jĕt'ĭ-sə-nĭng) *verb*

throwing off

The sailors made the boat lighter by **jettisoning** most of its cargo.

Kevlar® (kĕv'lär) *noun*

a brand of a special type of strong fiber

The boat captain ordered sails made of **Kevlar®** so that the sails would be strong and long-lasting.

laugh (lăf) *verb*

to show that something is funny

The comedian's jokes made the people in the audience **laugh**.

legacy (lĕg'ə-sē) *noun*

money, property, or power passed down from someone who came before

The king left his sons a **legacy** that included five castles and fifteen cities.

limestone (līm'stōn) *noun*

a kind of rock formed mostly from shells and other animal remains

The white cliffs above the river are made of **limestone**.

little (lĭt'l) *adjective*

small

There were two big dogs and three **little** ones chasing balls in the park.

local (lō'kəl) *adjective*

having to do with a particular place, like a neighborhood or town

Chris walked from home to the **local** grocery store to shop.

longitude (lŏn'jĭ-tōōd') *noun*

imaginary vertical lines that are used to measure distance and divide the Earth into time zones

When the sailors determined their **longitude**, they knew they were getting close to the island they were looking for.

look (lŏŏk) *verb*

to use your eyes

The explorers opened the door to the ancient tomb to **look** at what was inside.

looms (lōōmz) *verb*

appears very large

Even from a distance, the Sears Tower **looms** above downtown Chicago.

lurks (lûrks) *verb*

hides; sneaks

When the sun sets, the fox **lurks** around the pond, looking for ducks.

makeshift (māk'shĭft') *adjective*

temporary substitute

Dana couldn't find her sled, so she used a garbage can lid as a **makeshift** sled on the day of the big snowstorm.

mantle (măn'tl) *noun*

A layer of the Earth between the crust and the core

Most of the Earth's mass is contained in the **mantle**, the middle layer.

Vocabulary

marrow (măr'ō) *noun*

the soft tissue that fills the hollow center of most bones

The **marrow** in your bones is important to your body because it makes new blood cells.

marshes (här'shĭz) *noun*

swamps; bogs

The low-lying land by the river was covered with **marshes**.

may (mā) *verb*

to be allowed

Cars **may** enter the intersection when the light turns green.

Mediterranean (měd´ĭ-tə-rā'nē-ən) *noun*

an inland sea almost completely surrounded by Europe, Asia, and Africa

Ships carry cargo from port to port around the **Mediterranean**.

meteorites (mē'tē-ə-rītz´) *noun*

natural objects that come from outer space and land on Earth

The streaks of light in the sky called "shooting stars" are often **meteorites** hitting the Earth's atmosphere.

mocking (mŏk'ĭng) *verb*

making fun of; imitating

The children were **mocking** the seals at the zoo by clapping their hands together and barking like the seals.

moody (mōō'dē) *adjective*

temperamental; sulky

Chenda tried to cheer up her **moody** brother after he'd lost the softball game.

most (mōst) *adjective*

more than half, but not all

Most of the students left the room, but some stayed to ask the teacher questions.

motion (mō'shən) *noun*

movement

At the beach, the children were fascinated by the **motion** of the waves.

motto (mŏt'ō) *noun*

a short saying that explains a basic belief or goal

The running team's **motto** was "Try hard, run fast, and have fun!"

new (nōō) *adjective*

recent; made not long ago

The **new** computer lab gave students the chance to try the latest technology.

Nile River (nīl rĭv'ər) *noun*

a river in northeast Africa

The **Nile River** runs through nine countries and is the longest river in the world.

nobleman (nō'bəl-mən) *noun*

a man of high rank or title

The **nobleman** took charge of the castle while the king was away.

oil (oil) *noun*

a large class of liquids that have a slippery consistency and many uses such as for cooking or making machines run smoothly

Heat the **oil** in the cooking pot first and then put in the popcorn kernels.

orientation (ôr'ē-ĕn-tā'shən) *noun*

location or position

The students learned to use a map and compass to find their **orientation** in the park.

palace (păl'ĭs) *noun*

the official home of a king, queen, or other royal person

The emperor invited the explorers to his **palace** for a grand feast.

patented (păt'n-tĭd) *verb*

obtained the right to make, use, or sell an invention

The company **patented** Spring Walkers so that it would be the only company that could make and sell them.

peasant (pĕz'ənt) *noun*

a poor farmer

The **peasant** worked hard to raise enough food to last through the winter.

people (pē'pəl) *noun*

a group of more than one person

Lots of **people** lined the street to watch the parade.

perfectionist (pər-fĕk'shə-nĭst') *noun*

a person who tries to do things without making any mistakes

The artist was a **perfectionist**, so she worked to get every detail of the landscape into her painting.

perils (pĕr'əlz) *noun*

dangers

The professional skateboarder described to the class the **perils** of skateboarding without a helmet.

persistence (pər-sĭs'təns) *noun*

trying hard without giving up

Tom's **persistence** in practicing his spelling paid off when he got a perfect score on the test.

phoenix (fē'nĭks) *noun*

a mythical bird that lived for 500 years, set itself on fire, and was born again from the ashes; a thing or person who makes a remarkable comeback after difficulty

Although May was seriously hurt in an accident, she rose like a **phoenix** and was able to compete in the race the following year.

pigments (pĭg'mənts) *noun*

powders or pastes mixed with liquid to make colors

The painter used **pigments** to create the blues and greens he wanted to use in his painting.

plateaus (plă-tōz') *noun*

high, flat areas of land

Searching for gold, explorers traveled over the **plateaus** of Mexico and the southwest United States.

poor (po͝or) *adjective*

having little or no money

During the Great Depression, not many people had jobs, so many people were **poor**.

pounce (pouns) *verb*

to attack by jumping or swooping down quickly

The cat was ready to **pounce** on the mouse.

preceding (prĭ-sēd'ĭng) *verb*

coming before

The day **preceding** the test, Van studied for two hours.

precipice (prĕs'ə-pĭs) *noun*

a steep cliff or overhanging place

The hawk leapt from the **precipice** and soared above the valley.

precision (prĭ-sĭzh'ən) *noun*

exactness; accuracy

To paint the model airplane with **precision**, Gabriel needed a small paint brush.

prehistoric (prē'hĭ-stôr'ĭk) *adjective*

belonging to a time period before written history

Prehistoric people created art in stone on cave walls.

profitable (prŏf'ĭ-tə-bəl) *adjective*

beneficial; able to make money

Sean found that selling lemonade on hot days was a **profitable** business.

prolific (prə-lĭf'ĭk) *adjective*

very productive

The **prolific** author wrote one story every week for a year.

promoting (prə-mōt'ĭng) *verb*

contributing to; supporting

Hosting the international fair at school was the principal's way of **promoting** cultural diversity in the community.

prototype (prō'tə-tīp') *noun*

an original model used for testing before producing the final version

The engineers built a **prototype** of the plastic car so they could test it in the laboratory.

Puerto Rico (pwĕr'tō rē'kō) *noun*

a self-governing island of the United States in the Caribbean Sea

Explorers came to **Puerto Rico** in the 1500s looking for new trade routes.

rare (râr) *adjective*

not often found or seen

Abby found a **rare** old coin in the sand at the beach.

realm (rĕlm) *noun*

a region, often a kingdom

The king's **realm** stretched from the mountains all the way to the sea.

reconstruct (rē'kən-strŭkt') *verb*

to rebuild or recreate

From the clues he gathered, the detective was able to **reconstruct** what happened the night the painting was stolen.

reference (rĕf'ər-əns) *noun*

a source of information

The dictionary is the **reference** you need if you want to know how to spell a word.

referred (rĭ-fûrd') *verb*

known as

Normal vision is sometimes **referred** to as 20/20 vision.

relief (rĭ-lēf') *noun*

an easing of distress or pain

It was a **relief** when it finally rained after a long dry spell.

Renaissance (rĕn'ĭ-säns') *noun*

the time of a revival of art, literature, and learning that began in Europe in the 14th century and lasted into the 17th century

Michelangelo was a famous artist of the **Renaissance**.

revitalize (rē-vīt'l-īz') *verb*

to give new life or energy to something

The band planned to **revitalize** the town's interest in jazz by staging a big concert.

right (rīt) *adjective*

correct

Jon had studied for the test, so he got most of the answers **right**.

rotisserie (rō-tĭs'ə-rē) *noun*

a cooking device that turns meat while it cooks

They cooked the chickens on the **rotisserie** at the grocery store.

Sahara Desert (sə-hâr'ə dĕz'ərt) *noun*

a large North African desert

The explorer packed six camels with a week's worth of food and lots of water before he set out across the **Sahara Desert**.

say (sā) *verb*

speak

Every day after school, the students **say** "goodbye" to each other.

scholars (skŏl'ərz) *noun*

people who study things; students

The **scholars** presented the research they were doing on bats.

seals (sēlz) *noun*

designs or raised emblems showing that something is official

The queen used wax and a stamp to make **seals** on her official letters.

see (sē) *verb*

to use your eyes

The family went to the zoo to **see** the baby polar bears.

sensor (sĕn'sər) *noun*

a mechanical device used for identifying something by heat, motion, light, or sound

The **sensor** indicated that there was someone walking around inside the closed store.

skeptical (skĕp'tĭ-kəl) *adjective*

doubtful; uncertain

The track star said he could jump the high fence, but his sister was **skeptical** that he could.

solo (sō'lō) *adjective*

alone

The adventurer's **solo** trip around the world in a hot air balloon was a dangerous feat.

sound (sound) *noun*

something you can hear, such as words, music, or noise

The man could hear the **sound** of the marching band from down the street.

species (spē'sēz) *noun*

a group of individuals with common characteristics

There were two **species** of fox in the park: the red fox and the gray fox.

stance (stăns) *noun*

a position of the body when standing

The **stance** you take before hitting a baseball is different than the **stance** you take before hitting a golf ball.

striving (strīv'ĭng) *verb*

trying very hard

Hasan studied every night, **striving** to get good grades in math class.

though (thō) *conjunction*

despite the fact that

The tourists drank coffee, **though** they would have preferred tea.

through (thrōō) *preposition*

in one side and out the other

They opened the door and walked **through** it.

today (tə-dā') *noun*

the present day

The book report is due **today**.

tomorrow (tə-môr'ō) *noun*

the day after today

The mechanic said the car would be fixed by **tomorrow**.

transcontinental (trăn'skŏn-tə-něn'tl) *adjective*

spanning or crossing a continent

The **transcontinental** race was set to begin in San Francisco and end in Boston.

transfixed (trăns-fĭkst') *adjective*

held motionless in amazement

The students were **transfixed** by the stunning photographs of distant galaxies.

translucent (trăns-lōō'sənt) *adjective*

allowing light to pass through; almost transparent

We could make out the movements of the dancers on the other side of the **translucent** windows.

ultimate (ŭl'tə-mĭt) *adjective*

greatest possible

The trip to Hawaii was the **ultimate** vacation for people who wanted to visit a beautiful, tropical island.

unconventional (ŭn'kən-věn'shə-nəl) *adjective*

not ordinary; unusual

The tarantula was an **unconventional** classroom pet, but the students liked it.

venture (věn'chər) *verb*

to do something dangerous

The scientists planned to **venture** into the deepest parts of the ocean.

villain (vĭl'ən) *noun*

a bad or wicked person

The **villain** robbed the bank, but the police caught him afterward.

virtually (vûr'chōō-ə-lē) *adverb*

for the most part

The football player was so fast, he ran **virtually** untouched all the way to the end zone.

volunteers (vŏl'ən-tîrz') *noun*

people who perform a service for free

The **volunteers** picked up trash and trimmed the trees for the elderly neighbors.

vulnerable (vŭl'nər-ə-bəl) *adjective*

unprotected; open to harm

Before they grow up, baby crocodiles are **vulnerable** to attack from other animals.

want (wônt) *verb*

to desire; to wish for

The man at the counter asked his customer, "Which sandwich do you **want**?"

water (wô'tər) *noun*

a common chemical in its liquid state, which is essential to all life on Earth

Clean drinking **water** is one of the world's most precious resources.

way (wā) *noun*

path; direction; procedure

The tourist stopped to ask a woman the **way** to the bus stop.

windchill factor (wĭnd'chĭl făk'tər) *noun*

the cold experienced by people and other living things, based on a combination of wind and cold

It was 10 degrees Fahrenheit when they left for school, but it was so windy the **windchill factor** made it feel like 10 degrees below zero.

wits (wĭtz) *noun*

powers of understanding; intelligence

Keisha used her quick **wits** to solve the problem.

work (wûrk) *verb*

to use effort to accomplish something

The painters had to **work** hard to finish painting the house by sunset.

year (yîr) *noun*

a period of 365 or 366 days in the Gregorian calendar, divided into 12 months

Once a **year**, the students took a field trip to the natural history museum.

Category	Meaning	Location
Remember Units 7–8	Retrieve relevant knowledge from long-term memory	
list	state a series of names, ideas, or events	Unit 7
locate	find specific information	
name	label specific information	
recognize	know something from prior experience or learning	
state	say or write specific information	
describe	state detailed information about an idea or concept	Unit 8
recall	retrieve information from memory to provide an answer	
repeat	say specific infomation again	
retrieve	locate information from memory to provide an answer	
Understand Units 9–12	Construct meaning from instructional messages, including oral, written, and graphic communication	
conclude	arrive at logical end based on specific information	Unit 9
define in your own words	tell the meaning of something in one's own words	
illustrate	present an example or explanation in pictures or words	
predict	foretell new information from what is already known	
tell	say or write specific information	
identify	locate specific information in the text	Unit 10
paraphrase	restate information in somewhat different words to simplify and clarify	
summarize	restate important ideas and details from multiple paragraphs or sources	

Category	Meaning	Location
categorize	place information into groups	Unit 11
classify	organize into groups with similar characteristics	
discuss	talk about or examine a subject with others	
match	put together things that are alike or similar	
sort	place or separate into groups	
compare	state the similarities between two or more ideas	Unit 12
contrast	state the differences between two or more ideas	
explain	express understanding of an idea or concept	
Review **Remember** and **Understand** levels		Unit 12
Apply Units 13–15	Carry out or use a procedure in a given situation	
generalize	draw conclusions based on presented information	Unit 13
infer	draw a logical conclusion using information or evidence	
use	apply a procedure to a task	
show	demonstrate an understanding of information	Unit 14
Review **Apply** level		Unit 15
Analyze Units 16–18	Break material into its constituent parts and determine how the parts relate to one another and to an overall structure or purpose	
distinguish	find differences that set one thing apart from another	Unit 16
select	choose from among alternatives	
arrange	organize information	Unit 17
organize	arrange in a systematic pattern	
outline	arrange information into a systematic pattern of main ideas and supporting details	
Review all levels		Unit 18
*The last two levels of Bloom's Taxonomy, **Evaluate** and **Create**, are covered in Book D.*		

Glossary of Terms

Book C contains these terms. Unit numbers where these terms first appear follow each definition.

1-1-1 pattern. See **Spelling conventions.**

Abbreviation. A shortened form of a word. Examples: *Dr.*, Doctor; *Oct.*, October; *CA*, California (postal abbreviation). (Unit 12)

Abstract noun. See **Noun.**

Adding -es. See **Spelling conventions.**

Adjective. A word used to describe a noun. An adjective answers the questions which one? how many? or what kind? A prepositional phrase may also be used as an adjective. Example: *Six new kids from the school won the big game.* Adjectives can also signal a comparison between nouns or pronouns depending on their ending. **Comparative adjective.** Compares two nouns or pronouns by adding **-er** to the adjective and using the word *than*. Example: *He was shorter than his brother.* **Superlative adjective.** Compares three or more nouns by adding **-est** to the adjective. Example: *She was the shortest member of the band.* See **Prepositional phrase, Participle.** (Units 6, 14)

Adverb. A word used to describe a verb. An adverb answers the questions when? where? and how? A prepositional phrase can also be used as an adverb. An adverb can be moved within a sentence. Examples: *Julio ran in the park yesterday. Yesterday, Julio ran in the park.* See **Prepositional phrase.** (Units 4, 5, 6)

Antonym. A word that means the opposite of another word. Examples: *above/below; dead/alive; happy/sad.* (Unit 2)

Apostrophe. Punctuation mark (') that signals singular possession when used with the letter **-s** or the replacement of letters removed to make a contraction. Examples: the *man's map, Ann's pan, I'm.* (Units 2, 7)

Appositive. A noun phrase that follows a noun or a pronoun. It renames and tells more about the noun or pronoun that it follows. It is usually set off with commas. Example: King Tut, *an ancient pharaoh*, was buried in a pyramid. (Unit 17)

Attribute. A characteristic or quality, such as size, part, color, or function. Examples: *A windmill is tall. A windmill has a base and blades. Windmills are narrow. Windmills catch wind energy to make electric energy.* (Unit 5)

Biography. A type of literature that tells the story of someone's life. Example: *Leonardo da Vinci: The Inventor.* (Unit 14)

Blend. Consonant sound pair in the same syllable. The consonants are not separated by vowels, and each consonant sound is pronounced. **Initial blends** are letter combinations that represent two different consonant sounds at the beginning of a sound. Examples: **bl-**, *black, blink*; **br-**, *bring, brought*. **Final blends** are letter pairs that represent two different consonant sounds at the end of a word. Examples: **-nd**, *band, land*; **-st**, *last, mast*. **Clusters** consist of three or more consonants in the same syllable. The consonants are not supported by vowels. Each consonant is pronounced. Examples: **spr-**, *spread, spray*; **str-**, *stress, stray*. (Units 8, 11)

Capital letters. Uppercase letters used at the beginning of all sentences. Examples: **T**he cat sat. **W**here did it sit? **I**t sat on my lap! (Unit 1)

Comma. A punctuation mark (**,**) used to signal a pause when reading or writing to clarify meaning. Commas separate phrases at the beginning of sentences (e.g., *At the end of the song, Juan clapped*), adjectives of the same kind (e.g., *The big, black cat sat*), appositives from their modifiers (e.g., *Sam, my pet cat, is black*), the day from the year in a date (e.g., *December 1, 2008*), the city from the state in an address (e.g., *Denver, CO 80020*), and the greeting and the closing from the body of a letter (e.g., *Dear Uncle Tran, Thank you!*). (Unit 5)

Common noun. See **Noun.**

Compound word. A word made up of two or more smaller words. There are three types of compound words: (1) **closed**, which are written without a space between the words (e.g., *downhill*); **open**, which are written with a space between the words (e.g., *jump shot*); and (3) **hyphenated**, which are written with a hyphen between the words (e.g., *left-hand*). (Units 3, 13)

Concrete noun. See **Noun.**

Conjunction. A word that joins words, phrases, or clauses in a sentence. They also join sentences. **Coordinating conjunction.** Conjunctions that connect words that have the same function. Examples: *and, but, or*. The conjunction *and* relates two similar ideas. Example: *Ellen **and** her friends rested*. The conjunction *but* signals contrasting ideas. Example: *The hurricane hit land, **but** the people escaped*. The conjunction *or* signals an alteration or choice. Example: *An artist can carve **or** sculpt stone*. (Units 7, 10, 11)

Consonant. A closed sound produced using airflow restricted or closed by the lips, teeth, or tongue. Letters represent consonant sounds. Examples: <u>m</u>, <u>s</u>, <u>t</u>, <u>b</u>. (Unit 1)

Context cues. See **Vocabulary strategies.**

Contractions. Two words combined into one word. One or more letters are left out and are replaced with an apostrophe ('). Examples: **is** + **no/t** = *isn't*; **I** + **w/o/u/l/d** = *I'd*; **It** + **w/i/ll** = *It'll*. (Units 7, 9, 10)

Digraph. Two letters that represent one sound. Examples: / *ch* / as in *chop*, *such*; / *sh* / as in *shop*, *dish*. (Unit 8)

Direct object. A noun or pronoun that receives the action of the main verb in the predicate. Answers the question who or what received the action? Example: *Casey visits granddad.* **Compound direct object.** Two direct objects joined by a conjunction. Example: *The bugs infest crops and animals.* (Units 3, 4, 9)

Double consonants. See **Spelling conventions.**

Doubling rule. See **Spelling rules.**

Drama. A literary drama, it is a story written to be acted by character, such as a play, a musical, or an opera. Example: **"These Shoes of Mine."** (Unit 15)

Exclamation point. Punctuation mark (**!**) used to signal heightened expression or strong emotion. (Unit 1)

Expository text. Text that provides information and includes a topic. Facts and examples support the topic. It is organized using main ideas and supporting details. Expository text can be found in textbooks, newspapers, magazines, and encyclopedias. Example: **"Batty About Bats!"** Also called **informational text** and **nonfiction**. (Unit 1)

Expressions. A common way of saying something. They are similar to idioms. Expressions do not have a specific form. Examples: *all wet* = mistaken; *odds and ends* = leftovers. (Unit 7)

Final silent -e. See **Spelling conventions.**

First-person account. A type of literature, either fiction or nonfiction, in which the narrator recalls his or her own personal experiences. Example: **"King Tut: Egyptian Pharaoh."** (Unit 17)

Folktale. A type of narrative text characterized by fictional, everyday people, set in an imagined place and time. Example: **"The Spider's Thread."** (Unit 7)

Helping verb. See **Verb.**

Idiom. A common phrase that cannot be understood by the meanings of its separate words—only by the entire phrase. It cannot be changed, or the idiom loses its meaning. Examples: *be in hot water* = be in serious trouble; *hold your horses* = slow down. (Unit 4)

Homophones. Words that sound the same but have different meanings. Examples: *there/their/they're*; *our/hour*; *write/right*. (Unit 7)

Indirect object. A noun or pronoun often placed between the main verb and the direct object. It tells to whom or for whom the action was done. If a sentence has an indirect object, it must also have a direct object. Example: *Nikko gave granddad **a gift***. (Unit 17)

Informational text. See **Expository text.**

Irregular verb. See **Verb.**

Legend. A type of narrative text characterized by a particular person and a particular time and place in history. Example: **"Floki: Sailor Without a Map."** (Unit 2)

Letters. Two types of letters include the **informal letter** and the **business letter**. An informal letter is written to someone the writer knows well. A business letter is written to someone the writer does not know or who is in a position of authority. (Unit 16)

Meaning cues. See **Vocabulary strategies.**

Metaphor. A figure of speech in which a word or phrase implies a comparison or identity. Example: *Life is just a bowl of cherries.*

Narrative text. Text that tells a personal story of the writer. The writer uses "I" to tell the story. Narrative text includes a message, often a lesson learned from the experience that the author is writing about. The story has a beginning, middle, and end. Narrative text can be found in novels, anthologies, and magazines. Example: **"One Sport I Like!"** Also known as **Personal narrative.** (Units 7, 8)

Nominative pronoun. See **Pronoun.**

Nonfiction. See **Expository text.**

Noun. A word that names a person, place, thing, or idea. Examples: *children, campus, lemon, method.* **Abstract noun.** A word that names an idea or a thought that we cannot see or touch. Examples: *love, Saturday, sports, democracy.* **Common noun.** A word that names a general person, place, or thing. Examples: *man, city, statue.* **Concrete noun.** A word that names a person, place, or thing that we can see or touch. Examples: *teacher, car, pencil.* **Possessive noun.** Indicates ownership or possession. Formed by adding an apostrophe (') and an **-s** to signal singular possession. Examples: *Stan's stamps, the man's cap).* Formed by adding **-s** and an apostrophe (') to signal plural possession. Examples: *boys' cards, dogs' bowls.* **Proper noun.** A word that names a specific person, place, or thing. Examples: *Mr. West, Boston, Statue of Liberty.* (Units 1, 2, 3, 11)

Object of a preposition. A noun or pronoun that ends a prepositional phrase. Examples: *in the **cab**, during the **game**.* (Unit 4)

Object pronoun. See **Pronoun.**

Onomatopeoia. Literary device created when a word's sound suggests its meaning. Examples: *bam, bang, buzz, crash.* (Unit 16)

Paragraph. A group of sentences. Each sentence in the paragraph has a specific job. **Topic sentence.** Tells what the paragraph is about. Example: *Regular exercise benefits people's health in two important ways.* **Supporting details.** Give facts or reasons about the topic. Example: *One benefit is that exercise improves people's physical health.* **Transition words.** Link one supporting detail to the next. Examples: *one, also.* **E's, or elaborations (explanations, examples, evidence).** Sentences that support the topic and supporting details and add interest for the reader. Example: *It makes people feel better about themselves and calms them down when they are angry or stressed.* **Conclusion.** Ties the parts together. It often restates the topic. Example: *When people regularly do physical activities they enjoy, their bodies and minds stay fit, happy, and healthy.* **Introductory paragraph.** States the topic for the entire report. Example: *Exercise can benefit your health in two ways. Regular exercise improves your physical health and is good for your mind.* **Body paragraph.** Tells more about the topic. It often begins with a transition topic sentence and includes E's that support the topic sentence. **Concluding paragraph.** Links to the introductory paragraph

and ties the whole report together. Example: *It is clear that exercise is great for both the body and the mind. The benefits of exercise are just too important to ignore.* (Unit 7)

Participle. The verb form used with the helping verbs *have, has,* or *had* to indicate present or past perfect. **Present participle.** Ends in the **-ing** form of a verb and can be used as an adjective to describe nouns. Examples: *The sun is **shining**; The **shining** sun is hot.* **Regular past participle.** Ends in the **-ed** form of the verb and can be used as an adjective to describe nouns. Examples: *The athlete **injured** his foot; The **injured** athlete used crutches.* Many irregular past participles end in **-en.** Example: *eaten.* (Unit 16)

Period. Punctuation mark (.) used at the ending of all sentences or an abbreviation. Examples: *The cat sat. Mr. Jones came to the door.* (Unit 1)

Personal narrative. See **Narrative text.**

Personification. Figurative language that assigns human characteristics to an idea, animal, or thing. Example: **"Roberto Clemente: The Heart of the Diamond"** (Unit 16)

Phrase. A group of words that does the same job as a single word. Examples: *in the house; with a bang.* (Unit 4)

Plural. A term that means more than one. Nouns are usually made plural by adding **-s.** Examples: *bats, acts,*

cabs. Nouns ending in **-s, -z, -x, -chv,
-sh, -tch** use **-es** to make them plural.
Examples: *dresses, fizzes, boxes,
riches, dishes, matches*. (Units 1, 7)

Possession. Indicates ownership of
something. **Singular possession.** One
person or thing that owns something.
Adding **'s** (apostrophe and the letter **s**)
to a noun signals singular possession.
Examples: *Stan's stamps, the van's
mat, the man's cap*. **Plural possession.**
More than one person or thing that
owns something. Adding the suffix **-s'**
(letter **s** and an apostrophe) to a noun
signals plural possession. Examples:
boys', girls', dogs'. (Units 2, 11)

Possessive noun. See **Noun.**

Possessive pronoun. See **Pronoun.**

Predicate. The second of two main parts
of a sentence. It contains the main
verb of the sentence, describes the
action, usually comes after the subject,
and answers the question what did
they (he, she, it) do? Example: *The
man ran*. **Simple predicate.** The
verb that tells what the subject did.
Example: *The class clapped during
the song*. **Complete predicate.** The
simple predicate and all its objects
and modifiers. Example: *The class
clapped during the song*. **Compound
predicate.** Two simple predicates
joined by a conjunction. *The class
sang and clapped*. (Units 2, 8)

Prefix. A word part added to the
beginning of a word that can add to

or change the meaning of a word.
Prefixes include: **un-, pre-,** and **non-**.
Examples: **un**plug; **pre**set; **non**sense.
(Units 13, 14, 15, 16, 17, 18)

Preposition. A function word that
begins a prepositional phrase.
Prepositions show relationship. Most
prepositions show a position in space
(e.g., *inside, over, under*), time (e.g.,
during, since, until), or space and time
(e.g., *after, from, through*). (Units 4, 6)

Prepositional phrase. A phrase that
begins with a preposition and
ends with a noun or a pronoun. A
prepositional phrase is used either as
an adjective or as an adverb. Examples:
in the van; on Monday; to the class. See
Adjective, Adverb. (Unit 4)

Pronoun. A function word used in place
of a noun. Examples: *I, you, he, me, they.*
Nominative (subject) pronoun. A
function word that takes the place of the
subject noun in a sentence. Examples:
I, you, he, she, it, we, they. **Object
pronoun.** A function word that takes
the place of the object of a preposition or
a direct object. Examples: *me, you, him,
her, it, us, them.* **Possessive pronouns.**
Pronouns that show ownership.
Sometimes a possessive pronoun
functions as an adjective, or sometimes
the possessive pronoun replaces the
noun. Examples: *My desk is a mess.
Mine is a mess.* (Units 4, 6, 7)

Pronoun referent. See **Vocabulary
strategies.**

Proper noun. See **Noun.**

Punctuation. Marks that indicate the ending of a sentence (period, question mark, and exclamation point), a pause within a sentence (comma), or possession (apostrophe accompanied by the letter <u>s</u>). Examples: *The cat sat. Where did it sit? It sat on my lap! Yesterday, school was cancelled. Sam's map.* See **Apostrophe, Comma, Exclamation point, Period, Question mark.** (Units 2, 5, 7)

Question mark. Punctuation mark (**?**) used at the end of a sentence to indicate that a question has been asked. Example: *Where did the cat sit?* (Unit 1)

Regular verb. See **Verb.**

Report. A piece of nonfiction writing that focuses on one topic. The body paragraphs tell different points about the topic. Each point is stated in a transition topic sentence. A report does not include any personal details.

Schwa. A vowel phoneme in an unstressed syllable that has reduced value or emphasis. The symbol for schwa is / ə /. Example: *lesson* = / lĕssən /. The <u>o</u> in *lesson* is reduced to **schwa**, which sounds like / ŭ /, but is more reduced. (Unit 13)

Science fiction. A type of text characterized by fantastic or futuristic people and places. Example: **"Podway Bound: A Science Fiction Story."** (Unit 13)

Sentence. A complete thought that answers the questions who (what) did it? and what did they (he, she, it) do? Examples: *The cat sat. The players talked. Sam acted.* **Simple sentence.** A complete thought that contains one subject and one predicate. Examples: *The man ran. Casey batted. The bird hopped.* **Compound sentence.** Two sentences joined by a conjunction. Example: *Julio walked **and** Dan ran.* **Topic sentence.** States the topic of the paragraph. It is often the first sentence. Example: *"Batty About Bats" explains facts about bats.* (Units 1, 2, 10)

Simile. A figure of speech that makes a comparison. A simile always uses the words *like* or *as*. Examples: *as smart **as** Einstein; as artistic **as** Picasso.* (Unit 14)

Singular. A word that means one of something. Examples: *bat, act, cab.* (Unit 1)

Spelling conventions. Tips that help us remember how to spell words. **Words with <u>v</u> or <u>s</u> + <u>e</u>.** Almost no word ends with the letter <u>v</u>. The letter <u>v</u> is almost always followed by <u>e</u>. Examples: *have, give, live.* Often the <u>e</u> follows a single <u>s</u> at the end of the word. The <u>e</u> does not signal a long vowel. Examples: *promise, purchase.* **Double consonants.** Use double letters **-ss, -ff, -ll, -zz** at the end of many words, in many one-syllable words, or after one short vowel. Examples: *pass, stiff, will, jazz*. **Ways to spell / k /.** The sound / k / is spelled three ways. The position of / k / in the word signals how to spell it. First, use **c** at the beginning of words before the vowel **a**. Example: *cat*. Second, use **k** at the beginning of words before the vowel **i**. Example: *kid*. Third, use -**ck** after one short vowel in one-syllable words: Examples: *back, sick*. **Adding -es.** Nouns and verbs endings in **s**, **z**, or **x**, add -**es** to form plural nouns or singular present tense verbs. Examples: *dresses, boxes, presses, waxes*. **Using ch- or -tch.** The sound / ch / is represented two ways. The position of / ch / in a word helps you spell it. Use **ch-** at the beginning of words. Use -**tch** after a short vowel at the end of one-syllable words, with four exceptions: *much, such, rich, which*. / ŭ / **spelled o.** Some words keep an Old English spelling for the / ŭ / sound. In these words, the vowel sound is spelled with the letter **o**. Examples: *front, shove, ton*. **Final silent e.** The **e** at the end of the word is a signal to use the long vowel sound. The final **e** is silent. Examples: *mane, pine*. (Units 3, 4, 5, 7, 8, 9, 10)

Spelling rules. Can help us add endings to words. **Doubling rule.** This is also known as the **1-1-1 pattern**. When a one-syllable word with one vowel ends in one consonant, double the final consonant before adding a suffix that begins with a vowel. Examples: *hopping, stopping*. Do not double the consonant when the suffix begins with a consonant. Example: *slowly*. **Drop e rule.** When adding a suffix to a final silent **e** word, if the suffix begins with a vowel, drop the **e** from the base word. However, if the suffix begins with a consonant, do not drop the **e** from the base word. Examples: *hope + ing = hoping; hope + ful = hopeful*. **Words ending in o rule.** For words ending in a consonant plus **o**, add -**es** to form plural nouns and singular present tense verbs. The -**es** keeps the **o** sound long. Examples: *hero +es = heroes; go + es = goes*. For words ending in a vowel plus **o**, add -**s** to form plural nouns. Example: *video + s = videos*. **Change y rule.** When a base word ends in **y** preceded by a consonant, change **y** to **i** before adding a suffix, except for -**ing**. Examples: *try + ed = tried; try + ing = trying*. (Units 6, 10)

Subject. The first of two main parts of a sentence. The subject names the person, place, thing, or idea that the sentence is about. Examples: *The man made a map. The map helped the man*. **Simple subject.** The noun that the sentence is about. Example: *The blue egg fell from the nest*. **Complete subject.** The simple subject and all its modifiers. Example: *The blue egg fell from the nest*. **Compound subject.** Two subjects joined by a conjunction. Compound subjects require plural verbs. Example: *Ellen and her friends rested*. (Units 2, 7, 8)

Substitutions. See **Vocabulary strategies.**

Suffix. A word part added to the end of a word that can add to or change the meaning of a word. Suffixes include: **-ly.** Example: *quickly.* (Unit 17) **Inflectional suffix.** These suffixes are used to change number, possession, comparison, and tense. They are: **-s, -es, -ing, -ed, -en, -er,** and **-est.**

Summary. Tells the most important ideas from a text selection. **Simple summary.** Uses only the main ideas. Example: *"Batty About Bats!" explains facts about bats. Bats can fly. They eat a lot. Bats "see" with sound.* **Expanded summary.** Uses main ideas and some supporting details. Example: *"Batty About Bats!" explains facts about bats. Bats can fly. They are the only mammals that fly. Bats eat a lot of things each day. Bats "see" with sonar and other sound clues.* (Unit 1)

Syllable. A word or word part that has one vowel sound. Examples: *map, bend, ban • dit.* There are four syllable types: (1) **closed**, which ends with a consonant sound. Examples: *dig, trans • mit*; (2) **r-controlled**, which ends with a vowel followed by **r**. Examples: *car, mar • ket*; (3) **open**, which ends with a vowel sound. Examples: *she, my*; and (4) **silent e**, which is a syllable type and a spelling pattern in which the final **e** is silent and whose function

is to signal a vowel change from short to long. Examples: *de • fine; ath • lete.* (Unit 3)

Syllable patterns. Vowels and consonants follow certain rules when dividing into syllables. Divide VC/CV syllables between the consonants. Example: **ban** + **dit** = *bandit.* Divide VC/V syllables after the first vowel if the vowel is long. Example: **si** + **lent** = *silent.* Divide VC/V syllables after the second consonant if the vowel is short. Example: **rob** + **in** = *robin.* With VR/CV syllables, if the first vowel is followed by an **r**, the syllable is **r**-controlled. Example: **mar** + **ket** = *market.* With V/V syllables, divide the syllables between the two vowels. Example: **ne** + **on** = *neon.* (Units 3, 5, 15)

Synonym. A word that has the same meaning as, or a similar meaning to, another word. Examples: *big/large; slim/thin; mad/angry.* (Unit 3)

Tense. A category for verbs that expresses differences between periods of time. **Present tense.** A verb that shows action that is happening now. The **-s** or **-es** at the end of a verb signals present tense. Examples: *hops, drops, stops, wishes, pitches.* **Past tense.** A verb that shows action that is finished. Adding **-ed** signals past tense. The suffix **-ed** represents three sounds: (1) / *t* / after a sound that is not voiced. Examples: *blessed, chipped*; (2) / *d* / after a voiced sound. Examples: *spelled, checked*; and

Tense to Verb, Be

(3) / ĭd / after / t / and / d / so that we can hear the suffix. Examples: *ended, shifted.* **Future tense.** A verb that indicates future time. The verb **will** signals future tense. Examples: ***will** adapt*; ***will** connect*; ***will** finish.* **Progressive tense.** A verb form that indicates ongoing action in time. **Present progressive tense.** The **-ing** ending on a main verb used with **am**, **is**, or **are** signals the present progressive. Examples: *I **am** sitt**ing**. She **is** pick**ing**. We **are** sitt**ing**.* **Past progressive tense.** The **-ing** ending signals the past progressive verb form when proceeded by **was** or **were**. Examples: ***was** brush**ing***; ***were** brush**ing**; **were** cutt**ing**.* **Future progressive tense.** A verb that indicates the action is ongoing in future time. Examples: ***will be** pass**ing**, **will be** skat**ing**, **will be** camp**ing**.* (Units 4, 5, 7, 8, 9, 10)

Text features. Used by writers of expository text to provide clues to the topic and other important information. Examples: title, headings, pictures and captions, margin information, maps, charts, graphs. Also used by playwrights to guide the people who direct and act in the play. Examples: preface, list of characters, set, props, costumes, bold names, and parenthetical references. (Units 1, 15)

Trigraph. Three-letter grapheme that represents one sound. Example: *-tch*. (Unit 8)

Using ch- or -tch. See **Spelling conventions.**

/ ŭ / spelled o. See **Spelling conventions.**

Verb. A word that describes an action (e.g., *run, make*) or a state of being (e.g., *is, were*) and that shows time. Singular verbs are used with singular subjects, and plural verbs are used with plural subjects. Examples: *sits* (present tense; happening now), *is fishing* (present progressive; ongoing action), *acted* (past tense; happened in the past). **Helping verb.** A secondary verb that comes before the main verb in a sentence. Forms of **be** can be used as helping verbs when used with different personal pronouns to achieve subject-verb agreement in sentences. Examples: *I **am** looking. You **are** looking. He **is** looking.* **Regular verbs.** These verbs form the past tense by adding **-ed**. Examples: *I pass**ed**. You pass**ed**. They pass**ed**.* **Irregular verbs.** These verb forms do not end in **-ed** and have different endings and spellings. Examples: *be = was, were; say = said; bring = brought.* (Units 1, 4, 5, 8, 9)

Verb phrases. A group of words that does the same job as a single verb. It has two parts: (1) helping verb (e.g., *am, is, was, were, will*), and (2) main verb. Example: *the bus **is stopping**.* (Unit 9)

Verb, Be. Helping verb that takes the following forms: *am, is, are, was, were, be.* Different forms of **be** are used with different personal pronouns to achieve subject-verb agreement. Examples: *I am* packing; *he is* packing; *she was* packing; *they were* packing. (Unit 5)

Verb, Do. A verb that functions as a main verb or helping verb. Different forms of do are used with different personal pronouns to achieve subject-verb agreement. **Do** has these forms: *do, does, doing, did.* Examples: *I do my homework; he is doing his homework; he was doing his homework; they were doing their homework; he did his homework.* (Unit 2)

Verb, Have. A verb that functions as a main verb or helping verb. Different forms of **have** are used with different personal pronouns to achieve subject-verb agreement. **Have** has these forms: *have, has, having, had.* Examples: *I have a secret; he has a secret; I will be having a secret; he had a secret.* (Unit 3)

Visual information. See **Vocabulary strategies.**

Vocabulary strategies. Context clues to figuring out the meaning of vocabulary words. **Meaning cues.** These words provide cues to the definition of a word in context. Examples: *is/are, it means, which stands for, can be defined as.* **Substitutions.** Words or phrases that rename nouns. They are often synonyms or distinctive features of the noun. Example: *The internet links, or connects, computers around the world.* **Pronoun referents.** Use pronouns to identify meaning clues to

define unknown vocabulary words in context. Example: *Oliver Zompro is an entomologist. He is a scientist who studies insects.* **Context cues.** Clues to the meaning of an unfamiliar word. Example: *It is a movie review. The writer gives an opinion about a new movie.* **Visual information.** Pictures, charts, and other visual information that accompanies the text to help demonstrate the meaning of new vocabulary words. (Unit 7)

Vowel. An open sound produced by keeping the airflow open. Letters represent vowel sounds. Examples: <u>a</u>, <u>e</u>, <u>i</u>, <u>o</u>, <u>u</u>, and sometimes <u>y</u>. The sounds can be short (e.g., / ă / as in *cat*) or long (e.g., / ā / as in *cake*). The long vowel sounds for <u>a</u>, <u>e</u>, <u>i</u>, and <u>o</u> are the same as the names of the letters that represent them. The long vowel sound for <u>u</u> can be pronounced two ways: (1) / $\overline{oo}$ / as in *tube*, and (2) / $y\overline{oo}$ / as in *cube*. (Unit 1)

Words with <u>y</u>. See **Spelling conventions.**

Ways to spell / k /. See **Spelling conventions.**

<u>y</u> as a vowel. The letter <u>y</u> represents different vowels in different positions in words. At the end of a word, <u>y</u> represents a long vowel. At the end of a single-syllable word, the vowel sound is / ī /. Example: *deny.* At the end of a word of more than one syllable, the vowel sound is / ē /. Example: *happy.* In the middle position, <u>y</u> often represents / ĭ /. Example: *myth.*

Handbook Index

A

abbreviations, H14

abstract nouns, H35

adjectives
    comparative, H21, H54
    with conjunctions, H54
    defined, H52, H60
    participial phrases acting as, H54
    subject expansion with, H65
    superlative (adding -est), H21
    types of, H53

adverbs
    defined, H55
    moving in sentence, H64
    predicate expansion with, H63

antonyms, H29

apostrophes, H70

appositives, H41

athlete, history of, H33

attributes, H29, H31

audience awareness, H106, H107

B

be, correct use, H49

bird, history of, H32

blends, H5

Blueprint for Writing, H81

body paragraphs, H94–H95, H97

Bonus Words
    Unit 13, H118
    Unit 14, H119
    Unit 15, H120
    Unit 16, H121
    Unit 17, H122
    Unit 18, H122

business letters, H105

C

ch, using, H16

characters, in plays, H75

clues, for defining words, H71–H72

clusters, H5

commas, H70

common nouns, H34

compare and contrast paragraphs, H102–H103

complete subjects, H38

compound sentence parts, H66–H69

compound words
    chart of, H12
    defined, H12
    examples, H12
    types of, H27
    understanding meaning of, H26

comprehension questions, H76–H77

concluding paragraph, H94–H95, H97

conclusion, H88, H93

concrete nouns, H35

conjunctions, H59
    adjectives with, H54

consonants (c)
    blends, H5
    chart of, H4
    clusters, H5
    defined, H3
    digraphs, H5
    double, H15
    letter combinations, H5
    mouth position for, H4
    pronunciation key, H111
    trigraphs, H5
    types of, H4
    vc/cv pattern words, H11
    vc/v pattern words, H11
    v/cv pattern words, H11
    vr/cv pattern words, H11

continent, history of, H33

plural nouns, H19, H20, H35

plural possessive nouns, H20, H36

possessive pronouns, H58

predicates
    complete, H52
    compound, H67
    defined, H51
    expansion with adverbs, H63
    expansion with direct object, H63
    simple, H52
    writing sentences with, H86

preface, of play, H75

prefixes
    Bonus Words with, H118–H122
    chart of, H12, H24
    defined, H24
    Unit Words with, H112, H113, H114, H115, H116

prepositional phrases, H56

prepositions
    defined, H56
    objects of, nouns as, H41
    showing relationship, H56

present progressive phrases, H47

present tense verbs, H43

progressive form, of verbs, H47–H48

pronouns
    defined, H57
    meaning clues from, H72
    object, H58
    possessive, H58
    subject (nominative), H57

pronunciation keys
    consonants, H111
    vowels, H111

proper nouns, H34

props, for plays, H75

questions, answering, H76–H77
    multiple-choice questions, H77
    open-ended questions, H76
    signal words for, H76, H78–H79

reports
    body paragraphs, H94–H95, H97
    concluding paragraph, H94–H95, H97
    introductory paragraph, H94–H95, H96
    opinion essays and, H99
    parts of, H94–H97
    personal narratives compared to, H98–H101

revising paragraphs, H109–H110

's, adding, H20

s', adding, H20

-s, adding
    to plural nouns, H19
    to singular present tense verb, H22

s, words ending with, H15

schwa, H8

sentences
    beginning signals, H70
    compound, H66–H69
    compound parts, H66–H69
    defined, H61
    diagrams of, H61, H63–H69
    ending signals, H70
    expansion of, H63–H65
    fluency of, H106, H108, H110
    Masterpiece, H86–H87
    moving adverbs in, H64
    predicate expansion with adverbs, H63
    predicate expansion with direct object, H63
    signals for, H70
    simple, H61
    stages of writing, H86–H87
    subject expansion with adjectives, H65
    subject/verb agreement, H62

sets, for plays, H75

signal words, for answering questions, H76, H78–H79

signals, for sentences, H70

simple sentences, H61

adding **-s** to, H22
be, have, and *do,* correct use of, H49–H50
defined, H42, H60
endings, H22–H23
forms of, H43–H50
future progressive, H48
future tense, H46
irregular past tense, H45
past progressive, H48
phrases, H42, H46–H48
present progressive, H47
present tense, H43
progressive form, H47–H48
regular forms, H44
selecting, for topic sentences, H89
subject/verb agreement, H62
tense timeline, H43

vocabulary and morphology
adding **-ed** (past participle), H23
adding **-en** (past participle), H23
adding **-er** (comparative adjectives), H21
adding **-es** (plural noun), H19
adding **-es** (singular present tense verb), H22
adding **-est** (superlative adjectives), H21
adding **-ing** (present participle), H23
adding **-ing** (present progressive), H22
adding **-s** (plural noun), H19
adding **s'** (plural possessive noun), H20
adding **'s** (singular possessive noun), H20
adding **-s** (singular present tense verb), H22
meaning parts (adjective endings), H21
meaning parts (noun endings), H19–H20
meaning parts (verb endings), H22–H23
multiple meanings, H19
suffixes, H25

vocabulary strategies, H71–H72

voice and audience awareness, H106, H107, H110

vowels (v)
chart of, H6
defined, H3
long sounds, H7
pronunciation key, H111
short sounds, H7
sound of, when followed by consonant, H10
sounds of **y** as, H7
vc/cv pattern words, H11

v/cv pattern words, H11
vc/v pattern words, H11
vr/cv pattern words, H11
v/v pattern words, H11

W

water, history of, H32
word history
athlete, H33
bird, H32
continent, H33
curd, H32
hero, H32
third, H32
water, H32
why y?, H33

Word List
Unit 13, H112
Unit 14, H113
Unit 15, H114
Unit 16, H115
Unit 17, H116
Unit 18, H117

word recognition
abbreviations, H14
building words from sounds and letters, H9
compound words, H12
contractions, H13–H14
prefixes and. *See* prefixes
syllable patterns, H11

word relationships, H29–H31

words
choosing, H106, H107, H110
multiple functions of, H60
multiple meanings of, H19
transition, H88, H91, H98

writing
Blueprint for Writing, H81
checklist for Book C, H107–H108
effective, six traits of, H106
expanded summary, H83
opinion essays, H99
organizing. *See* organizing information
personal narratives, H98–H101
reports. *See* reports

Sources

Unit 13

Off-the-Wall Inventions,
Solving Problems, It'll Never Work

Griffiths, Nick. 1995. "It'll Never Work," from *Young Telegraph: Incredible Inventions*. Copyright 1995 by Two-Can Publishing, an imprint of Cooper Square Publishing. Reprinted by permission of Cooper Square Publishing.

Way to Go!

Miller, Steve. 1998. "Way to Go," adapted from *Odyssey* (May 1998) "Techno Travel" ©1998 Carus Publishing Company, 315 Fifth Street, Peru, IL 61354. All rights reserved. Reprinted with permission.*

Leonardo da Vinci: The Inventor

D'Alto, Nick. 2001. "From the Notebooks of Leonardo," adapted from *Odyssey* (November 2001) "Looking at Leonardo's Science" ©2001 Carus Publishing Company, 315 Fifth Street, Peru, IL 61354. All rights reserved. Reprinted with permission.*

Kralik, Milan, Jr. 2002. "Leonardo's Notebooks," adapted from *Calliope* (March 2002) "Leonardo da Vinci, Master Artist" ©2002 Carus Publishing Company, 315 Fifth Street, Peru, IL 61354. All rights reserved. Reprinted with permission.*

Museum of Science, Boston. 2003. "Renaissance Man: Scientist, Inventor, Artist." *Museum of Science*, Boston. http://www.mos.org/leonardo/inventor. html (accessed November 1, 2004).

Podway Bound: A Science Fiction Story

Werfel, Justin. 1998. "Podway Bound," adapted from *Odyssey* (May 1998) "Techno Travel" ©1998 Carus Publishing Company, 315 Fifth Street, Peru, IL 61354. All rights reserved. Reprinted with permission.*

Unit 14

Art at Home and Art in Caves

Newman, Patricia M. 2002. "Elisa Kleven: From Scraps to Magic," adapted from *AppleSeeds* (May 2002) "Becoming an Artist" ©2002 Carus Publishing Company, 315 Fifth Street, Peru, IL 61354. All rights reserved. Reprinted with permission.*

From Rock Art to Graffiti

Bahn, Paul G. 2001. "The Start of Art," adapted from *Dig* magazine (November/December 2001) ©2001 Carus Publishing Company, 315 Fifth Street, Peru, IL 61354. All rights reserved. Reprinted with permission.*

Gingold, Craig. 1989. "The Murals of Aztlán," adapted from *Cobblestone* (April 1989) "Hispanic Americans" ©1989 Carus Publishing Company, 315 Fifth Street, Peru, IL 61354. All rights reserved. Reprinted with permission.*

Gruen, John. 2002. "Keith Haring: the Authorized Biography." http://www. haringkids.com/keith/life/index.html (accessed November 1, 2007). Adapted with permission.

Becoming an Artist

Cummings, Michael A. "Michael A. Cummings: Artist and Quilter." http:// www.michaelcummings.com/biography. html (accessed November 16, 2007).

Greene, Louise L. 2002. "Action Artist," adapted from *AppleSeeds* (May 2002) "Becoming an Artist" ©2002 Carus Publishing Company, 315 Fifth Street, Peru, IL 61354. All rights reserved. Reprinted with permission.*

National Endowment for the Humanities Seminar of Kenyon College. 1997–98. "Augusta Savage." Kenyon College, Gambier, Ohio. http://northbysouth. kenyon.edu/1998/art/pages/savage.htm (accessed November 1, 2004).

*See page 174.

Sources (continued)

Wild, Patricia. 2002. "Famous Artists' Beginnings," adapted from *AppleSeeds* (May 2002) "Becoming an Artist" ©2002 Carus Publishing Company, 315 Fifth Street, Peru, IL 61354. All rights reserved. Reprinted with permission.*

Leonardo the Artist

Balch, Katherine S. 2001. "Leonardo: Engineer, Anatomist, Painter…Magician?" adapted from *Odyssey* (November 2001) "Looking at Leonardo's Science" ©2001 Carus Publishing Company, 315 Fifth Street, Peru, IL 61354. All rights reserved. Reprinted with permission.*

Budd, Denise. 2002. "The Master Works," adapted from *Calliope* (March 2002) "Leonardo da Vinci, Master Artist" ©2002 Carus Publishing Company, 315 Fifth Street, Peru, IL 61354. All rights reserved. Reprinted with permission.*

Museum of Science, Boston. 2003. "Leonardo da Vinci: Scientist, Inventor, Artist," *Museum of Science*, Boston. http://www.mos.org/leonardo/artist.html (accessed November 1, 2004).

Art in Space

Malina, Roger. 1999. "Space(y) Art," adapted from *Odyssey* (November 1999) "Science & Beauty" ©1999 Carus Publishing Company, 315 Fifth Street, Peru, IL 61354. All rights reserved. Reprinted with permission.*

Pietronigro, Frank. 2004. "Frank Pietronigro: Interdisciplinary Fine Artist." http://www.pietronigro.com/index.htm (accessed November 1, 2004).

Unit 15

Mythical Heroes

Columbia Encyclopedia (Sixth ed.). 2001–2004. New York: Columbia University Press. www.bartleby.com; http://www.loggia.com/myth/pantheon.html (accessed November 1, 2004).

Legendary Superheroes

Watts, Claire, and Robert Nicholson. 1995. "Super Powers" from *Super Heroes*. Copyright 1995 by Two-Can Publishing, an imprint of Cooper Square Publishing. Reprinted by permission of Cooper Square Publishing.

These Shoes of Mine

Soto, Gary. 1999. "These Shoes of Mine," play copyright ©1999 by Gary Soto. Used with permission of the author and BookStop Literary Agency. All rights reserved.

Navajo Code Talkers

Cluff, Nancy E. 2003. "Top Secret: An Interview with Sam Billison, Navajo Code Talker," adapted from *AppleSeeds* (March 2003) "American Heroes" ©2003 Carus Publishing Company, 315 Fifth Street, Peru, IL 61354. All rights reserved. Reprinted with permission.*

Watson, Bruce. 1999. "Human Code Machine," adapted from *Odyssey* (January 1999) "Code Breakers" ©1999 Carus Publishing Company, 315 Fifth Street, Peru, IL 61354. All rights reserved. Reprinted with permission.*

The Ride of Her Life

Andrews, Rose. 1998. "The Ride of Her Life," adapted from *AppleSeeds* (September 1998) "Great Adventures" ©Carus Publishing Company, 315 Fifth Street, Peru, IL 61354. All rights reserved. Reprinted with permission.*

Unit 16

The Complete Athlete, A Special Kind of Athlete

Crooker, Gary. 2003. "The Special Olympics," adapted from *Faces* (September 2003) "Rights of the Child" ©2003 Carus Publishing Company, 315 Fifth Street, Peru, IL 61354. All rights reserved. Reprinted with permission.*

*See page 174.

Hellickson, A.J. 2004. Adapted from "Marathon Madness" by A.J. Hellickson from SCHOLASTIC NEWS ONLINE, June 2003. Copyright ©2003 by Scholastic Inc. Reprinted by permission.

Tony Hawk: Extreme Athlete

Tony Hawk, Inc. 2003. Biography from *Tony Hawk's Official Website*. Tony Hawk, Inc. http://www.tonyhawk.com/bio.cfm (accessed November 1, 2004). All rights reserved. Used with permission.

Swifter, Higher, Stronger

Stalcup, Ann. 2000. "Swifter, Higher, Stronger," adapted from *Faces* (September 2000) "Greece" ©2000 Carus Publishing Company, 315 Fifth Street, Peru, IL 61354. All rights reserved. Reprinted with permission.*

Roberto Clemente: The Heart of the Diamond

Blair, Matthew K. 2003. "Roberto Clemente: The Greatest Right-Fielder Ever to Play the Game of Baseball." http://www.toptown.com/hp/66/roberto.htm (accessed November 1, 2004).

Loftus, Joanne. 1989. "The Heart of the Diamond," adapted from *Cobblestone* (April 1989) "Hispanic Americans" ©1989 Carus Publishing Company, 315 Fifth Street, Peru, IL 61354. All rights reserved. Reprinted with permission.*

Unit 17

The Pyramids, Building a Pyramid

Ayad, Mariam. 2001. "Building a Pyramid," adapted from *Calliope* (September 2001) "The Pyramids and Egypt's Old Kingdom" ©2001 Carus Publishing Company, 315 Fifth Street, Peru, IL 61354. All rights reserved. Reprinted with permission.*

Living in Egypt, Growing Up Egyptian

Anitei, Stefan. 2007. "Dentists Tombs from Ancient Egypt." Softpedia. http://news.softpedia.com/news/Dentists-039-Tombs-from-Ancient-Egypt-39079.shtml (accessed August 2007).

Haynes, Joyce. 1999. "School Days," adapted from *AppleSeeds* (February 1999) "Children of Ancient Egypt" ©1999 Carus Publishing Company, 315 Fifth Street, Peru, IL 61354. All rights reserved. Reprinted with permission.*

Wymore, Peggy Wilgus. 1999. "Growing Up in Another Time, Another Place," adapted from *AppleSeeds* (February 1999) "Children of Ancient Egypt" ©1999 Carus Publishing Company, 315 Fifth Street, Peru, IL 61354. All rights reserved. Reprinted with permission.*

The Study of Mummies

Haynes, Joyce. 1997. "The Story of the Manchester Museum Mummies," adapted from *Calliope* (September 1997) "Science and Medicine in Ancient Egypt" ©1997 Carus Publishing Company, 315 Fifth Street, Peru, IL 61354. All rights reserved. Reprinted with permission.*

King Tut: Egyptian Pharaoh

Malek, Jaromir, ed. 2002. "A.H. Gardiner's account of the opening of the burial chamber of Tutankhamen on February 16, 1923." From the *Archive of the Griffith Institute*. Copyright: Griffith Institute, University of Oxford. Reprinted with permission.

Scherer, Jane, and Susan Washburn. 1999. "The Boy King," adapted from *AppleSeeds* (February 1999) "Children of Ancient Egypt" ©1999 Carus Publishing Company, 315 Fifth Street, Peru, IL 61354. All rights reserved. Reprinted with permission.*

*See page 174.

Unit 18

Life at the Pole, Mysteries of Antarctica

Lewis, Karen E. 2001. "Mysteries of Antarctica," adapted from *AppleSeeds* (February 2001) "Amazing Earth" ©2001 Carus Publishing Company, 315 Fifth Street, Peru, IL 61354. All rights reserved. Reprinted with permission.*

The First Transcontinental Railroad

Gemmell, Charlotte. 1980. "The Builders of the First Transcontinental Railroad," adapted from *Cobblestone* (May 1980) "The First Transcontinental Railroad, 1869" ©1980 Carus Publishing Company, 315 Fifth Street, Peru, IL 61354. All rights reserved. Reprinted with permission.*

Continental Drift

Noyes-Hull, Gretchen. 1999. "Seashells on the Summit," adapted from *Appleseeds* (October 1999) "Exploring Mountains" ©1999 Carus Publishing Company, 315 Fifth Street, Peru, IL 61354. All rights reserved. Reprinted with permission.*

Reina, Mary. 2001. "The Pangea Puzzle," adapted from *Appleseeds* (February 2001) "Amazing Earth" ©2001 Carus Publishing Company, 315 Fifth Street, Peru, IL 61354. All rights reserved. Reprinted with permission.*

Rogers, John J.W. and M. Santosh. 2004. *Continents and Supercontinents*. Cary, NC: Oxford University Press, Inc.

The Quest for a Continent

Every Learner, Inc. 2007. "Europe Invades America." *KnowledgeNews*. http://knowledgenews.net/moxie/americana/exploration-age-3.shtml

Weston, Beth. 1992. "A Stranger to Foreign Shores," adapted from *Cobblestone* (January 1992) "The Legacy of Columbus" ©1992 Carus Publishing Company, 315 Fifth Street, Peru, IL 61354. All rights reserved. Reprinted with permission.*

Word Histories

The American Heritage Dictionary of the English Language (Fourth ed.). 2002. Boston: Houghton Mifflin Co. http://www.bartleby.com/61/ (accessed November 1, 2004).

Photo and Illustration Credits

Cover

Illustration

©Jonathan Till/Martin French

Unit 13

Photographs

4: www.sinclairc5.com. 6: Royalty Free ©Digital Vision. 7: ©Hulton-Deutsch/ Getty Images. 8: Purdue News Service Photo by Nick Judy. 9: Courtesy of DaimlerChrysler Corporation. 9: *bkgd.* ©Dennis O'Clair/GettyImages. 10–11: *Hovercraft.* ©Courtesy of Andreas Gronarz. 12: ©Denver Post. 16: ©Giuseppe Cacace/Getty Images.

Illustrations

3, 4–5: Steve Clark. 13–14: Phaidon Press/ ©2004 Jupiter Images. 15: ©Time Life Pictures/Getty Images. 17–22: Ivan Velez.

Unit 14

Photographs

26: Elisa Kleven 30: *top.* ©Bettmann/ Getty Images. 30: *bottom.* ©2008 Artists Rights Society (ARS), New York/ SOMAAP, Mexico City. 34: *top.* Van Vechten Trust. Yale Collection of American Literature, Beinecke Rare Book and Manuscript Library, Yale University. 34: *bottom.* ©Owaki-Kulla/Getty Images. 36: ©Michael A. Cummings. 44–45: *insets.* NASA. 44–47: *earth.* NASA. 46–47: *insets.* Frank Pietronigro "Drift Painting" in microgravity, original video footage courtesy of NASA. www.pietronigro.com/ NASA

Illustrations

23: ©2004 Dynamic Graphics. 24–25: ©2004 Jupiter Images. 27: From *The Lion and the Little Red Bird* by Elisa Kleven, ©1992 by Elisa Kleven. Used by permission of Dutton Children's Books, an imprint of Penguin Young Readers Group, a division of Penguin Random House LLC.

28: ©Fotosearch Stock Photography. 29: ©2004 Dynamics Graphics. 30: *bottom.* Schalkwijk/Art Resource, NY. 31: © The Estate of Keith Haring. 33: *easel.* Becky Malone. 37–42: Phaidon Press©2004 Jupiter Images.

Unit 15

Photographs

49: ©1999–2004 Getty Images. 50: Scala/ Art Resource, NY. 51: Royalty Free Creatas, NASA, Royalty Free Thinkstock, Royalty Free Photodisc, Royalty Free Thinkstock. 64: Photograph No. (NARA, 127-N-69889B);(Ashman); Official U.S. Marine Corps Photo USMC #57875. 68: ©United States Mint. Courtesy of Jeannie Sandoval. 74: Courtesy of Putnam County Historian.

Illustrations

52: Steve Clark. 53–54: ©2004 Jupiter Images. 55: ©Jonathon Earl Bowser. 56, 59-60, 62. Laura Lacamara. 64–69: map. Reproduced from *Natural Advanced Geography.* America Book Co., e. 1898, 1901. Public Domain. 70–73: Courtesy of Mark Mitchell. 72: ©United States Postal Service.

Unit 16

Photographs

76: ©Jonathan Nourok/PhotoEdit. 77: ©Tony Donaldson/tdphoto.com. 78: ©Matt A. Brown/X Games IX/ NewSport/CORBIS, *inset.* Courtesy THI. 78 *inset,* 79, 81: Courtesy of THI. 82: ©Jonathan Nourok/PhotoEdit. 84: Ray Ryan/SPORTSFILE *EDI*. 89: ©Tami Chappell/Reuters/Corbis. 90: Courtesy Carnegie Library of Pittsburgh. 90: bkgd. ©ArtVision. 92: ©Bettmann/Getty Images. 93: ©ArtVision. 94: Courtesy Carnegie Library of Pittsburgh, all rights reserved. Unauthorized reproduction or usage prohibited.

Illustrations

75: Martin French. 76, 78, 85, 86: Steve Clark. 87: ©Rykoff Collection/Getty Images. 88, 91, 94: Steve Clark.

Unit 17

Photographs

96: *top.* ©Picturequest LLC 1998–2003. 98: *inset.* ©Will & Deni McIntyre/ GettyImages. 101: ©Corel Corporation 1995. 102: ©The Granger Collection, New York. 104: ©2004 Jupiter Images. 105: The Minneapolis Institute of Arts, The William Hood Dunwoody Fund. 107–108: Image courtesy of The Manchester Museum, ©The University of Manchester. 110: ©Royalty Free/ Corbis., ©Roger Wood/Corbis, 1998- 2004 Picturequest LLC. 112: ©Royalty Free/Corbis. 116: ©Royalty Free/Corbis.

Illustrations

95: www.mapresources.com. 96–97: Steve Clark. 98–100: Steve Clark. 103: University of Pennsylvania. 105: *bottom.* Steve Clark. 113: Becky Malone.

Unit 18

Photographs

117: ©2004 PictureArts Corporation. 118: ©1999–2004 Getty Images. 119: Courtesy of National Oceanic & Atmospheric Administration/ Department of Commerce. 120: ©1999–2004 Getty Images. 121: ©U.S. Coast Guard Slide. 122: *top.* Courtesy of The Antarctic Meteorite Laboratory at the Johnson Space Center. 122: ©Sky Valley Pictures. 123, 125: Courtesy of Central Pacific Railroad Photographic History Museum, ©2005, CPRR.org. 126: Shuji Maeda 127: ©Royalty Free/Corbis.

Illustrations

123: *map.* Courtesy of Pacific Railroad History Museum, ©2004, CPRR.org. 128-130: ©Royalty Free/Corbis. 131: ©North Wind Picture Archives. 132: ©2004 Jupiter Images. 133: ©North Wind Picture Archives.©